Surrealism and Film

Surrealism and Film

by J. H. Matthews

Ann Arbor
The University of Michigan Press

For my children
Annette and Jonathan

Preface

Since the time when surrealism first became articulate, around 1920, its advocates have been particularly attentive to the cinema. They have asked what demands can be made of films in the name of surrealism, and have formulated some revealing answers to their own questions. But it is still not widely known that their evaluation of movies and the experiments in film they themselves have conducted point to a distinctive conception of the ideal cinematic form, constituting a highly original program for the cinema, well worth study by everyone interested in the medium.

The surrealist program has been neglected, by film critics and historians alike, for reasons not difficult to uncover. In the main, these reasons can be traced to confusion regarding the nature and significance of surrealism, and also about the influence it is capable of exerting, as much on the form of movies as on their content. As a result, most accredited commentators are extremely diffident when it comes to probing the concept of surreality in its relationship to reality. And that, basically, is what surrealism in films is all about.

Among the cinema's prime qualities, generally acknowledged even by those who would not accept this as its supreme virtue, is a remarkable aptitude for recording reality with admirable fidelity. The cinema can provide a much more convincing illusion of the real than its closest rival, the theatre, can attempt to give. In sharp contrast, the surrealists' approach to movies takes its point of departure in the conviction boldly summarized by one of their leading spokesmen on film, Jacques B. Brunius, that the cinema is "the least realist art." Hence the first step one must take, when dealing with the surrealist attitude to films, is to attempt to understand why surrealists look to the movies to question the fundamental conventions of realism, and why they are persuaded that films lend themselves to discrediting those conventions.

As soon as we set out to explore the subject of surrealism's connections with the cinema, we discover that all surrealists claim certain rights and privileges when they make films of their own and when they sketch movies in the form of scenarios and film scripts. Moreover, they invoke these same rights while watching films made by directors whose preoccupations and aspirations owe little or nothing at all to surrealist teaching. In consequence, before we can examine the surrealist viewpoint on film, some acquaintance with the surrealist outlook in general is essential. Without this, there is little chance of recognizing the consistent pattern of reaction and response that guides surrealist intervention in the cinema. Only after considering the basic principles of surrealism, as these promise to affect the surrealists' way of looking at movies, can we profitably ask which attitudes and elements to be found in the commercial cinema have appeared attractive to proponents of surrealist ideals. Then the discovery that the surrealist spirit manifests itself in movies where no surrealist intent is present will bring into focus certain important questions. How, for instance, have the surrealists set about handling some of the problems facing them in the cinema? How do they recommend that other problems be handled? And why should these be the problems given precedence by surrealism, in practice as much as in theory? Reliable answers to such questions can be sought only through analysis of typical surrealist film scripts and movies made under direct surrealist influence.

The present investigation is designed to show what the surrealists have looked for in films and to indicate, no less, what they have found in the movies. It aims, first of all, at identifying which features of film-making are accorded priority in surrealism. It aims, next, at directing attention to the means surrealists consider relevant to granting these appropriate prominence, often to the detriment of other aspects of the film-maker's art which, though commonly respected, are considered with disfavor or even open hostility in surrealist circles. Hence this study rests upon acceptance of the fact that every surrealist brings into the movie theatre a number of serious demands, persistently asking how successfully the film meets these, or in any case seems likely to do so. The central concern, throughout, is to clarify these demands, so as to shed light on their consequences for the cinema.

A grant-in-aid from the American Council of Learned Societies assured me freedom to complete my manuscript. It is a pleasure to acknowledge the Council's encouragement, for the second time. For courteous and prompt assistance my thanks go to Miss Cheryl Arnold, Corporate Information Department, Eastman Kodak Company, Rochester, N. Y.; Mrs. Mary Corliss, Stills Archivist, Department of Film, The Museum of Modern Art, New York City; Miss Sylvia Loeb, Editorial Department, *Sight and Sound,* The British Film Institute; Miss Sheila Whitaker, Chief Stills Officer, The National Film Archive, London; Mr. Bernard Lewis, The Bernard Lewis Company, New York City; Mr. C. Perry, Altura Films, New York City; Mr. Donald L. Velde, Donald L. Velde, Inc., New York City; and Mr. Myron Weinberg, Allied Artists Pictures Corporation, New York City. I am especially indebted to Jean-Louis Bédouin, Robert Benayoun, and Marcel Mariën for making available documentary material.

Grateful thanks go to the following, for permission to reproduce stills from the films cited in parentheses:

Allied Artists Pictures Corporation (*Belle de Jour,* an Allied Artists release); Altura Films (*Viridiana, El Angel exterminador;* photos kindly supplied by Messrs. Donald L. Velde, Inc.); Robert Benayoun (*Paris n'existe pas*); Luis Buñuel (*Un Chien andalou, L'Age d'Or, Las Hurdes;* photos kindly supplied by the National Film Archive, The British Film Institute); Léo Dohmen (*L'Imitation du Cinéma;* photos copyright by Léo Dohmen); Wilhelm Freddie and Steen Colding (*Spiste horisonter*); and The National Film Archive, The British Film Institute (*Violons d'Ingres;* copyright the National Film Archive).

But for my wife's support, this essay could never have been finished. Sharing in twenty years of film viewing, sometimes surviving three performances a day, she contributed actively and tirelessly to the preparation of the text that follows, prior to assisting in giving it final form. And she gave daily lessons in forbearance, all the more appreciated for being as familiar as they are necessary.

J. H. M.

Fayetteville, New York
September 1970

Contents

Introduction

During his military service in the First World War, André Breton was stationed for a time in Nantes. There he met Jacques Vaché, a man who affected his outlook profoundly. In Vaché's company, the future leader of the surrealists in France made the rounds of the movie houses, taking care not to ascertain in advance the names of the films they would be seeing. "When I was 'at the cinema age' [. . .] I never began by consulting the amusements page to know what film seemed likely to be the best. Nor did I inquire about the time when the film began. I agreed particularly well with Jacques Vaché in appreciating nothing so much as dropping in at a movie house when what was playing was playing, at any point in the show. And we would leave at the first sign of boredom—of surfeit—to rush off to another movie house where we behaved in the same way, and so on [. . .] ."[1] In this way Breton and Vaché made sure they confronted themselves with a succession of visual images, liberated from the formal arrangement imposed by a theme to which a pertinent title had been added. Their method protected them from knowing what the images they had seen were meant to convey, and juxtaposed these with images assembled by another film-maker for a totally different purpose. Breton explains, "I have never known anything so *magnetizing*."[2] The important thing was that he and his companion should come out, he says, "charged" for a few days.

While he talks of a method of film-going that rules out qualitative judgment, as this is generally understood, Breton begins to isolate the "lyrical substance" he sought and valued in the films he saw before 1920. Its discovery was evidently closely linked with a sense of visual, mental, and emotional dislocation which Breton himself sums up in the word *dépaysement*. Referring to the cinema, he remarks, "I think what we valued most in it, to the point of taking

1

no interest in anything else, was its *power to disorient* [*son pouvoir de dépaysement*]." Disorientation, here, is understood to allude to the power of the cinema to take man out of his natural surroundings, be these material, mental, or emotional. Hence it relates to "The *marvel* beside which the merits of a given film count for little." The marvel in question, Breton assures us, comes from a faculty which is the privilege of no one in particular to "abstract ourselves from our own lives when we feel like it." This privilege is granted anyone who passes through the doors of a movie auditorium. For he passes at the same time through a critical point for which the best analogy, Breton suggests, is that at which the waking state joins sleep.

Breton's analogy is valuable. It emphasizes the peculiar advantage of the cinema over books, or even plays, when it comes to facilitating the kind of release that surrealists seek from the discouraging spectacle of daily life. More than this, it makes clear that when a surrealist does find release this is largely because he seeks it so purposefully, uncovering the film's lyrical substance through the exercise of affective equipment which surrealism supplies. Breton leaves no room for further doubt on this score as he continues, "There is a way of going to the movies as others go to church and I think that, from a certain angle, quite independently of what is playing, it is there that the only *absolutely modern* mystery is celebrated."

Breton has just given a name to the process by which the substance of the film passing before the surrealist movie-goer's eyes is transmuted. While the miracle of a transubstantiation is paralleled, the presence of no celebrant is necessary here. In the cinema, the surrealist miracle calls for no intermediary other than the communicant himself. Interpretation becomes more a creative act than an evaluative one; or rather, evaluation is identified with creation in a manner proving beyond doubt that surrealism is less a style or a method than a state of mind which the film provides the occasion for externalizing. Because this is so, Breton is able to talk after *dépaysement* of *sur-dépaysement*.

When he wrote *Les Vases communicants* in 1932, Breton confessed that he was attracted by the "treasure of imbecility" to be found in the French cinema of the day. Recalling this in his 1951 essay "Comme dans un Bois," he remarks that attraction came from "the expectation of a super-disorientation," which he defines as "a discordance, deliberately as wide as possible, between the 'lesson' the film teaches and the manner in which the person receiving it disposes of it." Super-disorientation (*sur-dépaysement*) is the product of intentional exploitation of discordance between what is being shown and what the surrealist spectator chooses to see. The choice in this matter is his, just as its effects are significant in a very personal way. So far as these effects result from a selective process conditioned by surrealist thought and feeling, they warrant use of the adjective "poetic."

The surrealist sense of poetry in film will require analysis in due course. To begin with, the important thing is noticing how much faith surrealists place in the capacity of the movies to convey a poetic content that appeals to them. "What we ask of the cinema," Robert Desnos pointed out, when discussing "Mystères du Cinéma" in *Le Soir* on April 2, 1927, "is the impossible, the unexpected, dreams, surprise which efface the baseness in souls and rush them enthusiastically to the barricades and into adventures; we ask of the cinema what love and life deny us, that is mystery, miracles."

After citing some of the humorists, from Swift to Thurber, whose writings command the surrealists' respect, Ado Kyrou remarks, "the liberation of language due above all to Roussel, Brisset, and Marcel Duchamp, opens the way to the liberation of the image, and the cinema can see this job through much more completely than painting."[3] Kyrou evidently is alluding to certain natural advantages of the cinematographic medium—free association, unexpected visual juxtapositions, and the ability to arrange concrete images in an order alien to that of spatial and temporal reality. Surrealists see poetry in the cinema as coming from the ability, which no other medium possesses to quite the same degree, to "complete and enlarge tangible reality," as Luis Buñuel puts it.

"One would like not to have to return to this," observes Jacques B. Brunius, "but it is fitting to repeat that the film enjoys an incomparable facility for passing over the bridge in both directions, thanks to the extraordinary and sumptuous solidity it contributes to the creations of the mind, objectifying them in the most convincing fashion, while it makes exterior reality submit in the opposite direction to subjectivization."[4] Although no surrealist has defended this position so energetically in print as Brunius, none would repudiate his conclusions. Throwing off respect for everyday reality, surrealists welcome any effort to subject it to pressures coming from within man. So long as the cinema accepts as its role the mimicry of life, it appears valueless to them. But as soon as they are persuaded a movie has slipped the bonds of realistic control, they hold themselves ready to witness the emergence of a new universe.

The surrealists' ideal is the attainment of aspirations which current circumstances combine to deny us. This entails a review of reality, a revised sense of what is real. Even when they do not address themselves openly to the question of the role of the real in films, at the source of the concept of cinematographic poetry defended by all surrealists is anticipation of *une réalité rehaussée:* reality raised to a new level of significance, more in accord with the inner needs of man. Reflecting on what lies behind the conviction that reality can indeed be raised to a higher level of meaning (the semantic force of *surréalisme* is 'superrealism'),[5] one appreciates more readily how Brunius came to declare, "What is admirable in realism is that there is no more real, there is only the fantastic." He further insisted, "Although few authors seem to realize it, in spite of the few films that justify it, I believe this phrase can and must be considered as a fundamental cinematographer's law" (pp. 134–135).

Surrealists are adamantly opposed to compartmentalizing experience, and refuse to separate what they call dream from life. They are free, therefore, to subject reality to re-evaluation. They demonstrate that man's sensitivity to what is real is deeply influenced by his desires, which lend outline and consistency to what he wishes to see. As a form of protest against the mundane, poetry in film is for them the operation of the disruptive principle, working to reassess and to reclassify experience, against a background which is no longer realist (because alien and frequently antagonistic to man's desire), but surrealist (because sympathetic and attuned to his yearnings). Hence, inconsistent as it may sound, surrealists are persuaded that, as Breton observed in his first *Manifesto of Surrealism* (1924), "What is admirable in the fantastic is that there is no more fantastic; there is only the real."[6] Reconciliation of Breton's remark with Brunius' is facilitated by consideration of a declaration by the latter: "For the spectator, the mental representations provoked by the pictures on the screen tend to commingle with the habitual representations he has of the exterior world thanks to his perception of it. He is henceforth in a position to carry over into reality the fiction of the screen" (p. 112).

Breton assures readers of his *Second Manifeste du Surréalisme* (written in 1929) that the general question surrealism has undertaken to raise is *"that of human expression in all its forms"* (p. 183). Taken in conjunction with Brunius' remarks, Breton's statement helps reveal the surrealist film script for what it is: a sign of confidence in the adaptability of cinematographic language to surrealism's requirements. As in verbal poetry, the visual poetic effect foreseen results from the collision, to use Antonin Artaud's word, of elements uprooted from their normal environment and presented in uncustomary relationship to other elements, equally displaced. Through such a presentation, Artaud contends, one may hope to replace the "worn-out language" which is no longer pertinent to man's need to communicate with his fellows.

From surrealist scripts and scenarios the cinema emerges as a medium it is well worth the surrealist's while to explore. Artaud opened a scenario he wrote in 1927 "La Coquille et le Clergyman" with the words "The lens discloses. . . ." Although not every surrealist script writer draws attention to his method so explicitly, they all engage in composing scripts because of their faith that films can answer their demands. Ideally any way, practice of the language of surrealism in the cinema is identified with revealing something unprecedented, rising "subterraneously from the images," as Artaud put it graphically. Each scenario deserving of notice is an experimental exploratory rearrangement of nature. In it the categories to which we normally assign everything recognized as true to life are in danger of being dismissed as irrelevant to imaginative experience. Meanwhile, communication between author and reader is anticipated in that indeterminate zone where clear thought is forced to surrender its prerogatives and is acknowledged to be ineffectual.

A vital surrealist film script functions as a stimulant to the imagination, its existence giving weight to Paul Éluard's declaration in *Donner à Voir* (1939) that the poet inspires far more than he is inspired. Readers must be content to share the submissiveness of the hero in Artaud's scenario "Les dix-huit Secondes" before the display of contradictory images seen within. Only in such a state of receptivity can response to the surrealist script be profitable. Stilling any impulse he may have to heed reason's protest, the reader must be prepared to let his sensibility experience the osmosis of imagery. He will then enjoy the "pure play of appearances" recommended by Artaud, which can be appreciated only after effective inoculation against the contamination of strictly reasonable sequence.

The existence of a sizable number of film scripts, scenarios, outlines, and sketches makes it easier to understand why, in his essay "Comme dans un Bois," Breton deplored the "incontestable baseness" of cinematographic production only "on a secondary and accessory plane." Reading some of them, we can appreciate why, despite his disappointment with the movie industry, he retained his faith in the movies as among the best means of promoting what he called, out of respect for Arthur Rimbaud, "real life." Moreover, examination of surrealist scripts leaves us with a clearer impression of the following. In the passage from realism to surrealism, what matters above all is the direction the surrealist's glance takes. To all surrealists, their scripts and scenarios testify, the real is but the departure point for the unforeseen, the unknown, and even the unknowable.[7] So we are reminded that in his *Nadja* Breton speaks of "perpetual solicitations" which seem, he tells us, to come from "outside," immobilizing us for an instant or two before one of "those fortuitous arrangements of a more or less new character, to which it seems that we would find the answer by thoroughly questioning ourselves."[8] As we ask what we make of the scripts we read, we measure our own capacity for surrealist response. For if the poet "works by contagion," as the surrealist Éluard declared, the poetry of the surrealist script can have no effect upon someone immune to the "direct poison" which Artaud felt the film capable of transmitting.

Considering the script as indicative of how the cinema may be fashioned into an instrument for what Breton called "the auscultation of the imaginary," we situate it more accurately in relation to the surrealists' effort on all fronts to extirpate "the cancer of the mind" mentioned in the Second Manifesto—the cancer of thinking that "certain things 'are', while others, which so easily could be, 'are not'" (p. 221). To bridge the gap between what manifestly is and what could be: this is the purpose of the "dream of mediation" which all surrealists share with Max Ernst, whose undertaking Breton summed up in this phrase. In the movies, the mediative effort is designed to reconcile man and his unvoiced desires, rendered tangible through the concrete imagery of film. This is why the surrealist script lends weight to Breton's bold affirmation that surrealism is "what will be."

Whether as makers of movies, as authors of film scripts, or simply as members of a movie-theatre audience, surrealists share with Artaud the wish to create a world that results from imaginative transformation of elements supplied by objective reality. In surrealism purposeful play subverts appearances, lessening our trust in them by capturing an impression of the surreal, concealed behind the façade of the real. It draws us into a game in which minds like those of the surrealists, tired of mere "representational play," can hope to find pleasure and reward. Hence the surrealists' confidence in the cinema takes nourishment from the belief that one can look hopefully to the movie camera to disclose something previously undetected, or even unsuspected.

In surrealism, the film's function is to place before one of man's trusted senses—seeing is believing—the persuasive testimony called by Éluard *l'évidence poétique*. To begin understanding why such evidence qualifies as poetic, one can do no better than consult Breton, who has made a confession that every surrealist would gladly countersign: "For me the *only evidence* in the world is governed by the spontaneous, extra-lucid, insolent relationship established in certain conditions between this and that, which common sense would hold us back from bringing face to face."[9] In the degree that it denies common sense the right and power to restrain imagination, surrealism denotes a perspective upon the world and man's place in society having the effect, in the cinema perhaps better than anywhere else, of opening reality upon unreality, of raising the real to the level of the surreal. Everything thus depends upon the freedom with which the surrealist poetic spirit permits the spectator to make associations which rational thought processes would abjure or dismiss as impertinent. Hence Breton's first sentence in "Signe ascendant": "I have never experienced intellectual pleasure except on the analogical plane."

It will appear strange that the French surrealist leader should call his pleasure intellectual, until we recognize that in surrealism all man's faculties for response—intelligence no less than any of the others[10]—must be bent to opening forms and symbols, thanks to the "poetic influx" which, surrealists agree, gives meaning to effort in every field of creative activity. Typically, Breton prefaced his poems in the 1932 collection *Le Revolver à Cheveux blancs (The White-haired Revolver)* with the statement, "Imagination is not a gift but an object of conquest par excellence." No less typically, he asserted in his *Introduction au Discours sur le Peu de Réalité* (1927) that "everything depends on our power of *voluntary* hallucination."

Surrealists are not whimsical people, incapable of thinking consecutively or consistently. They are revolutionaries who want to unseat reason from the throne of the mind, requiring it to abdicate before the authority of imagination, to which they prefer to make obeisance. This is why hallucination—making contact with a private view of the world, imaginatively oriented—is to them a voluntary act. Just like the gallery-goer or the reader of a volume of surrealist poems, the movie-goer who places his trust in surrealist ambitions engages knowingly in this act, in a mood of confident anticipation. By doing this, he intimates that he refuses to be reality's dupe. If there is only one alternative open to him, he prefers to be imagination's dupe, since imagination seems to hold out more attractive rewards. Surrealism at all times emphasizes *image* rather than *word*, feeling rather than thought, instinct and desire rather than reasonable commonplace.

Dedicated to erecting bridges to a realm lying beyond the limits of day-to-day reality, surrealists center their hopes regarding the cinema upon faith that the film can poetically span the distance separating speculation from reality, desire from its realization. To understand better what desire means in this context, we must take into account certain themes favored in surrealism, which lend themselves especially well to illuminating it. These are themes frequently treated in the commercial cinema.

Since the form of desire that comes to mind most quickly is no doubt the one associated with love, it is natural that surrealists identify the pursuit of love in the movies, no less than in verbal poetry, with fulfilment of desire. "Give us films that come up to our torment," demanded Desnos in *Le Soir* on May 7, 1927. "What is the good of hiding any longer the surrealist torment of our time, in which the cinema has a big part to play?" Breton, for his part, refers to "turning our way of feeling upside down," and has in view, as much as anything else, a radical change in our manner of treating feelings, a reappraisal of their importance in our lives. At all times, the surrealists' attitude is one of revulsion for the limitations imposed by society upon the free play of feeling. It denotes rebellion against the controls imposed and maintained in our relationships with other people. This is why, under favorable circumstances which will call for definition below, surrealists see love in films as providing access to a privileged universe. When love—the least reasoned and reasoning of our responses, perhaps—takes over and guides behavior, it become a revelatory agent. It becomes a disruptive agent at the same time, severing ties of continuity, breaking the mesmerism of the past, and encouraging us to face the future optimistically. Meanwhile, thrown off equilibrium, the everyday world loses its stability, leaving man and woman the hope of controlling their own destiny.

In surrealism, faith in love, taken beyond the limits prescribed by reason, is a token of the conviction that, by placing trust in it, we shall benefit from its intervention in our lives. Love is considered a key to freedom, capable of overcoming all obstacles for those bold enough to bar the door, by whatever means are closest to hand, against oppressive restrictive influences. Breton's "Comme dans un Bois" states categorically that the *"absolutely modern* mystery" celebrated in the cinema rests mainly on desire and love. It asserts, further, that the advantage of the cinema over books and the plastic arts is its "ability to render the power of love concrete." And this alone, we are told, would suffice to sanction the movies, "the stimulant capable of peopling our deserted nights," as Desnos called them in *Paris-Journal* on April 27, 1923.

Surrealism betokens everywhere assimilation of the external world under the compelling attraction of creative imagination, bent on externalizing its dreams, aspirations, and ideals. Here love is not the only theme considered worthy of development on film. Among others, terror and comedy are particularly favorable forms of the commercial cinema, impressive to surrealists as illustrating the collapse of reasoning resistance, as well as dissolution of various inhibitions before the onslaught of desire. Both these are found to be poetic forms to the degree that they demonstrate the necessary removal of emotional, social, and moral obstacles which surrealists delight in seeing cast down. Antonin Artaud's summation of the achievement of the Marx Brothers as "an essential disintegration of the real by poetry" is exemplary and instructive here. Being far less restricted by the real than the theatre, in what it presents, the film is a mode of expression with immense poetic vitality. It gives us confidence to ask the impossible of the movies, as Desnos did. And when we do this, Brunius assures us (p. 114), the enlargement of reality reveals the marvelous.

Desnos defined the marvelous as surrealists speak of it when he wrote of it in the *Journal littéraire* on April 18, 1925, as "the supreme aim of the human mind since it gained possession of the creative power conferred upon it by poetry and imagination." The scarcity of films through which its spirit breathes is especially regrettable, Desnos affirmed, because the marvelous is the "admirable passport [. . .] for access to those regions where heart and mind liberate themselves at last from the critical and descriptive spirit that pins them down to the ground." Emergence from darkness to light at the end of a movie performance, surrealists are convinced, should mean confronting the problems which the film has raised, not escaping them. It is pertinent therefore that Desnos presented the marvelous as a passport, one which will enable us, hopefully, to "pass freely without let or hindrance" (as Her Britannic Majesty demands) between the everyday world we call reality and the domain of desire. To discuss surrealism in film is therefore to examine the surrealists' understanding of the marvelous, and to aim at comprehension of what they ask of it.

Had the film seemed unlikely to provide satisfactory answers to their questions, if there had seemed little chance of its meeting their demands, or projecting an exciting image of the marvelous, the earliest surrealists would not have been slow to turn their backs on the medium, dismissing it as unworthy of attention. However there is so much evidence that they looked to movies in a mood of optimism that Philippe Soupault can hardly be accused of exaggerating when recalling, "The cinema was for us an immense discovery at the moment when we were elaborating surrealism. [. . .] we then considered the film as a marvelous mode for expressing dreams. [. . .]

we thought the film would propose extraordinary possibilities for expressing, transfiguring, and realizing dreams. One can say that, from the birth of surrealism, we sought to discover, thanks to the cinema, the means for expressing the immense power of the dream."[11] Beginning with an examination of the surrealists' reaction to the avant-garde and commercial cinema will help us define the surrealist dream more clearly and establish to what extent surrealists regard the film as suitable for conveying it.

Surrealism and the Commercial Cinema

As a group, the first-generation surrealists were relatively slow to take formal notice of the cinema, and to voice faith in its capacity to meet their requirements. Around 1925, at all events, they were less prompt to formulate a consecutive theory of the film than of painting, for example. Strikingly lacking is any extended statement codifying surrealist opinion on the movies, comparable with Breton's series of essays on surrealism and painting. Reviewing his experience as a surrealist, during the period when Breton was preparing his *Surrealism and Painting*,[1] Georges Sadoul admits, "However doctrinaire we were, in many areas, we were far from being in agreement when it came to the cinema," adding emphatically that "surrealism did not have, properly speaking, a cinematographic doctrine."[2]

Unpromising as it sounds, this statement underscores one essential fact. In spite of the absence of general agreement upon the cinema, more than one of the original surrealists very soon came under the spell of films. Philippe Soupault and Louis Aragon were particularly fond of the movies, as of course was Desnos. Behind these major figures came certain younger men, who embraced surrealism during the years immediately following the appearance of Breton's 1924 manifesto. They included the Prévert brothers and a future historian of the cinema, Sadoul. Naturally the presence among the surrealists of men destined to become active in films after their separation from the group proves nothing, so far as the emergence of a specifically surrealist policy for the cinema goes. Without claiming otherwise, we can make a useful deduction from their participation in the surrealist venture. Among surrealists during the twenties, there were indisputable signs of curiosity about films. Already they were wondering about the relevance of the movies to the program they had in common, asking basic questions, and starting to look for answers. Opinions haphazardly expressed by individual members of the group, in their own publications and elsewhere, testify to growing responsiveness to the medium. Review of the movies they had seen was slowly leading to crystallization of a set of criteria serving to assist the surrealists in judging films coming to their notice. These criteria presented them with the occasion to discuss what they wanted of the cinema, and how they might attain their ends. They also provided the basis for a program eventually governing the surrealists' own experimentation in film production, and helped to clarify demands which have molded surrealist speculation around the theme of an ideal cinema, even better adapted to their requirements.

Although the *Manifesto of Surrealism* did not reach the bookstalls until late in 1924, several years in advance of Breton's summation of their aims those who were to be its active defenders were marked by a distinctive outlook upon reality and upon man's relations with the real. It is not immaterial, therefore, that the text hailed as the first specifically surrealist work, *Les Champs magnétiques (The Magnetic Fields)*, written in collaboration by Breton and Soupault in 1919, includes a direct allusion to the movies: "We were shown around factories producing bargain dreams and stores filled with dark dramas. It was a magnificent cinema in which parts were played by former friends. We would lose sight of them and then find them again at the same spot."[3] Although the cinema is not the central motif in *Les Champs magnétiques,* the passage cited is worthy of notice. It captures the wonder liberated in film audiences during the youth of the cinema, when movie houses were places of mystery to which the surrealists were naturally drawn.

"The eye exists in an untamed state. [. . .] It presides over the conventional exchange of signals apparently required by the navigation of the mind. But who will draw up the scale of vision? There exists what I have seen many times [. . .]. There exists also what I am beginning to see that is not *visible.*" So runs, in condensed form, the first paragraph of Breton's *Surrealism and Painting.* It points up the fascination of the film for surrealists, who could not remain for long incurious about a mode of expression with preeminently visual attractions, inviting associations which—they were quick to see—did not have to be rational. "One day," Soupault noted very simply in the magazine *Sic* in January 1918, "[. . .] man was endowed with a new eye."

By the early twenties, those supporting Breton were firmly convinced that literature had fallen into discredit. Might not the cinema assume the role of translating beliefs and aspirations which literature had become unfit to communicate? Asking this question, they soon realized it could not be answered until they had discovered how effectively the movies might be adapted to the requirements they must impose upon it. Hopeful of renewing modes of human expression, the first surrealists viewed with distrust any attempt to tame the eye. Hence the distinction drawn in one of Desnos' articles between "frenetic cinema" and "academic cinema." Hence, too, condemnation of those who confuse poetry with literature. This, Desnos pointed out, is the approach of the man of letters: "He declares that poetry is only literature; he declares that art is copying nature, naturally [sic]; he declares that the duty of the artist is to represent man in his dirtiest and most mediocre occupations; he puts his grubby fingers on the white apparitions or likeable phantoms of the night, on the pure faces of exceptional creatures, and everything disappears."[4] During the twenties the form of cinema that most completely fitted the definition "academic," as Desnos used it, was the so-called avant-garde cinema.

Foremost among those who have criticized avant-garde trends from the surrealist standpoint was Jacques Brunius, who has discussed its weaknesses at some length in his *En Marge du Cinéma français*. Detailed examination of Brunius' diatribe can be left to the interested reader. Only his general conclusion need be reproduced here, as distinguishing certain categories into which vanguard cinematic practice can be divided. Brunius identifies two tendencies within these: "the one toward renewal and broadening of subjects—the other toward investigation of the resources of language and technique, toward search for new photographic forms and awareness of rhythm." He points out, too, "This distinction has its importance, for the predominance of the second, then the final divorce of these two tendencies, originally mingled and indistinguishable, will inevitably signify the death of the avant-garde" (p. 68). Brunius does not deem it necessary to add that surrealism, placing its confidence in the tendency toward renewal of the cinema and toward the broadening of its subject matter, holds investigation of the language of the film in contempt. He finds it enough to note, "The cinema, which certainly was not an art, has definitely become one, with all that dignity implies" (p. 14). Brunius' irony emphasizes his viewpoint and shows it to be the same as Desnos'. In the *Journal littéraire* for December 24, 1924, Desnos spoke of Victor Sjöström's *Kölkarlen* (1921) as "a useful example proving that a technically perfect film is not necessarily a good film." Furthermore, he condemned it as lacking "poetic action." Writing in the same publication on January 10, 1925, he made clear once again that he had no more patience than Brunius with those who try to replace poetry with art.

Taking issue with the avant-garde as a technique-oriented, aesthetic-dominated form, the surrealists intimated from the outset that they were determined to defend a totally different conception of the film. Desnos' comments, like Brunius', indicate that they oppose the avant-garde primarily because of what it excludes from the cinema. These comments help us to estimate their opposition at its true value, and to appreciate how they came to promote a program for the cinema founded on ideals to which the avant-garde was patently indifferent.

Marguerite Bonnet is right in pointing out that purely technical and aesthetic problems concern the surrealists very little.[5] But indifference on this score is one of the strengths of the surrealist cinema, not its principal weakness, as Mlle Bonnet is tempted to believe. In the interest of accuracy, she should have added, as Ado Kyrou does when speaking from the surrealist standpoint, that "all technical means are interesting only in relation to the content expressed."[6] Kyrou, indeed, comes much closer to the mark than she, when declaring, "In themselves, they are only forms, therefore the arid ground on which aesthetes and other film hair-splitters find their daily food."

It is particularly useful to cite Kyrou at this point because of the noun he uses at the end of the sentence just quoted: *pâture*. This is a word with a special resonance for those who have read Charles Baudelaire's essay "Salon de 1859," in his *Curiosités esthétiques* of 1869. Here we find:

> The whole visible universe is but a store of images and signs to which imagination will assign a place and relative value; it is a kind of food [*pâture*] which imagination must digest and transform. All the faculties of the human soul must be subordinated to imagination which requisitions them all at the same time.[7]

Awareness of the surrealists' reverence for Baudelaire enables us to perceive where Kyrou is leading.

The ideal film serves the surrealist as a storehouse for visual images upon which, he anticipates, his imagination will satisfy its hunger for the marvelous. Exactly how these images are to be assembled, and with what display of technical finesse, is therefore less important to him than that their presence be felt, providing his imagination with something it can digest and transform surrealist-ically. So far as surrealists interest themselves in methods, they do so asking how the film-maker can best engineer the "irruption of poetry." This, we shall see, it is Robert Benayoun's declared wish to bring about in his *Paris n'existe pas*.

Considering the problems facing the painter, André Masson once spoke of the disparity between content and container.[8] Surreal-ists are convinced they have reason to believe this disparity of pressing concern for the film director also. To the surrealist mind, undue respect for the container—from which, surrealists believe, aestheticism is born—represents far more than formal preoccupa-tions only. Surrealists consider that it fosters a dangerous reluctance to test the container, to see if it can be made to carry more than it was designed to hold, or even something quite different from what it usually is expected to accommodate. To a man, surrealists are far more likely to be moved, therefore, when a film appears to be a vehicle for a content that overspills the mold in which it has been cast. To the extent that aestheticism directs attention away from the poetic potential of film material, it merits denunciation, they contend. They consistently reveal themselves too concerned with seeing things anew to tolerate practices designed to rearrange reality, per-haps, but never to disrupt its familiar orderliness. While contrivance is the hallmark of artistry, they allege, liberation is the consequence of poetry. Just as they distinguish between literature (the exercise of literary technique) and verbal poetry (the revelation of an aspect of the world, previously concealed, which the poet captures with words), so they separate the art of the cinema from the poetry of film. They align themselves with Desnos in regarding "poetic ac-tion," not technical skill, as the ingredient most likely to lend a movie distinction and give it lasting value.

Any move to restrict freedom and to establish limits in which surrealists have no trust is bound to provoke their resistance. Hence anyone whose main purpose appears to be marking technical boundaries and erecting aesthetic fences is the natural enemy of a group who realize that, while a fence effectively keeps out, it shuts in also. More interested in the benefits of freedom than in the virtues of constraint, the surrealists have no regard for directors who respect those boundaries. And there is no love lost between them and critics who assiduously maintain fences, repairing those that seem likely to collapse.

Surrealists make no secret of their contempt for anyone they find guilty of courting critical success. Soon losing patience with a director whose ambition appears to be leading where they do not care to follow, they reserve their approval for film-makers of quite different inclination. An original bias of taste has the effect of stimulating them to admiration of a special kind.

The ideals defended when surrealists praise Luis Buñuel while attacking Ingmar Bergman are brought into focus by a film that neither of these directors could have made: *King Kong* (1935) by Schoedsack and Cooper.

Seeing *King Kong* the year after it was made, one surrealist, Jean Lévy, reported experiencing no disappointment or disillusionment, while watching it in the company of a few technicians whose observations provided a running commentary on the special effects used in filming it. Lévy could see for himself that the quality of these effects is very uneven: "The animals show signs of painful stiffness," he observed, "all the more inexplicable because certain movements are strikingly true (I am thinking of King Kong's action in exploring the rocks with his hand and receiving a knife wound). As for the effects of back projection, if they fit in with the rest of the film with surprising virtuosity, the least skilled eye will not fail to be troubled by the confusion in perspective ignored by the camera men during filming. The first prehistoric monster felled, for example, sweeps away the hunters and a good part of the audience with its tail." Lévy concluded with an avowal backed up by his essay as a whole: "Nothing of all this, by the way, worries me."

Lévy's article on *King Kong*[9] says more than we need attend to, for the moment. It does not say, though, that surrealism bids us accept artlessness as a guarantee of the successful achievement of desirable ends in the cinema, or as a necessary prerequisite for them. Whether clumsy or skilful from the professional point of view, technical effects prompting the audience to ask how they were produced attract a surrealist less than others which leave him convinced they have results that his ideals justify regarding as beneficial. As a surrealist, Jean Lévy saw every reason to throw critical reserve to the winds, once persuaded that function takes precedence over aesthetics in the application of film methods in *King Kong*. All surrealists concur in this. What matters is not identification or professional evaluation of technical procedures like those by which special-effects man Willis O'Brien brought Kong to life, but how one can interpret the results to which film techniques may lead.

Breton insisted in the name of surrealism upon placing "the manifest content" of life second to its "latent content." In doing this he intimated that we must ask how films serve to convey the latent content of existence, so as to penetrate the reasons why surrealists give some aspects of film-making enthusiastic attention, while remaining quite unmoved by others. It is in this connection above all, then, that their responsiveness to movies like *King Kong* can provide invaluable assistance.

Surrealists turn without delay or regret from any movie where substance contradicts their beliefs or runs counter to their cherished hopes. Indeed, they have always seen it as their first duty to attack a film, upon finding its director guilty of using his artistry to plead implicitly for indulgence toward postures they reject as false or degrading to man. No surrealist could condone, for instance, the production of a film like Carl Dreyer's *La Passion de Jeanne d'Arc* (1928), of which Brunius wrote unequivocally in his *En Marge du Cinéma français*, "Here it's a question of affectation of style, of photographic Gongorism without any relationship to the meaning of the images, testifying to the silly pretentiousness of the author. It pleases me to repeat once again here that *The Passion of Joan of Arc* is one of the most *stinking* films I've ever seen" (p. 85). On the other hand, all surrealists unstintingly praise any movie in which they find some measure of agreement with attitudes and aspirations they defend. This is a sign that, through the film passing before their eyes, they pursue an ideal which surrealism has taught them to follow.

It is easy to see in *King Kong* "the very antithesis of the director's picture." In fact it was a non-surrealist who characterized it in this way.[10] Nor is it difficult to see that, for this very reason, surrealists would be predisposed in its favor. But to learn from this movie all it has to teach, one needs to understand still more. We cannot estimate how much more without grasping that *King Kong* stands as proof that, in surrealism, the director's handiwork may take on a significance he is a long way from foreseeing. Why mention a film like this one, surrealists give us to understand, if not to reveal its involuntary surrealist elements? And why discuss it in detail, unless analysis of its unintentional surrealist features confirms the vital presence of surrealism in the cinema?

"The pleasure one experiences in an 'open' film," wrote Robert Benayoun in the forty-ninth number of *Positif*, "in bringing out the imperceptible, and in elucidating the invisible thread of the story, corresponds almost to that of creation experienced by the author himself in his work." The film which prompted Benayoun to say this was Antonioni's *L'Eclisse* (1962). By any standards, this film is of a quality to prove that the surrealist method of discordance is not confined in its operation to movies which conventional critics feel safe in dismissing as unworthy of notice. But for surrealists the measure of value is not the technical competence of the director. Nor is it what we customarily call his integrity. It is, to borrow from Benayoun, the openness of the film he puts before us. Movies that are determinedly "closed," like those submissively attentive to the horror and misery of everyday life or simply to its dull monotony, cannot be expected to lend themselves to the process of re-creation by surrealist discordance. All the same, the surrealists have no reason to be discouraged. They find that many films are "open" to a man who identifies poetry with the manifestation through the world of reality of forces which surrealism has fitted him to detect and bring to light.

When surrealists talk of dreams and dreaming they refer to their ambition of bringing these forces to light. To them, dreaming means promoting an active program intended to facilitate the realization of distinctive aspirations. In other words, surrealists come to the cinema with the hope that films can be relied upon to play a positive role in helping them transform man's awareness of reality. For this reason, anyone who cannot enjoy *Peter Ibbetson* (1935) because it happens to have been a popular success will make slow progress with surrealism in the movies, and is likely to have serious trouble comprehending why Breton judged Henry Hathaway's "prodigious film" to be "a triumph of surrealist thought." On the other hand, admirers of Claude Lelouch's *Un Homme et Une Femme* (1966) will have to adjust their thinking, if they are to appreciate that, from the surrealist standpoint, this movie is no less irredeemably pernicious than David Lean's *Brief Encounter* (1945).

Search for evidence that reflects the surrealist spirit and identification of the nature of the surrealist dream demand that, by the side of films of less disputable value in the eyes of conventional critics, other films be examined which normally standards of good taste as well as of technical competence would eliminate from serious discussion. Flat denial of the charm exercised over the surrealist's imagination by an infantile film like Raffaele Matarazzo's *La Nave delle Donne perdute* [*The Ship of Lost Women* (1953)], hailed by Kyrou as "pure involuntary poetry," limits appreciation of what surrealism stands for in the cinema. Signs of involuntary surrealism may appear in an unexpected quarter like the American sex-movie business. To neglect such signs, because a film like Russ Meyer's *Mud Honey* (1964) offends intelligence as much as it lacks good taste and runs counter to the moral values of our society, would mean excluding valuable evidence which it would be shortsighted to discard.

The earliest surrealists were no more indiscriminate in their taste for films than the most recent members of the group have been. Neither were they inclined to impose or respect narrow limits upon the sector of the commercial cinema they would be prepared to examine. Doing this would have called for a systematized approach to the movies entirely lacking in Breton and his friends. They did not come to the cinema persuaded in advance that features lent value by their convictions could be sought with confidence here rather than there, detected without fail in this type of film rather than that. All the same, it was evident from the first that certain categories of movies held a special appeal for surrealists. Themes and treatment characteristic in three of these categories provide evidence sufficiently varied on the surface, yet significantly unified beneath, to enable us to ascertain what surrealists have never ceased asking of the commercial cinema and what they have found that it provides.

Terror

Not infrequently these days, revivals of so-called classic horror movies are accompanied by earnest or arch appeals to the public for a willing suspension of disbelief, as though viewing films of this type has become something of an act of charity. The tendency to excuse such movies, even to apologize for them, makes one think that audiences are assumed to have traveled far since the golden age of cinema horror, when the public could be counted on to surrender without reserve to emotions the director strove to liberate in them. Time and again we witness the effect of a propensity to condescend, shared by director, producer, distributor, and exhibitor alike. Supposedly it is born of some feeling of superiority in which present-day cinema-goers are presumed to share. Whatever the origins of the attitude of reserve now displayed before filmed horror, one clear consequence is dissipation of the mood essential to enjoyment of its characteristic atmosphere. Apparently no longer thinking it wise to rely on uncritical receptivity, nowadays stigmatized as a sign of naïveté, film directors, while not invariably intending to debase the genre, very often imply they propose to modify its function. The methods adopted by current practitioners of horror in the movies stem from a fundamental revision of attitude. This has reached the stage where the term "horror film" denotes an arrangement of conventional devices, presented in stock situations, with little pretence to novelty. All in all, the net result, however obtained, is total loss of the genre's paramount virtue, its sincerity.

Those inclined to believe current practices are making us

witnesses to the collapse of a form, once respected but now outworn, are mistaken. It is more fitting to talk of a new emphasis, likely to modify that form radically. The new emphasis is enlightening because it shows the effect of a dual influence. Audiences have become so inured to the application of well-tried formulas that directors have been quick to realize there is today little chance of any but the most unsophisticated enjoying a horror movie except as detached observers. So far as most reasonable people still feel some interest in filmed horror, they have accustomed themselves to take pleasure from the skill evidenced in the orchestration of proven effects. In the circumstances, directors attracted to the horrific mode can be sure of having no need to seek originality in theme, since they can rely on being judged, rather, upon their technical expertise. Film-maker and audience agree on one important thing: horror has engendered a fixed cinematographic form, as respected but oddly dated as the sonnet in poetry, and no less distant from us.

Distance is the essential revelatory feature making the new emphasis visible to everyone. It gives prominence to a significant characteristic of horror, as now used in the cinema. No one expects it any longer to captivate an audience as it once did. Instead it is treated as a convenient frame, within which the virtuosity of a practiced master can be displayed for admiration. In France especially, where film directors customarily receive more notice than the stars they control, horror movies tend to elicit a kind of response universally detested by those least reasonable of men, the surrealists.

Surrealists deprecate the fashionable approach tending to empty the horror film of content the better to concentrate attention of form. The term "horror movie" has changed in associative meaning. It no longer serves to evoke the mode of cinematographic creativity they consider capable of contributing substantially to the satisfaction of some of their needs. We advance appreciably to where the surrealists await us, if we adopt the less familiar term "film of terror" as identifying more accurately certain movies that take on special value in the context surrealism creates. This is because surrealists treat terror as a welcome and propitious emotion, admirably communicable through film and particularly suited to highlighting fundamental preoccupations from which their aspirations take strength.

More than one French surrealist has recalled a shiver of delight felt upon reading a caption flashed on the silent screen during *Nosferatu, eine Symphonie des Grauens* (1922). As Sadoul reports it, the whole surrealist group in Paris, including the unfrocked priest Jean Genbach, attended a revival of this film in 1928 or 1929.

Already *Nosferatu* enjoyed an enviable reputation among members of the band, although they were still unacquainted with F. W. Murnau's name. What is more, they were unperturbed by the possibility that the caption they found so exciting ("On the other side of the bridge, the phantoms came to meet him") might have been absent from the original version. What mattered was that this phrase typified the compelling fascination of *Nosferatu* and of all the films of terror surrealists judge worthwhile—the evocation of the marvelous, "heart and nervous system of all poetry," as Benjamin Péret has described it.[11]

When Desnos lauded *Nosferatu* in *Le Soir* on May 21, 1927, it was because he felt none of its technical innovations to be arbitrary. "Everything," he noted with pleasure, "was sacrificed to poetry and nothing to art." On March 5 of the same year, he had remarked, also in *Le Soir,* "We witness, in the cinema, the great struggle which, in every domain, opposes intelligence to sensibility (and I intend to oppose here only two words taken strictly in their exact meaning), poetry to literature, life to art, love and hate to scepticism, revolution to counter-revolution." All the technical advantages of the cinema seemed meaningless, then, so long as they did not express the very spirit of the cinema as Desnos defined it, "the links binding it to the solemn elements of disquiet."

Mention of the aspect of poetic protest surealists call the marvelous, as it touches upon the theme of terror, sends us back for clarification to *King Kong,* and to Jean Lévy's assessment of this film.

King Kong is a movie about an oversized gorilla, which carries off a white woman who takes his fancy. Subsequently captured, the animal is brought to the United States, only to escape from the New York theatre where it is being exhibited as a freak. Searching the city for the young woman, it spreads destruction everywhere, before finally climbing with her to the top of the Empire State Building. Here it provides a squadron of fighter planes with welcome target practice, apparently much needed, before falling to its death. "I had so definitely given up the idea of seeing a poetic film," begins Lévy's one-page article on this pot-boiler, "that, beyond any attempt at criticism, I cannot help pointing to the appearance of this rare phenomenon, greeted, as one would expect, with howls of derision and contempt. I hasten to say that what gives this film value in my eyes is not at all the work of the producers and directors (they aimed only at a fairground attraction on a grand scale) but flows naturally from the involuntary liberation of elements in themselves heavy with oneiric power, with strangeness, and with the horrible."

Despite ludicrous elements meticulously noted in his article,

Lévy insists upon the profound effect *King Kong* had upon his sensibility, relating this to a fairly common nightmarish dream. He suggests that those who scoff at this naïve movie are merely taking refuge behind criticism of its technical unevenness so as to avoid giving in to a feeling of disquieting strangeness (*étrangeté inquiétante,* he calls it) which, he says, speaking on the surrealists' behalf, "we cherish and cultivate, for our part, so carefully." Whether the monstrous Kong was to be taken for a real animal or for an automaton, it makes no difference to Lévy. "In any case," he explains, "whether the monster is true or false, the terror he provokes takes on no less of a frenzied [*délirant*] and convulsive character through its very impossibility."

Readers who have read Péret's *Anthologie de l'Amour sublime* (1956) and Breton's *L'Amour fou* (1937), with its stress upon love as *délirant,* noting too that the surrealist leader's *Nadja* (1928) closes with the words "Beauty will be CONVULSIVE or will not exist," will appreciate that we have not finished with *King Kong* yet. They will know, too, how to weigh Lévy's words when he speaks of the essential feature of terror as its capacity to release in us a sense of the marvelous.

Lévy insists that elements he finds admirable in *King Kong* are present in spite of directorial supervision, not as a result of it. It is not going too far to say, therefore, that the interference surrealists abhor in the movies can come no less from the film director than from his audience. Just as they may underestimate his accomplishment, so he may underrate his own achievement and, more to the point, may work against it. When a director goes so far as to impede communication of the surrealist potential of his movie, he must expect to hear the surrealists protest loudly.

With its studied artistry and a manipulative technique taken to the level of pure ostentation, Roger Vadim's version of Sheridan Le Fanu's *Carmilla,* called *Et Mourir de Plaisir* [*Blood and Roses* (1960)], shows what can happen under such conditions. Seeking to impress with his undeniable artistic command, in one visually striking dream sequence Vadim divides our attention between what he is doing and how he is doing it. Thus he reduces our feeling of involvement in the disturbing mood he has undertaken to create. Reproving Vadim's method, surrealists argue as follows: so long as there must be technical command, then let it be of the kind practiced in Roger Corman's *The Fall of the House of Usher* (1960). Here, at least, it serves to heighten the atmosphere of terror, not undermine it by intrusive emphasis upon the presence of the director.

Unfortunately, this is exactly what occurs in a more recent film of Corman's, *The Trip* (1967), which has done much to improve his reputation with French movie critics. The lamentable collapse of *The Trip*, in which a trite dénouement confirms the flimsiness of plot structure which the director's professional dexterity cannot conceal, underlines the immediate risks only too well.

Nothing should be allowed to distract audiences from the prime qualities of terror films, as these are identified by members of the surrealist circle. Surrealists gladly surrender reasonable resistance, out of a desire to see the non-reasonable and anti-rational triumph in every aspect of their lives. Their desire colors their responsiveness to terror movies. They are touched by elements exerting a more subtle pull than those surface features stridently advertised by commercial distributors, who know from experience that receipts are swelled by provocative allusions to "shock" effects. However, this is a long way from saying that, in their way, surrealists preach the sterling virtues of restraint and good taste. On occasion, the very opposite is true, and with good reason.

Those interpreting taste and restraint as society demands are bound to note the absence of both from many movies which surrealists admire far more than examples of stylized elegance such as *Et Mourir de Plaisir*. One film in particular comes to mind, since it captures excellently a heady atmosphere more congenial to them than the chilling climate of Vadim's movie. Whereas *Et Mourir de Plaisir* is assured a place in film club programs, this movie is more likely to run at a drive-in theatre, as often as not heralded by advertising appealing unblushingly to the prurient: *L'Orribile Segreto del Dottor Hichcock* (*The Abominable Dr Hichcock*), made in 1962 by Riccardo Freda, using the pseudonym Robert Hampton.

The Abominable Dr Hichcock does not keep its audience waiting long before treating them to the sight of the surgeon interrupted when about to remove a sheet to gaze at a nude female cadaver. Soon after they are introduced to the world where the surrealist adjectives *délirant* and *convulsif* take on dark hues, as Hichcock draws others with him like a nightmare—first his wife: with every sign of pleasure, she allows herself to be injected with fluid producing symptoms like those of death, so that her husband may fulfill his desire, after ritualistically laying her out on an ornate bed, bedecked as in a funeral home; then his second wife, married after the first has apparently departed this life, presumably having succumbed to an overdose of anti-elixir.

We find here no sign of the gentlemanly good taste characteristic of Terence Fisher, putting to intelligent use the superior qualities of Peter Cushing, the uniquitous cerebral hero of a succession of English horror movies. All the same, Freda spares us the sensationalism of by-products of American puritanism like Herschell G. Lewis' *Blood Feast* (1963), through which the hideous consequences of moral pressure, substituting perversion for sexual normality, find expression. True, the final sequence of Freda's film is extremely violent. But it is redeemed by a note of humor, parodying the suspense dear to the heart of a successful director whose name, suitably misspelt, is borne by its hero. Hichcock suspends his second wife by the feet, with the intention of cutting her throat, so as to use her blood to rejuvenate his first spouse. The latter, very much alive after all, but grotesquely disfigured and evidently demented, stands ready to assist him. Luckily a fire rids the world of both of them, so that Barbara Steele may live to play another role.

Freda is content to end his film with a horror-movie cliché, ironically providing the standard happy ending for people who need to go home believing everything comes out right in the end. Not being among those, the surrealists are more inclined to enjoy the "black humor" of the closing scene than to be displeased or disappointed by the conventionality of its ending.[12] From the very first shot they have been alerted to a distinctive mood, by the sight of a grave-digger struck down by a shadowy figure, who proceeds to open a coffin beside a half-completed grave, and to embrace the beautiful female corpse inside.

Reviewing *L'Orribile Segreto del Dottor Hichcock* in *Positif*, Gérard Legrand called it "a hymn to necrophilia."[13] A surrealist well aware of the element of parody involved, Legrand might have let us parody an old song ("All the nice surrealists love a necrophiliac . . . "), were it not that parody would be no excuse for false conclusions. To the surrealist, perverse passion assumes a special function here. Those who misconstrue it fail to grasp the meaning surrealists read into this tale of terror.

Always confusing eroticism with the salacious, Vadim has not even succeeded in transporting to the screen the uncomplicated fascination with sexual taboo of Zola's *La Curée*. Abetted by Roger Vailland, he has made a disastrous attempt to adapt Sade, trying to combine both *Justine* and *Juliette* in his *Le Vice et la Vertu* (1963). Disregarding the emphasis given *Carmilla*, he uses Lesbianism in *Et Mourir de Plaisir* simply to hint at the forbidden, never treating it as more than a titillating adornment. Freda acts quite differently, when he makes necrophilia the principal motivating force of Hichcock's conduct. He deliberately places his main character's passion outside the bounds of socially acceptable behavior.[14] The result is a mode of conduct entirely controlled by what Legrand accurately calls "a mysterious passion, of a type far more oneiric than morbid." As a picture of human existence dominated by a dream of possession, this film uses terror to provide an object lesson no surrealist can regard with indifference. To all who have been touched by surrealism it must appear of the greatest significance that Hichcock takes his perverse pleasure in a room accessible through a door concealed by a full-length mirror. Freda holds out the prospect of passing through the looking-glass, without demanding of us the tribute to Victorian inhibitions exacted by Lewis Carroll. The respectable erotic of the commercial cinema, where desire is threatened with summary emasculation the moment it becomes necessary to bring about reconciliation with bourgeois values and religious teaching, offers little stimulus to the surrealist's imagination. Fortunately for him, the erotic force of *L'Orribile Segreto del Dottor Hichcock* makes its effect felt at quite another level, and works in a different direction. It presents the equivalent of the marvelous frenzy which in eighteenth-century English Gothic literature opened the door on suggestive symbols of desire and conquest.

Like those of *King Kong*, the overt themes of *L'Orribile Segreto del Dottor Hichcock* command the surrealists' attention far less than its depiction of inner forces, releasing upon the outside world a dream of possession externalized in sexual deviation. This is offensive enough to respectable social feelings to isolate Hichcock, investing him with a curious grandeur, best explained, no doubt, by Desnos:

> Lost in a deep forest, whose floor is made of moss and pine needles and where the light, filtered by high eucalyptus trees with hanging bark, by pines as green as the meadows promised the souls of good and free wild horses, by oaks with knotty bodies tortured by infernal maladies, sometimes is yellow like dead leaves, sometimes white like the edge of woods, the modern traveler seeks the marvelous. [. . .] He seems to recognize the domain promised his dreams by night. Night falls thick and full of mysteries and promises. A great searchlight pursues fabulous creatures. Here is Nosferatu the Vampire; here is the asylum where Cesare and Dr Caligari met memorable adventures; here, rising up from poetic caverns, are Jack the Ripper, Yvan the Terrible and their old friend from the *Cabinet des Figures de Cire*.
>
> The modern traveler, at last carried away by the powers of poetic tragedy, is at the heart of the miraculous regions of human emotion.[15]

It is going too far, of course, to ask that Hichcock be granted tragic status. Indeed, from the vantage point of surrealism he appears a singularly free representative of human endeavor. His presence in Freda's film reminds us that Desnos wrote in *Le Soir* for February 26, 1927, to praise two early French serials, much admired by surrealists in Paris during the twenties (*Fantômas* and *Les Vampires*) as well as an American serial starring Pearl White (*The Exploits of Elaine*), boldly asserting, "There are no vices except to the impotent; sensuality, on the contrary, is a justification for all forms of life and expression. To the former belong literature, art, and all reactionary manifestations; tradition, classicism, the shackling of love, the hate of liberty. To sensual persons, on the other hand, belong the profound revolutionary pleasures, the legitimate perversions of love and poetry."[16] Desnos' article is not designed to enter a plea for pornography. Instead, it leads to a concluding statement of policy for the cinema, worth reproducing in full:

> This is why we refuse to consider the spectacle on the screen other than as the representation of desired life just like our dreams; this is why we refuse to believe that any rule, any constraint, any form of realism can reduce it to the level to which writing has fallen since the novelists, those good business men, brought public discredit on poets; this is why we ask the cinema to exalt what is dear to us; this is why we want the cinema to be revolutionary.

In following Desnos, we have left behind as immaterial the question of the moral values seemingly defended in *L'Orribile Segreto del Dottor Hichcock*. No less definitely excluded, now, is the argument that would decry the lack of realism in its script. Desnos is talking about the standards by which surrealists condemn movies that present a constant menace to their ambitions, because the director either seeks to placate those we call, for want of a better term, serious film-goers, or decides to appeal instead to sensation-seekers.

Wondering in *Le Soir* on February 5, 1927, whether it was not natural that the cinema should have tried to project dreams, Desnos asked rhetorically, "But if the attempts are rare that have not failed completely, is it not from misconception of the essential characteristics of the dream, sensuality, absolute liberty, the baroque even, and a certain atmosphere which evokes as a matter of fact the infinite and eternity?" He used a comparison to stage lighting when, utilizing the adjective "surreal" for the first time in his film reviews, he blamed the failure of movies purporting to communicate dreams on their not being situated in a "surreal light." Any film in which this

light does shine claims and holds the surrealists' notice. The famous
Caligari, for example.

Desnos praised Robert Wiene's *Das Kabinett des Dr Caligari*
(1919) for the poetic virtues of its script. In the *Journal littéraire* for
January 31, 1925, he defined these virtues as the absence of scepticism and acceptance of the reign of mystery, giving intensity to the
dramatic action of Wiene's movie, making it "one of those in which
emotion comes closest to terror." Desnos was not alone among the
early surrealists in commenting favorably on *Caligari*. When he
called its plot perfect, one of his friends, René Crevel, agreed. However, while Crevel, too, judged *Caligari* "une œuvre parfaite," he
made this important proviso: "on condition one arrives in the middle
of the film and avoids the preface."[17] The premise of *L'Orribile Segreto del Dottor Hichcock* is no less unsound than *King Kong's*, while
the plot structure erected on it is no more resistant to intelligent protest. In the circumstances, it is noteworthy that Crevel found *Das
Kabinett des Dr Caligari* to be marred by a "préface d'une sottise
si raisonnable." The very purpose of the film's introductory section
—to supply a reasonable explanation for all that follows—made it
silly to him. Thus his response allows us to draw the moral which
Cavalcanti's *Dead of Night* (1945) holds for surrealists.

In *Dead of Night* an architect, invited on business to a
country house in Kent, discovers that the house and the people he
meets there are familiar to him. They all figure in a nightmarish
dream he has had several times. Punctuated by tales of mysterious
happenings recounted by the other characters, the architect's nightmare is re-enacted once again. It is brought to a close when, awak-
ened by his wife, he finds himself safe in his own bed. A phone call
invites him to come down to Kent to advise on remodeling a country
house. The film closes as he is admitted to the house he has visited
in his dreams. It leaves us anticipating the terror from which we
thought the morning light had released him.

By an interesting coincidence, Desnos wrote in *Paris littéraire*
as far back as April 27, 1923, before the word "surréalisme" had be-
gun to be current in the sense Breton's associates reserved for it, "I
should like a director to take a fancy to this idea. In the morning
after a nightmare, let him note exactly all he remembers and let him
reconstruct it with exact care. It would no longer be a matter of
logic, of classic construction, or of flattering the incomprehension of
the public, but of things seen, of a higher reality, since it opens a
new domain to poetry and to dreaming." Curious as it is to notice
how closely Desnos' instructions seem to have been followed in the
final sequence of *Dead of Night*, we should not be giving the latter's

achievement full credit, if we omitted to note that this film goes further still, to provide a remarkably effective lesson in the terror one wakes up to, not from.

Freda's Hichcock is no surrealist Perceval. Whatever the motives behind the filming of *L'Orribile Segreto del Dottor Hichcock,* they most certainly were not surrealist in origin. Desnos' extended reference to Perceval's quest emphasizes something else. Following the line of thought surrealism dictates, had he lived to see *L'Orribile Segreto del Dottor Hichcock,* Desnos would have been bound to regard Hichcock's conduct as paralleling that of the surrealist hero, on the trail of the marvelous. The results of preconditioning upon a surrealist's reaction to those terror movies which fire his imagination may be anticipated with confidence. Their very predictability underlines what surrealist interest in the terror film serves to prove.

Pandering to vulgar taste, mere sensationalism offers no better outlet from oppressive reality in a film of terror than elsewhere. Surrealists became attentive only when they are satisfied the director has accepted honestly the task of inducing through terror a salutary state of anxiety. This sharpens sensitivity to the presence of unsuspected forces in life, and to the possibility of unprecedented solutions to life's problems. The regard they have shown for movies like Paul Leni's *The Cat and the Canary* (1927) rests upon appreciation of films which show how anxiety takes root in terror, so intimating that terror is infinitely preferable to the depressing burden of acceptance in the world of mundane reality. By the same token, good taste denotes ready conformity with society's values, sometimes closing the door upon cinematic effects of great promise, while bad taste seems more appropriate to the ends they have in mind: militating against hypocrisy in censorship, for instance, instead of treating the latter as added spice for questionable purposes.

All surrealists are convinced the cinema should disturb, not reassure. It should bring attention to a disquieting aspect of life, rather than to its familiar face. More, it must accept responsibility for challenging the validity of the real, in the interest of uncovering the surreal. Hence terror strikes the surrealist as one of the emotions most apt to release responses it is the province of the cinema to elicit. The terror film does not exemplify all the qualities surrealists call poetic. But in its invitation to disregard reasonable reserve before the cinematic image and in its ability to hint at a mode of human existence normally concealed by everyday contacts, it sets us on the road to appreciating the surrealist sense of the poetic in films. Terror prompts surrealists to evidence a special sensitivity to movies, which becomes clearer as we examine the other extreme of response, evoked by comedy.

Comedy

In Desnos' article "Mack Sennett Libérateur du Cinéma," printed in *Le Soir* on April 15, 1927, two sentences especially suggest at first that nothing could be less representative than this text of the tone and emphasis now familiar to us in surrealist film criticism: "We well know the madness presiding over his scripts," wrote Desnos of Sennett, "It is the madness of fairy tales and of those dreamers whom the world holds in contempt, and to whom the world owes what is delightful in life." Nothing here seems likely to persuade the objective witness that Desnos takes his stand at a notable distance from reputable historians of the cinema, nostalgically looking back to the days when, as the sentimentalizing phrase goes, comedy was king. Nor can his essay on Mack Sennett lay claim to signal independence of judgment by rescuing some forgotten comic from obscurity. Like later surrealists commending the Marx Brothers or saluting the prodigious W. C. Fields, Desnos paid homage in his film reviews to the same comedians as the professional critics of his day.

Superficial scanning of the available evidence seems to point to the conclusion that specifically surrealist ambitions really count for nothing, when comedy comes under consideration. But more careful scrutiny shows the surrealists asserting their individuality in subtle ways. Speaking of comedy, they do not convince us of the independence of their views by championing the neglected or the unknown, from tilting valorously at windmills in order to claim validity for arguments which few outside their group would accept without demur. Their originality lies in a special angle of vision, shedding the light of surrealism upon the work of some of the most successful comedians in the movies. For this reason, identification of the salient features of surrealism's attitude to film comedies calls for sensitivity to profound differences, very often concealed beneath surface agreement with professional critics of unimpeachable respectability.

When we turn, say, from the surrealists' admiring comments on a striking essay in terror, *The Most Dangerous Game* (1932) by Schoedsack and Pichel to ask how they react to Chaplin or Buster Keaton, much of what we have learned to recognize as characteristic of surrealist response bears reiteration. Clearly, comedy shares with filmed terror qualities that a surrealist regards as of the greatest promise. The comic film impresses him as much more than an amusing movie when it liberates impulses capable of changing life's pattern, nullifying controls exercised in the everyday world by reasonable conjecture.

From the beginning, the struggle in which they have been engaged with convention and with conditioned reflexes in thought, feeling, and attitude has made surrealists respond with alacrity to humor. Impressed by the subversive potential of humor, they have tried wherever possible to turn this to account. Through word games like *Exquisite Corpse* and *Si . . . Quand,* for example, they have submitted the mechanism of laughter to analysis, so as to discover how it relates to their purposes.[18] Since the founding of the surrealist group, games of this kind have typified determination to put comic effect to use, in protest against a soberly reasonable universe. Considered against the background of surrealist jokes—expressed as memorably in the pictorial collages of Heisler as in the verbal play of Desnos' *Rrose Sélavy*[19]—film comedy promises to be a noteworthy form of involuntary surrealism; so long, that is, as it steers clear of the sentimental.

At the very most, films indelibly marked by sentimentality take politely timid liberties with social convention, carefully confining these to the level of whimsy. Since sentimentality denotes compromise, and sometimes even blind acceptance, society can afford to tolerate movies of this variety. In fact, it encourages their production, because, in the long run, they argue for acceptance of social values, often rehearsing them in the last reel, for the audience's edification, just in case some misunderstanding subsists.

Any comedy is totally alien to surrealism in which comic effect functions as a safety valve for a boisterous restlessness that social custom finds it safer to release than repress. The films of Fernandel in France or Norman Wisdom in England, for instance, represent an attitude toward society that can best be described as placatory. As for Laurel and Hardy, their comedy holds an important lesson. The very "purity" for which it is generally esteemed—the absence of dedication to any other cause than amusement—attractive though it is to some film authorities, denies most of their work relevance to surrealism in the film. Their *Two Tars* (1928) never faces the consequences of its heroes' destructive activity in a traffic jam, any more than it supplies an explanation for it. On the contrary, every care has been taken in this film to deprive violent behavior of social significance: it comes from nowhere, and leads nowhere beyond indulgent laughter. By conventional standards a classic comedy, *Two Tars* leaves no impression on the surrealist's mind. It makes no appeal to his imagination, because it does not exemplify an attitude toward the world in which he can place his trust and with which he can identify.

Surrealism defends a comic mode which necessarily appears impure, next to the typical Laurel and Hardy vehicle. This is because, without imposing hard and fast rules, surrealists demand one condition at least, whatever form comedy takes on film. Rather than bolster society's usages, the movie must supply proof that it stands for a critical attitude before social custom. Whenever a comic film questions social conventions or accepted modes of conduct, it enters regions where surrealists demand proof of the comic hero's commitment to combat repressive forces, ranging all the way from common sense to social, political, or religious obligation. Because he deems these forces a hindrance to the expression of the spirit of poetry, a surrealist tends to associate poetry with their rejection. In the measure that a film offers resistance to forces surrealism considers repressive, it will merit respect and warrant examination designed to bring its poetic content to light. And so evaluation of a filmed comedy worthy of serious attention consists in assessing its poetic virtue. In its turn, the latter can be defined best, surrealists argue, by someone sensitive to the protest embodied in the movie he is watching.

Brunius indicated what is at issue here when recommending that certain American comedy shorts be called poetic or lyrical films. As defined by Brunius, the characteristic of these short features is that they "incite us to question logic and reason all over again" (p. 67). By mentioning Chaplin, Keaton, Langdon, and Sennett among the leading comedians in whom he had faith, Brunius testified that his standards were those which had induced Desnos to call Sennett a liberator of the cinema. And there is no question but that Desnos spoke for all surrealists when declaring in the *Journal littéraire* on February 14, 1925, "It is remarkable indeed that the comic film tends to become uniquely poetic."

A celebrated scene in *Modern Times* shows Chaplin as a factory worker pursuing a fat woman with the evident intention of using his spanner to loosen her nipples.[20] Surrealists interpret this sequence as going beyond gratuitous laughter to relate a ludicrous impulse to criticism of the oppressive monotony of the Little Man's role in production-line industry. Furthermore, they view the accompanying release from inhibition, admirably suggested in Chaplin's diabolical expression, as a token of healthy revolt.[21] A comparable effect is produced in *Putting Pants on Philip* (1927), reportedly Laurel's favorite among the films he made with Hardy. Stanley is cast as a compulsive kilt-wearing woman-chaser, whose erotic impulses Oliver is incapable of curbing. Having lost an undergarment without knowing it, Stanley inadvertently steps over a grating. A rising gust of air treats two ladies to a sight that throws them into a faint. Emphasized by Oliver's prudish embarrassment, and even more by the look of beatific contentment on Stanley's face, the implications of this scene (shot, in a Los Angeles street, by the way, instead of a studio lot) are not lost on the audience. Without the laughter provoked during this incident, many would share the disapproval which makes Oliver tug frantically at Stanley's kilt.

Stanley's self-satisfied expression shows him to be more than an unintentional exhibitionist—a contradiction in terms, after all. It conveys an unambiguous message, in much the same way as the mental derangement causing Charlie to confuse nipples with nuts. By their behavior, both Laurel and Chaplin challenge common inhibitions, just as Harpo Marx often does. In full view of two audiences, we remember—the one in the film *A Night at the Opera* (1935), the other in the movie house—Harpo reaches out to tear off a dancer's tights, his attention having been caught by a pose he finds provocative. Or would it be more accurate to say that the pose is, for him, merely an inviting one since, throughout his film career, Harpo enjoys a full measure of the innocence which made Stanley flagrantly violate decency in *Putting Pants on Philip*? Almost immediately and unreservedly responsive to his desires, Harpo Marx has provided surrealists with one of their great screen heroes.

Harpo, Stan, and Charlie all provoke laughter and contravene sexual taboos at the same time. Comedy, they show, is capable of releasing feelings which good manners usually demand we suppress. Resembling in this the terror movie, the comic film creates a privileged domain, offering the chance of surrender to desire, instead of restraint. When Harpo withdraws from a concealed pocket of his voluminous coat first one leg taken from a window dresser's dummy, then a horse-collar, and finally the other leg, he hints so unequivocally at the sexual motivation of kleptomania that it is doubtful anyone would dare make such a direct allusion except within the framework of comedy.

The comic focus makes us witnesses to the cinematic equivalent of the operation of an essential creative process in the surrealist verbal poetic image. Here, as Breton has emphasized, the word *like* functions as a verb—the creative element making something unforeseen result from a bold comparison. At the same time, the world of comedy guarantees the verbal revolt of Groucho Marx and W. C. Fields complete freedom. Outside its limits, their offensive outbursts would be subject to penalty as infractions of society's code of acceptable behavior. Within these limits, Fields' aggressive rejection of the niceties of human contact—finding expression of hate for children among its most impressively uncompromising forms—allies with the magnificence of Groucho's insults, reserving their most corrosive sarcasms for wealthy matrons.

Following a rhetorical pattern established when Breton listed forerunners of surrealism in his first manifesto, Kyrou pronounced W. C. Fields "surrealist in everything" in *Le Surréalisme au Cinéma* and called the Marx Brothers "his worthy continuators" (p. 98). Looking to Antonin Artaud, we find corroboration of Kyrou's estimate of the significance of the Marx Brothers for surrealism.

Artaud has left an important note on the Marx Brothers, appended to his *Le Théâtre et son Double* (1938). In it he singles out as the distinguishing feature of *Animal Crackers* (1930) "the liberation through the medium of the screen of a particular magic which the customary relation of words and images does not ordinarily reveal." Artaud continues, "If there is a definite characteristic, a distinct poetic state of mind that can be called *surrealism, Animal Crackers* shares in it to the full." According to Artaud, the poetic quality of a film like *Animal Crackers*—better still, we might suggest, *Duck Soup* (1933)—would fit his definition of humor as "essential liberation" and "destruction of all reality in the mind." Going further, he sees the originality of *Animal Crackers* in "the notion of something disquieting and tragic, a fatality (neither happy nor unhappy, difficult to put a name to) hovering over it like the cast of an appalling malady upon an exquisitely beautiful profile."[22]

Is Artaud reading into a movie of his choice his private sense of tragic destiny? Not necessarily; for he is not the only one among those whose outlook has been marked by surrealism to relate comedy to a tragic sense, mingling sad and laughter-provoking elements. All surrealists tend to see the essential contribution of comedy as deriving from a combination of gaiety and sadness—the supreme gift of Chaplin and Keaton. In "Mack Sennett Libérateur du Cinéma," Desnos speaks for the group, when declaring that Sennett "has introduced into the cinema a new element that is neither the comic nor the tragic, but, to be accurate, the most elevated form of the cinema, on the plane of ethics, of love, of poetry, and of liberty."

The amalgam of amusement and seriousness identified by Desnos is a form of gravity, taking its coloration from surrealist ambitions. Those ambitions deny a pessimistic view of the ultimate potential of man, faced with a universe hostile to his desires. Never-theless, they reflect at the same time a clear-sighted appraisal of everything that tends to oppose man's fulfillment of his desires, or tempts him to give them up and settle for more accessible satisfac-tions of an ephemeral nature. Anything working against the at-tainment of surrealist ideals must be discredited without delay. Wherever it persists in intruding, it must be eliminated, no less from comedies than from other films. Hence the surrealists' swift condem-nation of any film comedian they find guilty of placing artistic ac-complishment before the expression of the revolutionary spirit they call poetry.

In 1925, the Vieux-Colombier theatre offered a program of three films to illustrate the evolution of Chaplin's comedy. Desnos was enthusiastic about the first two, reaffirming the surrealist viewpoint in the *Journal littéraire*, on January 10. "Everything turns to en-chantment. It is not a matter here, of seeing a film well made, or well photographed, but of following the heroes' adventures fever-ishly." Of the last film, *The Kid* (1921), he was critical, speaking in terms similar to those he had reserved for Buster Keaton in the same publication, the previous November 29. In late 1924, Desnos char-acterized Keaton's development as a movement "from genius to talent," linking the former with the absence of technical concern, with imaginative freedom, and delightful eroticism, while defining the latter as the surrender of these virtues. What is more, the tech-nical command displayed in Keaton's most recent work struck Des-nos as an alarming sign: "We sense the work of art, that is patience. Henceforth the actors are incapable of carrying us along with them. They simply move about before us: this is literature." Alluding to his earlier statement, he wrote on January 10, "I have already said, with regard to Buster Keaton, what discomfort we experience at seeing those we used to be accustomed to see live now acting. From the moment when Charlie Chaplin and Malec [the name by which Keaton was known in France during the twenties] became con-scious of what they were doing, they lost their creative power. Art then replaces poetry." All surrealists agree, as they agree that Bena-youn's observation regarding animated films applies generally in the movies: "Formal research, it is permissible to believe, is incom-patible with the spontaneous exercise of humor."[23]

In spite of significant reservations about Chaplin's work, the surrealists' respect for him remains deep and abiding. Within a few months of expressing alarm at tendencies exemplified in *The Kid*, Desnos was writing in the *Journal littéraire* on June 13, "It is com-monplace to speak of genius with regard to Charlie Chaplin: it is difficult not to do so." However, Desnos' reasons for admiring Chaplin took him beyond recognition of the virtues critics usually extol. He specifically stressed the social significance of Chaplin's comedies, basing his estimate of this comedian's greatness on the social consciousness reflected in his films. Indeed, for Desnos the superiority of Chaplin over Keaton, the Keystone Cops, and others who unwittingly communicate the spirit of surrealism is that he, "their master, is a moralist."

Those who prefer *City Lights* (1931) to *Modern Times* (1936) are out of sympathy with the surrealists' preference for a form of comedy that assesses life as it comments upon man's place in the world. Anyone wanting to understand better why surrealists prize the latter movie has only to contrast it with René Clair's *À Nous la Liberté* (1932). This is so not only because, as Kyrou observes, like all Clair's comedies, this one is too intellectual. Essentially *À Nous la Liberté* is a "charming" movie, with all the elements of compromise and acquiescence the adjective implies. After the fashion of Hollywood musicals, it ends its protest against obligatory work with a song. The lulling quality of Clair's film confines it to the level of significance intended for it. In contrast, when Chaplin walks away down the road with his girl, he leaves us at the end of *Modern Times* with an idealized optimistic view of protest against industrialization, and against everything else that stands between man and the achievement of complete happiness.

Where Chaplin seems most at ease in society his satire loses much of its force, as well as its direction. In *Limelight* (1952), the touching pathos that endeared Charlie to the public is replaced by an insidious sentimentality, typified in the theme song which Chaplin unwisely has admitted to writing. On the other hand, when he keeps clearly in sight the need to oppose social custom, his later work finds once again the mood of iconoclasm from which surrealists see his comedy as taking its strength. Two movies represent the revival of this mood. Significantly, neither of these has escaped censure—a sure sign of the hypocrisy Chaplin has made it his task to uncover.

Those whom these movies attack most directly are sharply critical of them. In the United States, and Great Britain too, *A King in New York* (1957) has not fared well, while in France *Monsieur Verdoux* (1947) is considered Chaplin's failure. The word "failure" is invoked to conceal a sense of grievance, easier for the Anglo-Saxon critic to recognize in his Gallic colleague than in himself, and vice versa. The vulgarity used to bait complacent, materialistic American society in *A King in New York* is condemned as a sign of bad taste. Hence it serves its purpose, provoking the injured party to revealing retaliation. Meanwhile the French film critics, bourgeois by instinct, refuse to see Verdoux as funny. Ado Kyrou reports that pupils of the Institut des Hautes Études Cinématographiques in Paris are informed of the technical weaknesses of *Monsieur Verdoux*.[24] Their instructors' stratagem, transparently obvious, is quite ineffectual, so far as surrealists are concerned. By far the most meaningful feature to the latter is the conclusion of the film. Verdoux, an artist in his original way, leaves his cell for the scaffold, after accepting a drink because he has never tasted rum. Abandoning the pose of pretentious affectation assumed with biting satire as the movie progressed, Chaplin is led off to execution, shoulders bowed, feet turning out— a reminder of the Little Man adding its poignant comment as the film closes.

For the surrealist, the poetry of the last shot in *Monsieur Verdoux* eludes identification by analysis of the composition of the frame, by consideration of the camera angle, or use of lighting. The elements which hold the formalist critic's attention are there, to be sure. And they make their effect. But the dominant element, to surrealists, is identification of Verdoux, the wife poisoner, with the victim of society habitually impersonated by Chaplin.

In the silent shorts of the twenties, Charlie, the aggressively impudent rebel, kicked backsides and slapped corpulent dowagers. His early films, like those of Sennett, lent substance to Desnos' claim in "Mack Sennett Libérateur du Cinéma" that slapstick is, "in short, but the most disconcerting form of lyricism." During the thirties Chaplin created another character, more disturbing because less self-assertive, yet sharing with his predecessor one essential feature. As a social outcast, he becomes an outsider—a representative of the category to which Verdoux also belongs: judging the society that has judged him and found him unacceptable. The poetic nature of the *persona* continues to be uncontaminated by social intercourse, and still takes definition from opposition to society's practices. Sadness is a constant ingredient in the characters Chaplin plays, hinting at the elimination of individuality under the weight of social demands. It is a contributing factor in the "metaphysical humor" that, an article by Desnos in the *Journal littéraire* (February 28, 1925) reminds us, is the form of humor surrealists will always find profoundly moving.

The critical point where comedy commands the surrealists' respect is that at which it defeats the vigilance of censorship, whether this be the censorship exercised by the Hays Office or the deep-seated censorship within, sometimes making us unwilling participants in our own liberation. Some will not hesitate to accuse

Artaud of exaggeration for calling the end of the Marx Brothers'
Monkey Business (1931) "a hymn to anarchy and wholehearted revolt." And perhaps indeed full response to this hymn can come only
from surrealists in whose name Artaud wrote apropos of the Marx
Brothers, "and when the poetic spirit is exercised it always leads
toward a kind of boiling anarchy, an essential disintegration of the
real by poetry." In any case, Desnos said much the same in the
Journal littéraire on December 6, 1924: "It seems that, from its very
invention, the cinema found perfection in the comic," intimating that
all surrealists see the cinema as perfectly adapted to the function of
projecting a revolutionary content which attains the value of poetry
while combatting reality.

Placing side by side *The Exploits of Elaine, Les Vampires, Caligari,*
and the work of Chaplin, Keaton, and Sennett, Desnos insisted in
the *Journal littéraire* on March 21, 1925, that these are all "equinoxes
of the human mind since the time when it succeeded in recreating
dreams, in endowing its imagination with a life as real as that of
matter." In fact he first used the term "metaphysical humor" to de-
scribe Clair's *Le Fantôme du Moulin-Rouge* (1925) which is not a
comic movie at all. Never concerned with genres or with distinction
between them, all surrealists share with Desnos an overriding passion for the poetic. As Desnos puts it in his review of *Le Fantôme
du Moulin-Rouge,* the poetic "naturally, commits [*engage*] all that
is deepest in man." Although this review was edited to a third of
its length, before being turned over to the printer, it still makes its
main theme very plain. By giving to the idea of *engagement* a sense
which no existentialist would entertain even for a moment, it shows
why comedy is so highly regarded by the surrealists. All of them
would subscribe to Desnos' evaluation of Sennett as the "true genius of the cinema" because all agree that nothing can elude the
restraining force of our reasonable universe so efficiently as film
comedy. All therefore share the optimism underlying Desnos' pre-
diction: "The time is close when the cinema will escape for good
from the real, as the comedies of Mack Sennett already allow us to
foresee."

Love

The privileged locale of the terror film leads the surrealists to anticipate special rewards. So does the privileged universe of comedy.
But privilege has its price. Many will claim that the worlds of terror

and comedy are too remote from everyday experience for us to find in them benefits that will directly enliven our humdrum world. Elements ensuring man full liberty of action in comic and terror movies may well seem to stand as obstacles between the audience and complete identification of their destiny with that of characters on the screen. To argue that the latter's conduct is merely of symbolic value for surrealists does not resolve the difficulty entirely. They will be dangerously exposed to the accusation of escapism unless they can show that surrealism applies itself without prevarication to meeting the challenge of life. To give full force to the opinions we have seen advanced so far and to protect these from misrepresentation, advocates of the surrealist program must confront detractors who question their deep concern with man's situation in the world of today. They need to provide incontrovertible evidence that their point of view takes into account important and pressing aspects of the human predicament. This they undertake to do when they discuss love and its place in the movies.

When the influence of the cinema upon other arts was being discussed, Robert Desnos advised in 1925, "Let us speak if you will of the influence of the cinema on mores; it is a real one. Modern love comes from the cinema and by this I do not mean only the spectacle on the screen, but also the auditorium, the artificial darkness." Desnos was repeating himself, taking up one or two points made in an article published in *Paris-Journal* on April 20, 1923. Beneath the title "L'Érotisme," this article had advanced a plea for eroticism, "one of the most admirable factors in the cinema," culminating in the words, "Admitted by Nazimova or Pauline Frederick to an anxious headlong life, we would not know how to satisfy ourselves any longer with banal reality. During the intermission we shall seek out someone among our neighbors who can draw us into an adventure equal to the cinematographer's twilight dream."

Breton related in *Nadja* seeing a woman divest herself of her coat and walk nude up and down the aisles of the Electric-Palace in Paris. Almost a decade later, in 1937, Paul Éluard entered a theatre following a woman who had appealed to him, as she passed on the street. It is easy enough to conclude from evidence of this kind that, following Desnos' recommendation to the letter, surrealists were not averse to seeking amatory adventures in the movie houses they frequented. But there is something more important to notice. Reporting what happened to Éluard, Ado Kyrou declared himself envious of the manner in which Éluard had discovered by chance "that exceptional work" *Peter Ibbetson*, not of his luck in finding female companionship in the theatre where it was playing.[25] Breton, meanwhile, mentions what he saw in the Electric-Palace by way of conclusion to a paragraph of *Nadja* beginning, "I have always wished to an incredible degree to encounter at night, in a wood, a beautiful nude woman, or rather, such a wish no longer signifying anything, once expressed, I regret to an incredible degree not having met her."[26] While Breton expresses his preference for unvoiced desires, his friend Éluard demonstrates *his* responsiveness to desire when an unknown woman unwittingly serves as his guide to one of the most remarkable illustrations of the surrealist concept of love.

To define the special quality of love for surrealists, and to understand how they see its role in human affairs, one has to ask several questions about the nature of desire, asking too about the ways in which it manages to find expression, in the face of what obstacles, at what price, and with what consequences: questions to which surrealism's evaluation of love in the movies helps supply answers.

Citing Desnos with approbation in *En Marge du Cinéma français*, Jacques Brunius recalls how he and Jean-George Auriol followed his lead, when entitling their 1928 series of contributions to *La Revue du Cinéma* "Le Cinéma et les Mœurs" ("Cinema and Mores"). Their intention was to dissociate themselves openly from a fashionable tendency to analyze the form of the film at the expense of all its other aspects. Taking their cue from Desnos and from the Communist Moussinac, they set out to give prominence to the poetic, moral, and sociological significance of films. It seemed to them high time to introduce into film commentary a stress indicative of surrealism's attitude toward love in the movies.

In 1927, just before Auriol and Brunius began their column, the English-language Parisian periodical *Transition* printed a text called "Hands Off Love." It was signed by the surrealists, who reprinted it in their own magazine, *La Révolution surréaliste,* in October of the same year. "Hands Off Love" was designed to defend Charles Chaplin against attacks by his wife, as summarized in statements she and her divorce lawyer had just published in *Le Grand Guignol.* It fulfilled its function by ridiculing Mrs. Chaplin's outraged feelings and taking issue with bourgeois morality, as the surrealists spoke glowingly of an aspect of Chaplin's films they esteemed highly: the manner in which he represented and responded to love. "We think of that admirable moment [. . .]," it said, "when suddenly at a party Charlie sees a very beautiful woman pass by, as tantalizing as can be. Suddenly he abandons his adventure to follow her from room to room and onto the terrace, until she disappears. At the beck and call of love, he has always been at the beck and call of love, and this is what his life and all his films proclaim with one accord."

Foreshadowing the conduct of Harpo Marx, whose instinct for self-preservation, however mad the chase in which he is the quarry, is never proof against the charms of a pretty face, Chaplin's behavior in his movies unremittingly testifies to a faith in love going far beyond reasonable limits. The optimism of the last shot of *Modern Times* gives more than an inkling of what surrealists mean when they refer to love as a poetic experience.

Surrealists in the twenties did not have to rely on Chaplin's films alone to convey the lyrical quality of love. Breton, who once remarked that people too often forget how much surrealism is given to love, adding that "what it stigmatizes passionately is exactly that which may damage the cause of love,"[27] advised his associates to see Frank Borzage's *Seventh Heaven* (1927). Soon afterward, in 1929, he worked with Albert Valentin on a screen adaptation of Jules-Amédée Barbey d'Aurevilly's strange tale of love, *Le Rideau cramoisi (The Crimson Curtain)*. From the first, as head of the surrealist group in France, Breton gave careful attention to love in the movies, and to considering the manner in which the surrealist view of love can be transmitted by film.

There were numerous films in which the early surrealists could find their approach to love reflected, at least in part. All the same, their viewpoint made Chaplin's case a special one. Off screen as well as on, he appeared to personify protest in the name of love against social customs and moral values that seem to all surrealists to have a hollow ring. Hence "Hands Off Love" testifies that they are moved by love only when it impresses them as enjoying or militating for freedom from the contamination they attribute to social, moral, and religious custom. They do not balk at characterizing such contamination as a sign of hypocrisy, and therefore as the negation of love in the form they find most inspiring. Thus they are quick to express distaste for all movies in which love is used to reinforce prejudice, buttress convention, or otherwise persuade gullible audiences to respect and accept the status quo.

As in the sentimental comedy, the happy ending of the love film is treated with suspicion when it leaves society unaffected by the lessons surrealists believe love has to teach. This is particularly so when love is depicted as a weak emotion, capable of inducing those it governs to hold out only momentarily against social, moral, religious or political forces dubbed repressive by surrealism. In such circumstances, reconciliation through compromise besmirches the

image of love. And so surrealists see no reason to concern themselves with movies in which an ill-starred love takes its depressing
course to an inexorably unhappy conclusion. However, a film on
this theme which succeeds with conventional critics—*Brief Encounter*, for instance—provokes them to protest against a degrading picture of love, defining and supporting limitative pressures before
which love is forced to capitulate.

In the surrealists' estimation, love stories of the sort that provides the masses with temporary relief from their dreary lives, while
carefully refraining from offering them any stimulus to rebel against
their mode of existence, have the same defects exactly as sentimental comedies. On the other hand, a film that presents love as expres-
sive of an outlaw spirit which society makes every effort to suppress
frequently earns their acclaim. This is so even when it ends in the
defeat of the lovers, showing them paying the penalty reserved for
their anti-conformity. The theme of Stuart Heisler's *I Died a Thousand Times* (1955) seems hackneyed—that of the lone gangster
efficiently hunted down by the law. Even the admixture of the outlaw's love for a woman, touchingly played by Shelley Winters, appears trite. But to a surrealist this movie is anything but banal.
Kyrou, for example, sees it as the story of a man, "sublime in his
solitude," who finds a love that allows him to "die like a man, rather
than live in chains."[28]

Even more impressive in this context is Alf Sjöberg's *Fröken
Julie* [*Miss Julie* (1950)], where desire irresistibly follows its course,
undeterred even by the inevitable prospect of death.

The surrealist's greatest concern is not so much the outcome
of the plot as the image of love transmitted by the movie he is
watching. Lelouch's *Un Homme et Une Femme*, for instance,
deeply offends surrealist susceptibilities largely because it is im-
bued with a moral atmosphere that every surrealist finds revolting.
Contradicting surrealist convictions, it argues that passion can be
rewarded only after it has submitted to the requirements of a moral-
religious code for which surrealists can have nothing but disdain.

Astruc's *Le Rideau cramoisi* (1952) casts light on the complexities
of surrealism's relations with filmed love from another angle. Com-
paring this movie and an adaptation of Stendhal's *Mina de Vanghel*
by Maurice Clavel and Maurice Barry, Breton expressed admiration
for the heroines of both films. In them he saw "dangerous creatures"
bringing "all the shadows and all the perfumes of the jungle," superior in every way to the familiar movie vamps. But he went on to
comment, "If, with reason, Alexandre Astruc has been praised for

the great respect he has shown for Barbey's text, I am obliged to say that the 'climate' of *Le Rideau cramoisi* did not seem right to me: the scabrous, which is the mainspring of the tale, is sacrificed (perhaps out of fear of censorship?) and the Medusa side of the woman is lost." Missing in Astruc's version the style which gives Barbey's story its heady quality (replaced, it seemed to him, by the dry tone of a theoretical report), Breton was much more taken with *Mina de Vanghel,* "where the passionate tension does not weaken," and where, incidentally, concern for literal transcription of the source material counts for much less. All the same, seeing both films together impressed Breton as an unforgettable experience. "Love," he noted with satisfaction, "takes fire here in the wind which it likes, the wind of perdition."[29]

It was far from Breton's mind to stir up thoughts of guilt and sin, in speaking of perdition. He was alluding instead to the liberation love is instrumental in bringing about, both in *Le Rideau cramoisi* and in *Mina de Vanghel.* Certain films of terror and movie comedies have made clear that surrealists applaud the spectacle of the release of erotic instinct through the shedding of sexual inhibition. So we need expect no hesitation on the part of Breton's companions in confessing to fascination with the erotic.[30]

Gladly acknowledging its influence on their own work, surrealists have no reason to minimize the appeal of eroticism in the mode of love that commands their respect in the cinema. One of their number, Desnos, recalled in *Paris-Journal* on April 27, 1923, "I have already said how much I deplored the prohibition of eroticism.[31] Just imagine the remarkable effects that could be drawn from nudity and what admirable works the Marquis de Sade could produce in the cinema." Later, another, Lévy, was to highlight the "monstrous eroticism" of *King Kong*—not the least mitigated by the disparity in size between Kong and the woman he loves.[32] Kyrou, for his part, discussing "the admirable scene" in which Kong strips away Ann's clothing, remarks, "Sadism-protest which leads to revolt after passing through love is the only one that has value for man."[33]

Kyrou makes it plain that a surrealist is not likely to be persuaded to countenance scandal for scandal's sake. His point becomes even clearer when he refers to Bergman's *Virgin Spring* (1959) and *The Silence* (1963): "These are not love films just because in *Virgin Spring* we see a rape and in *The Silence* one woman masturbates and another makes love in a not very Catholic (or Protestant) way."[34] In *The Silence,* the scene of autoeroticism, to borrow Havelock Ellis' word, is a sterile act, accomplished in isolation. How different is the impression of frustrated desire communicated in an incredible film of Kaneto Shindo's, *Onibaba* (1965). Here a woman, who knows her daughter-in-law is preferred by a virile young man she herself would like as a lover, resorts to rubbing herself against a tree trunk.

The Silence portrays the tragic effects of loneliness through the inability to communicate, presented as our hopelessly irremediable condition. The elements of eroticism introduced to underline this theme serve the very opposite function from the one surrealists reserve for the erotic. In *Onibaba,* an erotic fairy tale terminating in an admirably irrational dénouement in which surrealists will be quick to detect a touch of the marvelous, autoeroticism is a valid sign of a remarkable mood of violence, giving the whole movie unreasoning momentum. In *The Silence,* on the contrary, it brings temporary relaxation and relief of tension to the person on the screen, while casting the audience in the role of voyeurs. Utilized with a cold detachment that makes it difficult to exonerate the director of charges of perverse cruelty—Bergman's sense of scandal being rooted in his obsession with sin—the scene of masturbation we witness leaves us with a variety of uncomfortable feelings, provoking revulsion and disgust, perhaps, but above all guilt. Whatever our response, it turns our thoughts back upon ourselves. And this is far different from the rebellion one feels when seeing the lovers of Buñuel's *L'Age d'Or* (1930), rolling on the ground in sexual embrace, brutally separated by onlookers. If, as Kyrou believes, Bergman's message is "Look at them; like dogs, like dogs," then Buñuel's message must be read as one of protest against the treatment of sexual union as no more than an act of animal coupling.

Commenting on *L'Age d'Or* in his *L'Amour fou,* Breton proclaimed it the only film up until then to exalt total love as he envisaged it. However he corrected himself immediately in this footnote: "No longer the only one, but one of the two since that other prodigious film has been revealed to me, a triumph of surrealist thought, *Peter Ibbetson.*"[35] It is tempting to believe Éluard revealed Hathaway's movie to Breton. But however the latter actually came to see it, he noticed at once how well it transposed his ideas on mad love to the screen. Kyrou, too, has praised the film's "explosive vigor," summarizing its theme as "victory over time and death,"[36] illustrated in "the dazzling union of the couple," Peter and Mary.[37]

Kyrou's is a typically surrealist reading of a screen-play adapted quite faithfully from a novel by George du Maurier. Childhood sweethearts who meet again as adults, Peter and Mary recognize one another thanks to a dream both of them have had. Soon after, having killed Mary's husband in self-defense, Peter is imprisoned for life. His back broken during a beating at the hands of his prison guards, he is confined to bed in a miserable cell, to the end of his days. But he continues to meet Mary in their dreams—no distinction being drawn between daydreaming and nocturnal dreams. Their happiness is unaffected by the distance between them, by the social distinction separating a duchess from a condemned killer, or even by the passage of time. Here especially the advantage Breton saw in the cinema over the written word and over the plastic arts is impressively demonstrated. We are given visual evidence of the miraculous power of love to overcome all obstacles. And we see for ourselves that, in their dreams, the lovers remain as young as on their last meeting, the drabness of their "real" lives effectively obliterated, once they have crossed over into a world where love is subject to no limitations. One day, Mary does not keep their appointment, leaving Peter to search his dream for her in vain. Realizing she is dead (only in their dreams are lovers protected against old age), Peter prepares to die also, in order to live entirely in a world created by love.

Considered on the level of plain common sense, *Peter Ibbetson* is ridiculous. Even Gary Cooper's tight-lipped performance can do little to lend it credibility. However, spared common-sense objections, surrealists can see this film as representative of the form of the cinema praised in *L'Amour fou*, and can give it a meaning born of their deepest convictions. The cinematic form in question is the one which, Breton contended, helps "turn our way of feeling upside down." Hence Hathaway's success in *Peter Ibbetson* rests for Breton and his friends on his ability, for once, to create a universe comparable with Joseph von Sternberg's.

Enthusiastically, Kyrou has characterized Sternberg's cinema universe, "made up of the strange and of eroticism," as purely surrealist, a universe whose creator "burns away the visible envelope to explore all its latent richness" (p. 119). To surrealists, Sternberg's *Der blaue Engel* (1930) is a hymn to the erotic appeal of the Blue Angel, Lola-Lola, played by Marlene Dietrich. They laud Marlene's thighs, and praise her director for caressing them time after time with his camera. So far as they pay any attention to the sad character played by Emil Jannings, it is to express delight at his downfall —a tribute to the disruptive force embodied in Lola-Lola which makes its effects felt by bourgeois society. Naturally, they do not fail to note that Marlene Dietrich has played a similar role in *Dishonored* (1931), where Victor McLaglen commits treason for her.

Surrealists see no fundamental difference between the destructive effect of the Blue Angel's passage through the sorry life of her school teacher and the passage of Kong through New York, leaving a trail of wreckage behind him. The angel and the gorilla both give the word *convulsive* the thrilling quality surrealists all recognize in it. As for elements in *King Kong* which Lévy gladly acknowledges as absurd, several of these may be interpreted as signs of the marvelous potency of love, exceeding reason's power to comprehend, just as it exceeds the school teacher's capacity to resist Lola-Lola's attraction: Kong, in pursuit of Ann, breaking down the great door which, up to now, has kept him outside the native village; or breaking his chains in a New York theatre, so as to search once again for Ann, despite apparently having been shackled quite adequately on board ship; or unerringly finding his way to the woman he loves, seeking her out against the unfamiliar urban background of Manhattan.

None of the films of love mentioned so far owes anything directly to surrealism. They all illustrate some of its attitudes only coincidentally. Albert Lewin's *Pandora and the Flying Dutchman* (1951) on the other hand, reflects a conscious effort on the part of a director—never a member of any surrealist group, it is true—to capture something of surrealism.

Lewin's collection of paintings includes several surrealist canvases. His earlier movies, *The Moon and Sixpence* (1942) and *The Picture of Dorian Gray* (1945), were concerned in some degree with painters and painting. Recalling these facts, Lewin himself has stressed that the first time we meet the Flying Dutchman he is painting the portrait of a woman he has never seen. Insisting this is a purely surrealist aspect of his character, Lewin has explained:

> It was therefore, for me, natural to try to make a deliberately surrealist film. This desire took form in *Pandora*. The surrealist habit of juxtaposing old and new images, which is particularly noticeable in the work of Chirico and Paul Delvaux, has always disturbed me. I found in the character of the Flying Dutchman, who was condemned to live for several centuries, a symbol of this juxtaposition of periods.[38]

The source of Lewin's idea of surrealism is pictorial, not cinematic. This makes no difference to his achievement in *Pandora and the Flying Dutchman*. In fact, all the scenes which he himself singles out as possessing surrealist content or atmosphere meet with unreserved approval from the surrealist camp. And, while incorporated in the movement of the film, almost all of them can be isolated and immobilized as stills, having the disturbing quality reminiscent of the very painters who appear to have inspired Lewin— de Chirico, and above all Delvaux.

In *Pandora* dream experience spills over into waking life in one exemplary sequence. The Dutchman, unable to commit suicide in a dream, awakes to find the dagger he has cast aside lying on the floor beside him. Thus contamination of the real by the oneiric is accepted as one of the basic elements of plot structure and character motivation. The whole film, Lewin tells us, grew out of one image, that of a fire-ball moving quickly in front of the statue of a Greek goddess standing on the sand. This Chiricoesque image he insisted on retaining, despite his backers' belief that it was superfluous. Like Breton in *L'Amour fou*, Lewin showed himself sensitive to the "catalysing role of the find [*la trouvaille*]." And like Breton, he showed himself well able to take advantage of it. Another sequence shows men in evening dress dancing with girls in bathing suits, to the music of "You're Driving Me Crazy," played by a jazz group "erotically arranged" among pieces of old statuary. Each of these sequences contributes directly to the mood of the film and sustains the atmosphere which makes the story of the Flying Dutchman's love a haunting one. Nowhere is the surrealist myth of the redemptive power of love more forcefully expressed than in this movie about a beautiful woman who voluntarily accepts death, so as to release the man she loves from the curse which condemns him to wander the world. And nowhere is the anti-Christian basis of that surrealist myth—so pointedly inverting the religious theme of the Wandering Jew—more aggressively played out before our eyes.

In their adaptation, *Manon* (1950), of the Abbé Prévost's *Manon Lescaut*, Henri-Georges Clouzot and a surrealist, Jean Ferry, transposed an eighteenth-century novel to contemporary society. The conduct of the hero loses none of its significance in the process. Like his predecessor, Des Grieux, Robert Desgrieux sacrifices his faith and neglects his duty so as to give himself over to love. As obligations to the Church (Des Grieux had taken orders) are replaced by obligations no less compelling (Desgrieux, as a member of the Maquis, sets free the prisoner Manon, and leaves with her), Ferry's influence on the treatment of love changes the very texture of a story originally intended to stress the enigmatic nature of its heroine. Hence, while *Manon* was attacked for infidelity to its source and Claude Autant-Lara's *Le Diable au Corps* (1947) condemned for showing what Radiguet's novel concealed under its veneer of aestheticism, the surrealists enthusiastically acclaimed both films, and for the very reasons which offended those who attacked them.

What makes *Manon,* in Kyrou's view, "one of the most daz-

zling images of *mad love*" (p. 131) and links it with the other films
we have been examining is that it testifies to a belief expressed by
Breton in *Point du Jour* (1934): "There is no solution outside love."
As they cannot solve the problem of living outside love, man and
woman must do so within and through love. Following their destiny,
they discover that bourgeois morality is one of the forces to be stigmatized for damaging the cause of love. And they learn that, like
Harpo Marx and Charlie Chaplin, they must be prepared to follow
wherever love may lead.

Because every surrealist movie-goer has come to think and feel in a
special way, no obstacles delay or impede his response to films on his
own terms. In his *Le Surréalisme au Cinéma*, Kyrou, for example,
refers without irony to "deliberately and sublimely idiotic films"
which are to him "the often involuntary equivalent of surrealist collages" (p. 91). Movies falling under this heading range from Richard
Thorpe's *The Prodigal* (1956), which Kyrou finds "far more crazy
than Biblical," to examples—though not necessarily typical examples
—of the sexy-movie mode. The latter are no less interesting for being exceptional exercises in a genre no one may take seriously without risk of censure. They help shed light on surrealism in the movies
from an unexpected quarter.

The debased form of commercialism known contemptuously
as the exploitation film often runs parallel to the ideal surrealist
pattern. For it frequently pays little attention to common-sense sequence in its impatience to precipitate situations which its devotees
find especially rewarding. Naturally, it would be foolish to equate
the display of sexual appetite to which a movie of this sort treats
us with the satisfaction of desire, as surrealists pursue it through
film. But it would be no less foolish to dismiss what movies of this
type have to offer on the grounds that their vulgarity divests them
of all significance and denies them relevance. The surrealists' disregard for good taste saves them from the necessity to argue this
point. Meanwhile the appeal the erotic holds for them ensures that
they will feel no reluctance, guilt, or indignation when watching
events on the screen. Detained by neither reasonable nor emotional
reserves, undismayed by blatant evidence of bad taste, free of the
inhibitions inculcated by moral, social, and religious teaching, surrealists enjoy complete liberty to take from the sexy movie whatever
suits their purpose.

Yet in this area, as everywhere in the cinema, responsiveness
on the surrealists' part is not automatic. It is not guaranteed, because
it does not originate in blind confidence. The surrealist sensibility
requires stimulus so that its capacity to enter into a productive re-

lationship with a film may be demonstrated. Thus the particular value of the exploitation movie is that it claims the surrealist's notice, holds his attention, and exemplifies the power of the film to be a stimulant to his imagination, all at a level which is patently not the level at which it is intended to appeal. Examination of films in this class provides us with a valuable opportunity to witness the operation of the process by which a surrealist can re-create the film he is watching, according to exigencies welling up from within: the process by which, thanks to the admixture of elements that can be traced directly to surrealist influence, reality precipitates poetry.

One film in which poetic precipitation is effected with remarkable efficiency is Russ Meyer's *Mud Honey* (1964). Purporting to relate incidents taking place against a realistic background, the action of this movie is set in the farmland of Missouri, during the early thirties. Yet the characters and their activities are far removed from the normal. Meanwhile the acting frequently falls into the exaggeration typical of movies of this type, as histrionics become a contributing factor to an air of unreality that sets its stamp on the film. Released from the realistic convention, *Mud Honey* is set on a track that promises to take it away from reality, rather than running parallel to it.

The most precious quality a surrealist can find in *Mud Honey* is its excess, the manner in which inner turmoil spills over corrosively into the everyday world. Hence the film crystallizes into moment of extreme emotional tension. Because the characters are pasteboard imitations of real people, the surrealist viewer's attention is drawn obsessively to the expression of feelings which no longer need the support of character or rationally explicable situation to justify his giving them sympathy. He finds the effect it communicates vertiginous, for the very reason that it does not depend upon credibility to convey its message. For the surrealist, the last fade-out marks the explosion of the movie's virtualities, the moment when its latent content displaces its manifest content once and for all.

At the end of Matarazzo's *La Nave delle Donne perdute* women on a prison ship revolt against their captors, subduing them by the novel but practical procedure of stripping, and then seducing them. Regrettably, the end of this film falls short of our expectations. Instead of closing on this level of "sublime idiocy," Matarazzo has his crewmen and girls kneel before the ship's cook (an ex-priest), who prays as the ship goes down. The last sequence of *Mud Honey* shows no sign of such decline. On the contrary, it is at this point that the film takes its full effect for the surrealist, through parody, not through reconciliation. He is alerted to what is implied as the close-up of the victim of a lynching puts us in mind of the Crucifixion. Just as the death of an evil man parodies the sacrifice of the Savior, so the latter's miracles are parodied in the miraculous manner in which a mute prostitute, the film's Magdalen, finds her voice.

Every surrealist who engages in film commentary makes clear that his comments are directed to defining his view of the world and defending it against all others. Robert Desnos, for example, spoke without prevarication when he confessed in *Paris-Journal* on May 13, 1923, "I have always tried not to write criticism. In what touches on the cinema, I have confined myself to emitting desires, to formulating feelings of repugnance, knowing that, if it suffers from art and literature, it also participates even more in human agitation." All other surrealist commentators could say as much. Each of them is an interested witness, not an objective observer. Film commentary in surrealism, then, is an act of commitment, taking direction from the commitment it reflects. And this is as true when surrealists express their opinions collectively as when they speak individually; in "the irrational enlargement of a film" [Joseph von Sternberg's *Shanghai Express* (1932)], published in the sixth number of *Le Surréalisme au service de la Révolution* (1933), for instance, or in the tribute to Mario Soldati's 1942 version of *Malombra*.[39]

From the first, surrealists have been content to communicate their enthusiasm for certain films at the expense of critical detachment. An early representative text by Philippe Soupault seeks above all to communicate the mood released in the writer by a Chaplin short:

> It's rain that greets us in these deserted streets. Birds and hope are far away. In all the towns the restaurant dining rooms are warm. We no longer think, we look at the clients' faces, the door or the light. Do we know now whether to leave or to pay? Doesn't the present minute suffice? All we can do is laugh at all that disturbs us.[40]

Later, though, when they deliberately undertook to "enlarge" *Shanghai Express* by interpreting it irrationally, a group of surrealists proved they were inclined to bring to the consideration of movies something very much like Salvador Dali's paranoiac-critical method. As with Dali, whose critical paranoia Breton esteemed as his greatest contribution to surrealism, they demonstrated the following conviction, which underlies surrealist film criticism. Detection of virtualities concealed from the eyes of others is possible when a surrealist refuses to allow his responsiveness to movies to be limited by surface features of the material under examination.

One can understand, of course, why critical paranoia appeared so significant to Breton and his fellow surrealists and why it exerted a telling influence upon surrealist writing about films. Dali's was a "spontaneous method of *irrational knowledge* based upon the critical and systematic objectification of delirious associations and interpretations."[41] Its effect was to pass through the manifest content of reality in order to probe the latent content that commands the surrealist's attention. "Enlargement" of J. von Sternberg's movie was designed to produce comparable results: a profoundly subjective interpretation in which irrationality displaces reason, desire ousts banal reality.

Desnos has characterized the phenomenon we face when dealing with surrealism film commentary, in an article written for *Le Soir* on April 2, 1927. Speaking of two mirrors facing one another, Desnos was intent above all upon suggesting by his analogy the infinite potential of film projection. However, examining the inferences to be drawn from his comparison, we find it points to a common factor underlying and giving direction to all film commentary of surrealist inspiration.

Before two mirrors can reflect infinity, they must be parallel. Furthermore, to demonstrate the infinite possibility of parallel mirrors to reflect, one has to place an object between them that will render their power visible to all. In the cinema, too, the relationship between spectator and film needs to be regulated just as strictly. Otherwise the phenomenon of surrealist poetry—the object giving meaning to their confrontation—will not be manifest. For this reason, although the comparison Desnos draws is not so close as he would have us believe, it is an instructive one.

Because his outlook on life has preconditioned him to certain responses more readily than to others, making him prize the former far more than the latter, the surrealist takes care to position himself before the film only as it suits his purpose to do. He is not concerned to know whether others would agree that the position he has chosen is either authorized or even permissible. His first duty is to reflect something that becomes visible only when he makes capturing its reflection possible. At all times, he remains totally indifferent to those who protest they cannot see things the surrealist sensibility reflects and who would go so far as to question the existence of what surrealist beliefs enable him to bring out in films. Surrealist film commentary, quite simply, expresses its author's deepest convictions and most compelling needs. This being the case, the surrealists' response to the commercial cinema gives the scope and function of surrealist movie scripts clearer definition.

Surrealist Film Scripts

From the very origins of the surrealist movement, the cinema appeared to all its participants as, in a phrase used by Desnos in the *Journal littéraire* on April 25, 1925, "a perfect opium." Its prime appeal was the ability to release the imagination from pedestrian limitations. Evidence that surrealists viewed the movies in this way comes not only from their published comments on films, but also from private letters like one Jacques Vaché wrote André Breton, containing a passage beginning, "What a film I'll act out."[1] It comes most significantly in the form of texts directly inspired by the movies. These concern us initially, as we take up the question of surrealist speculation around the theme of an ideal cinema, fully adapted to the demands members of the group felt entitled to voice.

"I remember having written as early as 1917," Philippe Soupault tells us,[2] "cinematographic surrealist poems: I considered that the cinema could permit me to express more rapidly and more intensely than writing a sort of surrealist lyricism." One may quibble about the applicability of the adjective "surrealist" to writing dating from 1917. But we cannot overlook the importance of this manifestation of interest in the movies on the part of one of the founders of surrealism. Soupault's "Note 1 sur le Cinéma," published in the magazine *Sic* in January 1918, merits quotation in its entirety:

> One day on a piece of waste ground in Vincennes an individual called Pathé presented to a group of rubber-necks a cinematograph invented by the Lumière brothers: man was endowed with a new eye.
>
> Those who from then on gave their attention to this extraordinary invention made a great mistake: they made the cinema the colorless mirror and mute echo of the theatre. No one has stopped making this mistake yet.

However since the means the cinema places at the artist's disposal are very different from those with which the theatre provides him, it is therefore important to establish a difference between the screen and the stage, to *separate cinematographic art from the art of the theatre.* That is the important point in this first note.

Already the richness of this new art appears to those who can see. Its strength is impressive since it reverses natural laws: it ignores space and time, upsets gravity, ballistics, biology, etc., . . . Its eye is more patient, sharper, more precise. It is therefore the creator's job, the poet's, to use this hitherto neglected strength and enrichment, for a new servant is at the disposal of his imagination.

And without however exceeding the limits of this note, I propose to those who have the material means that they realize this first essay.

CINEMATOGRAPHIC POEM

Indifference

I am climbing a vertical road. At the top extends a plain where a violent wind is blowing. In front of me rocks puff out and become enormous. I bow my head and I pass between them. I arrive at a garden with monstrously high flowers and weeds. I sit down on a bench. There suddenly appears beside me a man who changes into a woman, and then into an old man. At this moment another old man appears who changes into a child and then a woman. Then soon, and little by little, a mixed crowd of men and women, etc., gesticulate, while I remain immobile. I get up and all disappear, I take a seat on the terrace of a café, but all the objects, the chairs, the tables, the spindle-trees in the barrels, gather around and worry me, while a waiter circles around the group with ever-increasing speed; the trees lower their branches, the tramway and the cars pass at top speed, I take off and leap over the houses. I am on the roof facing a clock which grows and grows while its hands revolve faster and faster. I throw myself down from the roof and onto the sidewalk where I light a cigarette.[3]

Beside scenarios and scripts by certain other surrealists, Soupault's text has more historical than intrinsic interest. Indeed, it deserves comparison with poems like his *Westwego,* written between 1917 and 1922, more than with explicit proposals for surrealist films. But he does not purport to have written "Indifférence" with cinematographic adaptation in view. Rather Soupault wished to illustrate some of the benefits the cinema seemed so much better able to offer than the theatre. In consequence, his text exemplifies the kind of stimulus to creative imaginative freedom Soupault believed those looking upon the world with the eye of a surrealist could find in movies. While Walter Ruttmann did adapt two of his cinematographic poems, the significance of Soupault's experimentation with his new literary form is not so much that it serves as an example to film-makers but that it testified to responsiveness among the earliest surrealists to the cinema as an inspirational force.

"Indifférence" takes more from films than it contributes to them. It is a literary text in which freedom from time, space, and gravity—to name only one of the liberties the film-maker can enjoy, if he chooses—guarantees the writer a greater sense of mobility. Texts like this one demonstrate how the movies can aid the creative surrealist writer in breaking down the barriers limiting our perspective upon reality.

We touch here on an interesting feature of the earliest surrealists' response to the cinema. The latter's influence directly affected their approach to prose narrative, as well as to poetry. It coincided with increasing displeasure on their part before the novel as a literary mode conventionally dedicated to realism. There can be no doubt, for example, that American slapstick comedies deeply influenced the form of Desnos' *La Liberté ou l'Amour!*[4] All the same, Desnos' intention was not to write a film scenario. As disrespectful as any other surrealist to categorization in literary endeavor, he saw the movies as a valuable disruptive force to be turned to account in devaluing a literary genre. By and large, then, when we examine material like Soupault's poems or Desnos' *La Liberté ou l'Amour!* we find among surrealist writers quite a number eager to learn from films. We do not find, though, in writers such as these much evidence of ability to bring anything to the cinema in return. Looking to surrealist writing for proposals which will clarify our understanding of the cinematic form considered ideal in surrealism, we progress best through examination of texts by authors, stronger in this respect than Soupault, who have it in them to make a genuine contribution to film. This contribution takes the form of plans for the cinema going further than mere imitation of existing models provided by commercialism. Among the first-generation surrealists three stand out as possessing the necessary qualification. They are Benjamin Péret, Robert Desnos, and Antonin Artaud.

Written in 1922, "Pulchérie veut une Auto" ("Pulchérie Wants a Car") is a scenario Péret published in the magazine *Littérature*

(Nouvelle série, N° 10), in May 1923. Pulchérie is a nanny who loves cars so much she leaves the children for whom she is responsible, to be able to ride in an old automobile owned by Glouglou. During her absence, the children are kidnapped, leaving Glouglou to undergo many trials in his effort to find and rescue them. As a reward for tracking the children down and returning them to their parents, he accepts a new car in which he and Pulchérie drive off.

Summarized in this way, "Pulchérie veut une Auto" seems to hold little interest for us. Only in incidental details are there signs of surrealism. These consist in intermingling effects which suggest influence from a variety of films popular in the twenties. Mack Sennett appears to have inspired one section, Harold Lloyd another, and adventure serials a third. One sequence has Pulchérie at the wheel, driving several times over Glouglou, and ending up in a field with cattle. Here a bull tosses the vehicle and its driver to the other end of the field, where a second bull tosses them back again. This maneuver is repeated five or six times before a third bull throws Pulchérie and her car into a pond. Later, attempting to escape from a burning building, Glouglou jumps on the belly of one of the kidnappers he has killed. As the man's body is swollen with the heat, it bursts, permitting the hero to use his intestines ("There are yards and yards of them and they stretch like rubber") to let the children down to the ground, through an open window. True, one of the children falls, and has to be dug out piece by piece from the hole he makes in the ground. But this being one of the "fairy-tales for grown-ups" Breton advocated, the pieces can be stuck together again with glue, just as the parts of Glouglou's body can be joined again when it breaks in two.

Wherever we have occasion to notice in Péret's scenario evidence of possible influence from the commercial cinema, we recognize at the same time that he goes further in the direction of absurdity and improbability than Harold Lloyd, shall we say, or the Keystone Cops. Péret differs from Soupault in definitely wanting to go beyond the models provided by movies he has seen. While the commercial cinema accounts for "Indifférence," it merely marks a stepping-stone in the direction taken by his "Pulchérie veut une Auto," which antedated the first surrealist manifesto by two years.

More than twenty-five years later, Péret wrote another scenario called "Midi" ["Midday" (1950)], even more uncompromisingly defiant of reasonable preconception regarding the cinema's potential. Here plot is placed second to startling visual and auditory effects. The effects foreseen are blatantly unrelated to narrative sequence such as screen-plays conventionally advance: a double agent working for the police has two bodies, joined at the hip. These speak at the same time, in different voices. The text provides also for a double priest, joined by the buttocks, and a double dog urinating on a double lamp standard.

For our purposes, there is no need to summarize Péret's scenario. Quotation of its first and last paragraphs is sufficient to communicate its flavor:

> A room for music classes with platform and podium. From time to time, the podium sighs. On one side a little narrow-gauge railway runs from the platform to the back of the room, disappears and comes back in the opposite direction. It runs on five rails which are the music clef, where notes stand out in relief. Passing over these notes, the train gives a little jump and emits the sound corresponding to the note. Near the platform, a grand piano, half open, seems to be chewing something, its tail wriggling. The students, men and women, all have different musical instruments and are wearing derby hats. The women are all pretty and wear a fixed smile. The men are ugly and wear strange beards [. . .]. They are making a terrible racket. Some are fighting with violins, guitars, and mandolins. A chair kicked close to the piano, accidentally, is gobbled up by the instrument. Wriggling, the latter brays. A mandolin explodes above the head of one of the combatants whose derby bursts into flames which are fanned with a cornet. When the flames are high enough, a violinist takes a chicken from his case, skewers it on his bow and roasts it on his companion's head. The piano brays.

After such a beginning, we look in vain for plot development that will make sense of all that Péret invites us to visualize. Reconciliation with reason is the last thing he seeks:

> Dying, the students' souls escape in two halves, and each half rises in the air in its turn. The musical instruments also. The students' halves arrive before a double Saint Peter who has the double keys to the gates of a park filled with double trees in blossom. He shows them in. They follow a pathway bordered by double trees from which all the blossoms fall at once before them. The pathway leads to a castle in front of whose drawbridge stands the double god. He is soldered by the ears and has only one beard for his two chins. He is surrounded by double saints wearing double haloes arranged in every possible manner. Above the double god

flies a double dove linked by the tail. In fury, the students join together again and massacre everybody with their musical instruments. The god and the saints fall down to earth and become a shower of hailstones that falls on a procession and breaks it up.

Examination of the short stories written by Péret[5] reveals that "Pulchérie veut une Auto" and "Midi" do not differ essentially from his short narratives collected under the title *Le Gigot sa Vie et son Œuvre*. In fact, both texts are included in that 1957 volume. If there is a distinction to be made between the stories and texts we have been examining it comes from absence of elaborative detail in the latter and from insistence upon visual effect to the exclusion of everything else except sound. In short, it rests on the impression we bring away from our reading that, writing "Midi" and "Pulchérie veut une Auto," Péret is thinking of the cinema, asking us to imagine how they would look on film.

So far as they would lend themselves profitably to screen adaptation, Péret's two scenarios mark a notable advance upon the cinematographic poems of Soupault. But we still have to assign them to an intermediary position between literary exercises and concrete proposals for the cinema. While Péret writes from a standpoint movies have led him to adopt, he does not write as a filmmaker. To locate material more deserving of classification as film scripts, one has to look elsewhere.

When we turn from the writings of Péret to those of Desnos, a major difference is immediately observable. Among the latter are texts that follow much more closely the form associated with the shooting script of a movie. In one case, however, Desnos' aim appears to differ from Peret's only on the surface. This is a script called "Les Mystères du Métropolitain" ("Mysteries of the Metropolitan Underground Railroad"), published in *Variétés* on April 15, 1930.

In comparison with Peret's texts, this scenario for a sound film in color is presented in a manner that might be called businesslike. But, while it is set out like a shooting script, it does not depart very noticeably from the pattern of Péret's "Midi." The tone is very similar, and the same attention is given to outrageous incident detrimental to realistic effect. As an example, the presence of a fish which has escaped from a shopping basket might be cited. It flies through the air along the underground passage ways, as though guiding the subway trains. On balance, we cannot escape the conclusion that,

although he may be considerably more alert than Péret to the technical implications his script has for the movie medium, Desnos too is
making use of the cinema more than he is serving it, in "Les Mystères du Métropolitain." Of the four scripts he published, only one
really accepts the priority of the cinema over literature. This is his
"Minuit à quatorze heures," subtitled "an essay in the modern marvelous."[6] Only in this, his first published script, does Desnos reveal
the ability to project a surrealist view of the world while displaying
a noteworthy instinct for the cinema.

A discussion of the work of Max Ernst once gave Desnos
the occasion to remark, "For the poet there are no hallucinations.
There is the real."[7] To Desnos himself, the real is "a reality that is
more extended than is commonly recognized." Hence the structure
of "Minuit à quatorze heures." It begins in the most conventionally
realistic fashion. A couple meet a guest at the railroad station and
bring him back home. During the absence of the host, the woman
and the guest are seen kissing. The next day, while the host is fishing, the other two go off for a walk. Attempting to release his line
from weeds, the host falls into the water and is drowned. After his
body has been retrieved from the water, the guest and the woman
return to the house.

While the plot has been developing methodically, according
to proven narrative patterns, the script has been emphasizing
circular shapes which claim our attention everywhere: rings in the
water, the setting sun, round circles of light from a lamp, the full
moon, etc. Everything, then, seems reassuring and appears to be
working out in a manner calculated to gain and hold the audience's
trust in Desnos' intention of telling a familiar tale by familiar film
techniques. But now something inexplicable takes place:

> 36. The round door handle turns slowly. The door opens.
> The two lovers watch it open. No one enters.

Each of the two lovers has a disturbing dream in which circular patterns are intrusively present. And both feel they are drowning
—he in a river current, she under a heap of coins—before their
dream ends. Now the following incident is introduced:

> 59. The apparition of a big ball like a croquet ball.
> 60. The ball comes down the stairs, step by step, slowly.
> 61. The ball moves across the landing on the floor where
> the two lovers are sleeping.
> 62. It continues to descend.

> 63. The man awakes. He listens. He gets up.
> 64. The ball, reaching the ground floor, goes out through
>   the door.
> 65. It disappears into the garden.

Interpretation of the ball is left to our imagination: it grows larger
and larger on a diet of birds, rabbits, reptiles, and even trees in an
equatorial forest. Desnos' concern is to avail himself of cinematographic technique in bringing its menace home to us:

> 132. The ball at the top of a hill overlooking the villa.
> 133. The villa.
> 134. The ball rolling down the hill.
> 135. It arrives at the house.
> 136. At the moment when it arrives at the house, everything,
>   the ball and the house, disappears, as though swallowed
>   up.
> 137. The round moon.
> 138. At dawn. Instead of the house, a vast crater.

Moreover, he takes advantage of one of the favored techniques of
the vanguard cinema—insistence upon formal imagery—to increase
our awareness of the mysterious, not to explain it away. His script
ends:

> 158. The little boy with the hoop.
> 159. The spherical shape in the sky.
> 160. Rings in the water.
> 161. The spherical shape in the sky.

All in all, "Minuit à quatorze heures" impresses as a text in which
full attention is granted the cinema, its demands, and its capabilities,
while fidelity to surrealism remains beyond question. There seems
little reason to be sorry that no director came forward in 1917, when
Soupault invited professionals of the cinema with sufficient means to
make a movie of his "Indifférence." It is regrettable, though, that no
one attempted to derive a film from "Minuit à quatorze heures."
Desnos' script showed that as early as the mid-twenties, surrealism
had something to contribute to the cinema which only surrealism
could give.

Possessed of imaginative powers that surrealists could appreciate and admire, as well as a real grasp of the suitability of the
film to surrealism's requirements, Robert Desnos was well equipped
to bring surrealist modes of thought and feeling to the cinema. So
was a fellow surrealist of the first generation, Antonin Artaud.

Believing the movies to be "a remarkable stimulant," Artaud

set out, around the same time as Desnos, to propose an original conception of the cinema. He referred to this when presenting his scenario "La Coquille et le Clergyman" in *La Nouvelle Revue Française* in November 1927, declaring the film to be "essentially revelatory of a wholly occult life with which it places us directly in contact." And he demonstrated what he meant by writing "Les dix-huit Secondes" ("The Eighteen Seconds"), posthumously published in the spring number of *Les Cahiers de la Pléiade*, 1949.

In "Les dix-huit Secondes," Artaud establishes his position *vis à vis* the temporal demands of conventional reality. He places a close-up of a man's watch at the very beginning, slowly ticking off the seconds. His film, he informs us, will end when eighteen seconds have gone by. But we are asked to note that "The time going by on the screen is the inner time of a man who is thinking":

> This is not normal time. Normal time is the 18 seconds that are real. The events you are going to see unfold on the screen will be made up of the man's inner images. The whole interest of the scenario resides in the fact that the time during which the events described take place is really 18 seconds whereas the description of these events will take up to an hour or two to project on the screen.
>
> The spectator will see unfold before him the images which, at a given moment, will begin to pass through the man's mind.

The man in question suffers from a strange malady, we learn. He is "incapable of attaining his thoughts." While he continues to be lucid, he can no longer translate any thoughts that may come to him into appropriate gestures or words:

> He lacks the necessary words. They no longer respond to his call. He is reduced to merely seeing images pass within him, a large number of contradictory images, without much relation to one another.
>
> This makes him incapable of mingling in the lives of others, and of engaging in any activity.

Artaud's hero is the victim of an acute sense of dissociation which he finds exceedingly distressing. Nostalgia for intelligence has taken possession of him. Going unsatisfied, it leaves him no alternative when his eighteen seconds are up but to blow his brains out.

Like the hero of "Les dix-huit Secondes," the central character of "La Coquille et le Clergyman" ("The Seashell and the Clergyman") finds himself in a time vacuum, benefiting from complete freedom from limitations of space. But he does not experience the distress that finally costs Artaud's other hero his life. Although he obviously faces problems peculiar to his situation—presumably induced by enforced celibacy—he is in touch with things enough to relate to them. He does this so directly that his conduct lends itself ideally to carrying through his creator's plan: "to realize this idea of a visual cinema in which even psychology is eaten up by action."

Central to the conception of the scenario entitled "La Coquille et le Clergyman" is the primacy of images. Artaud comments:

> Images are born, are deduced from one another as images, imposing an objective synthesis that is more penetrating than any abstraction, creating a world that asks nothing of anyone or of anything. But from this pure play of appearances, from this sort of transubstantiation of elements is born an inorganic language which moves the mind by osmosis and without any kind of transposition into words. And by the fact that it plays with matter itself, the cinema creates situations which result from a simple bumping together of objects, forms, repulsions, attractions.

Behind Artaud's plea for exclusive attention to film images lies the following theory:

> A certain agitation among objects, forms, expressions cannot be well translated unless through the convulsions and involuntary starts undergone by a reality that seems to be destroying itself with an irony in which one hears the extremities of the mind cry out.

The importance he attaches to his theory is evidenced in its prominence at the very end of the essay "Cinéma et Réalité," prefacing his scenario in *La Nouvelle Revue Française*. Its relation to Desnos' definition of the cinema as "a perfect opium" is made clear by a statement of Artaud's made in another context: "The cinema has above all the virtue of an inoffensive direct poison, a subcutaneous injection of morphine. This is why the object of the film can never be inferior to the film's power of action—and must partake of the marvelous."[8] The text of "La Coquille et le Clergyman" will reveal what Artaud means by the film's "power of action."

Looking back in 1933, Artaud wrote, "We knew that the most characteristic and most distinctive virtues of the cinema were always, or almost, the effect of chance, that is of a sort of mystery and we could not manage to explain how it came about."[9] On the authority of this statement, "La Coquille et le Clergyman" might be described as a scenario written to create the sort of mystery that appealed to Artaud, who had discovered that the cinema "reaches a turning point in human thought, at the very moment when worn-out language is losing its power as symbol, when the mind is tired of representational play."

"La Coquille et le Clergyman" exemplifies its author's firm belief that "Clear thought is not sufficient for us."[10] It opens with a reference to the central character, shown titrating liquid from glasses of unequal height and volume by means of "a sort of oyster shell," and breaking his flasks after using them. Are we to understand that his behavior indicates sexual frustration? Is his main protagonist, a uniformed officer whose sabre drags to the ground, the bearer of a giant phallic symbol? Perhaps; but not necessarily, since Artaud has pointed out, "The first degree of cinematographic thought seems to me to be using objects and existing forms which can be made to say everything, for the possible arrangements of nature are profound and truly infinite."[11] It would be a disservice, then, to read his scenario as meant for interpretation in one sense only. Indeed, Artaud makes it difficult for us to do this, unless we are prepared to disregard details which would interrupt the smooth course of our interpretation: for instance, the presentation of the officer as "like a sort of spider," at one moment lurking in dark corners, at another on the ceiling.

From the first sentence of his scenario, Artaud insistently demands that we watch rather than elucidate. Following the officer and a beautiful white-haired woman, the clergyman finds them in a church confessional. He throws himself on the man. The officer's face now "cracks, burgeons, opens like a flower," before its owner unaccountably changes into a priest. Finding himself next on the top of a mountain, the clergyman throws his victim down into the valley. As Artaud tells us, "The priest falls from the clergyman's arms like a millstone, like a fisherman's float exploding, and falls vertiginously into space." Artaud concentrates in this fashion on visual effect, without imposing an interpretation upon us. Thus he is true to the viewpoint on films expressed in a note on "La Coquille et le Clergyman," written for the eighth number of the *Cahiers de Belgique* in October 1928. Here he asserts that the "truly magic, truly cinematographic, specific element" of film "emerges, subterraneously from the images, and comes not from their logical, linked sense, but from their mingling, from their vibration and collision."

An article of Artaud's on "Cinema and Abstraction" emphasizes that his scenario "seeks to reach the essence of the cinema itself, and is not concerned with any allusion to art or to life."[12]

Instead, it aims at communicating an inescapable impression of fluidity, of movement, and of metamorphosis, in which the technical advantages of the movies over the theatre are turned to disturbing account.

The clergyman's coat-tails grow out of all proportion, and then, illustrating the instability of matter, change into darkness, into which he and the woman run. Their flight is punctuated by shots of the woman in various attitudes: now with a swollen, enormous cheek; now sticking out her tongue, which stretches away endlessly, the clergyman clinging to it, as to a rope. Her breasts balloon horribly. At the end of the race, we are to see the clergyman entering a corridor, while the woman is behind him "swimming in a sort of sky." Very soon, the officer, presumably back from the dead, is on the scene once again. Here, as throughout the scenario, Artaud expresses his belief that "innovation does not consist in multiple technical discoveries, in external and superficial formal play but in the profound renewal of the plastic material of imagery, in a true liberation, not a hazardous liberation, but a precisely related one involving all the sombre forces of thought."[13]

The officer once again intervenes between the clergyman and the woman, whom he kisses while she floats horizontal in the air. A paroxysm of rage takes possession of the hero as he reaches out to grasp a throat, which changes to sky and phosphorescent landscapes between his fingers. Is the ship on which this incident takes place the symbol of chastity, as in medieval times? And is the carapace of shells which the clergyman finds protecting the woman's breasts, when he tears her clothing away, a symbol of unattainable sexual fulfilment? It is easy, no doubt, to persuade oneself to think so. But doing this takes us only a very short way toward a rationally satisfying explanation of Artaud's scenario. So much more defies explanation than invites it: Artaud's comments on the clergyman's head, for example.

While he and the woman are praying in the confessional just before he tears at her clothing, the clergyman's head is described fairly realistically as "swaying like a leaf." Later, we recognize him by his physiognomy, so discovering that he is already in a ballroom when he arrives there, carrying his carapace of shells. Soon afterward, we see him strangling an invisible woman "with expressions of unbelievable sadism," before thrusting her severed head into a glass globe. Next comes a close-up of the clergyman's head:

> From deep inside his half-open mouth, in between his eyelashes something like shimmering smoke emanates, piling up in a corner of the screen, forming a town scene, or extremely

luminous landscapes. In the end the head disappears and houses, tangling and untangling, form a sort of unbelievable firmament of celestial lagoons, of grottos with incandescent stalactites and beneath these grottos, between these clouds, in the middle of these lagoons, we see the silhouette of the ship passing back and forth, black against the white background of the towns, white against the backcloth of visions which suddenly turn to black.

But on all sides doors and windows open. Light comes flooding into the room. Which room? The room with the glass globe.

This is the room in which the clergyman was seen earlier to be strangling an imaginary victim, before consigning her head to the globe. Thus, whether it makes sense to us or not, we have literally passed through the clergyman's head into a place already visited.

The globe is still there, filled with water. As servants cleaning the room pass it from hand to hand, "momentarily it seems that a head can be seen moving inside." Apparently the priest is about to marry the clergyman and the woman, at this point. But the screen is cut in two by the appearance of an immense ship. As this disappears, the clergyman is seen descending a staircase which seems to reach up to heaven. He is headless, and carrying a package wrapped in paper, from which he takes the globe. Breaking it open, he takes out a head. It is his own:

> This head makes a hideous grimace. He holds it in his hand like a hat. The head rests on an oyster shell. As he brings the shell up to his lips the head melts and is transformed into a sort of blackish liquid which he imbibes, closing his eyes.

The head serves as a recurrent motif in "La Coquille et le Clergyman," just as circular patterns do in "Minuit à quatorze heures." Like Desnos, Artaud dispenses with explanations when utilizing a motif selected for emphasis and development. His text ends with the words we have just read, so denying the reader (and ultimately the spectator) any interpretation other than the one he may feel inclined to supply for himself. If this interpretation should lean heavily on psychology (is narcissism the key to the closing shot, for example?), that is his affair. Artaud does not hold himself responsible. Defining the "ambitious thought" informing his scenario, Artaud wrote in the *Cahiers de Belgique* that it "goes in any case beyond the framework of simple narration, or problems of music, rhythm, or aesthetics usual in the cinema, in order to pose the problem of *expression*, in all domains, and in its full scope."

For the reasons outlined above, the scenario called "La Co-quille et le Clergyman" denies its readers the reassuring hypothesis that the collapse of logical sequence is a sign of merely humorous intent. The word "comedy," Artaud realizes, might serve to minimize the revolutionary motivation behind his text. Hence his insistence that "La Coquille et le Clergyman" was not conceived as a comedy—a point stressed in an introduction written for another of his scenarios, "La Révolte du Boucher" ("The Butcher's Revolt"). Presenting the latter in *La Nouvelle Revue Française in* 1930, he emphasized at the same time that his new scenario rests on the same ideas and reflects the same attitude as "La Coquille et le Clergyman."

So far as there does seem to be a difference between the two scripts, it lies here: elements only potentially present in "La Coquille et le Clergyman" are accorded some development in "La Révolte du Boucher." "Eroticism, cruelty, taste for blood, search for violence, obsession with the horrible, dissolution of moral values, social hypocrisy, lies, false witness, sadism, perversity"—these implicit features of the first text reappear in the second "with maximum legibility." Even so, Artaud's introductory note points out, the *raison d'être* of "La Révolte du Boucher" is not in the free expression of feelings usually kept under control, offered as an insight into psychological motivation. On the contrary, we are advised, "Sexuality, repression, the unconscious have never appeared to me a sufficient explanation for inspiration or the mind." Placing "La Révolte du Boucher" next to "La Coquille et le Clergyman," we detect no evidence of a change of outlook in their author, for whom "clear thought" never ceases to be less than sufficient for dealing with the questions raised by human existence.

All the same, side by side the two texts do reveal one other difference, and an imporant one. The second foresees the use of sound. By stressing images, not ideas, in "La Coquille et le Clergyman," Artaud demonstrated that he shared with Desnos suspicion about the use of sound in films, questioning that the arrival of sound must lead to the enrichment of the medium of the cinema. As Soupault defined it, "the cinema is a superhuman eye, much richer than the human eye, which is of doubtful fidelity."[14] If this is so, both Artaud and Desnos argued, would not the special powers of the cinematographic eye, as surrealism taught them to identify these, be subject to compromise by the spoken word? Even subtitles were of questionable utility, when they appeared isolated from the action "like the commentaries of a dominie below a fine poem," Desnos pointed out in *Paris-Journal* on April 13, 1923.

In the circumstances, Artaud's decision to use sound in "La

Révolte du Boucher" is surprising, at first. However, examination of "The Butcher's Revolt" shows there is no intention here to question the principles upon which "La Coquille et le Clergyman" rests. Indeed, there is nothing paradoxical in Artaud's statement that his "La Révolte du Boucher" is "silent in principle," using words and sounds from time to time only "with a view to seeking certain effects."[15] Scrutiny of his text reveals the nature of these effects, indicating that sound separates "La Révolte du Boucher" from "La Coquille et le Clergyman" much less than might have been anticipated.

"La Révolte du Boucher" opens on the Place de l'Alma in Paris where, at 2 a.m., a madman is nervously waiting for a woman. A butcher's cart, turning at speed, loses a side of beef which is hastily loaded once again. Now the scene changes to a café. Here the madman is torn between hatred and desire for a woman, whose gigolo provokes him:

> The madman considers him with a baleful air, and as the gigolo advances, he punches him right in the face, saying without raising his voice:

> | Take care, your head to the butcher's. |
> | --- |

> At this moment the waiter drops his tray. The thunderous noise of the tray makes a terrible impression on the madman. The gigolo becomes of no account in his hands; and as everyone in the café is on his feet, coming toward him, the madman suddenly has a blank spell during which everything stands still, and *we hear* the sound of the butcher's cart grinding the asphalt in the morning, to the sound of hoofbeats.

> Then the *sounds* of the café resume. The madman recovers his senses, but has before his eyes the vision of the cart passing by, rolling along in one corner of the screen like those tiny images that move about on the ceiling, in a camera obscura, by the chink of light from the drapes. He cries out, looking at the people in the café who are staring at him like animals:

> | To the slaughter-house. |
> | --- |

"La Révolte du Boucher," Artaud asserts, is a talkie film in the measure that "the words pronounced in it are so placed as to make the images rebound." Thus, when at a later stage in the scenario the master butcher has laid the woman out as though he intends to cut her up like a carcass, he opens his mouth, but does not utter a sound. Instead, a magnified voice announced over a loudspeaker, "I've had enough of cutting meat without eating it," while the text specifies that the loudspeaker is heard *during a break in the images.*" The effect is far from accidental, then: "The voices here exist *in space,* like objects," Artaud affirms. What is more, the consequence of using this effect is anticipated: "And it is on the visual plane that one must, if I may say so, *accept* them." Hence no case can be made for the argument that, planning "La Révolte du Boucher," Artaud set aside or conveniently forgot earlier reservations about sound in movies. Spoken words, and sound effects also, are introduced into his scenario to deepen the spectator's involvement in a non-rational experience. They are certainly not there to make the author's peace with reason.

The statements Artaud plans to use are even fewer in number that one might expect to see communicated through subtitles, had sound been excluded altogether. Isolating these in his text, by setting them in little boxes, he draws attention to his avoidance of consecutive dialogue. Like the sound effects used in "La Révolte du Boucher," the words spoken will interrupt the film far more than they will supply continuity. There is no exaggeration, therefore, in Artaud's claim:

> You will find in this film an organization of voices and sounds, taken in themselves and not as the *physical consequence* of a movement or an act, that is without concordance with the facts. Sounds, voices, images, the break in the images, all these are part of the same objective world in which it is above all movement that counts.

Artaud presents the world he is creating in "La Révolte du Boucher" as objective. Just as in all his scenarios, attention to visual effect is proof that he wishes the audience to enter into the reality his movies present. Such an entry entails approval of an act of defiance against the reality we know, a challenge which—from the very first—is directed to the senses (and principally to the eye), instead of to the reasoning process in which the mind tends to take refuge from the unfamiliar. "And it is the eye that finally pulls together and under-scores the residue of all the movements," he declares at the end of his prefatory note to "La Révolte du Boucher."

With little prospect of seeing their proposals adopted, some surrealists have continued to write for the cinema. Jacques Brunius collaborated with Jacques Prévert and Maurice Henry on the script of an adaptation of *Baron Munchhausen* which Hans Richter would have directed, but for the outbreak of war in 1939. Earlier, he had worked with Paul Gilson on a script called "Un Peu moins de Bruit" ["A Little Less Noise" (April 1929)], subsequently published in the second issue of *Bizarre* in October 1955 over the subtitle "model of a scenario for a talkie film." This is an amusing short subject in which the influence of Louis Feuillade's serial about Fantômas is discernible: a mysterious masked criminal called Subtilas emerging from and taking refuge in a billboard advertising poster.[16] All the same, it does not contribute anything noteworthy to our understanding of what the surrealists ask of the cinema. The same can be said of the synopsis by J. V. Manuel, *Celui qui n'a pas de Nom (He Who Has No Name)*, published in 1942 as Number 7 in the collection "Les Pages libres de la Main à Plume," and of Joseph Cornell's *Monsieur Phot.*[17] More adventurous are Léon Corcuff's "D'un Procédé funéraire utile à la Défense passive" ("On a Funeral Procedure Useful in Passive Defense") a *"film à thèse"* reproduced in the thirteenth number of the surrealist magazine *Minotaure* in 1939, and the scripts of Henry Storck.

Storck's "La Rue" ("The Street") appeared in the special issue of *L'Age du Cinéma* devoted to surrealism, in 1951. The most significant aspect of this synopsis is that it offers a rebuke to all who tend to identify surrealism with evasion and assume surrealism cannot survive where reality is present. "La Rue" is situated in the world we all know. In fact, it is situated in a street; "that is," Storck specifies, "the houses have been emptied of their contents, and furniture and accessories clutter the middle of the street." The set includes a drawing room complete with chandelier and a hostess presiding over an elegant reception at which the daughter of the house plays the piano and sings, while everyone behaves as though indoors. And yet space is reserved in the street for traffic to pass through. Realism is not excluded, as it might be in a pure fantasy. It is deliberately allowed to intrude in a manner that defies its power to limit human experience. Realistic details are used *against* realism; for example, in the operating theatre functioning in the roadway: "When the patient is dead under the combined efforts of the surgeon's art and nursing care, all that has to be done is have a hearse come along and carry the cadaver away without handling by a middleman."

Storck relies upon the dominant impression of life proceeding normally and calmly in the middle of the street while "a few infrequent passers-by move very busily about on the sidewalks." True, the windows of the houses are crowded with curious spectators. But some of these have fallen asleep. They rest undisturbed by either the revolver shots of gangsters shooting people down or the cries of a little girl whom a man is raping in a dark corner. The impression is one of displacement and disorientation, involving the disruption of habitual response. Habit and normal behavior are especially ridiculed when servants on duty in the drawing room put up umbrellas to protect the guests from mud sprayed on them intentionally by a fire truck.

An army tank passes, equipped with an altar on which Mass is being celebrated; a bus also goes by, in which a court trial is going on, as does a garbage truck collecting taxes from trash cans. Meanwhile violence continues in the street (murder of children, lynching of bearded Christs), without causing any concern. Nevertheless, it does not seem to be Storck's intention to provoke us to moral indignation. When he speaks of a reporter who is describing events to a radio audience, in conventional terms which falsify the truth, he insists upon the "comic effect" of man's actions. Meanwhile scientific detachment is subject to mockery as the script describes people inside the houses rushing out to gather various objects which they carefully seal in labeled bottles: a passer-by's shoe, a blind man's dark glasses, a child's rattle, cards belonging to a fortune-teller. Moreover, nothing that happens seems to have a lesson for those who should learn from life. Children in school are denied direct contact with events, being obliged to sit with their backs to the scene. As their teacher describes what is going on, everything he mentions is deprived of movement and life.

The only person whose conduct is normal is a young man. He is struck by the beauty of a young woman as she lies asleep in bed (in the street), her bosom bare. For him it is love at first sight. He carries her off in a taxi, after she has dressed before him with no sign of shyness, imagining herself in her own bedroom. Together they drive to the seaside, where the taxi driver is paid off with the young man's clothes, and presented with the young woman's dress as a tip, before the couple swim out to sea and over the horizon.

Later, we see the young man dressed for their wedding. His efforts to contact the young woman by television are frustrated by technicians, who gag him to prevent him speaking. During the night he staggers drunk into the street, where he finds a yellow tramcar, which he manages to set in motion. The vehicle emits musical sounds as it bears him over sand into the sea. Here he undresses and begins to swim in slow motion, with great effort "as though in an agonizing dream." His fiancée swims to meet him, from over the horizon, also in slow motion. With difficulty they meet and embrace, as fish swim in slow motion around them. And the scenario is over:

> Close-up of the fishes' tails fanning out in slow motion and decorated with changing colors which create a delightful effect. We can hear the tramcar still singing.

The realistic details studding "La Rue" make this script an unequivocal attack upon the fallacy that surrealism thrives only in films where realism is eschewed. Furthermore, Storck's hero and heroine are shown to escape the fate—indifference, routine, callousness, and so on—of those living lives we consider normal. In a world where passion has been replaced by insensitivity, their love has the power to unite them, even in circumstances which seem, as in a nightmare, opposed to their finding unity in the desire they share.

The fidelity of Storck's scenario to surrealist ideals is never in doubt for one moment. Like Artaud, he uses sound to stress the surrealist perspective of his film, not to justify it reasonably. What is more, his treatment of love testifies to the moral principles surrealism inculcates. Above all, he gives proof of possessing an instinct for the cinema of a kind that submits cinematography to the demands of surrealism.

The same instinct is reflected in the scenario "Am-ster-dam" which Storck wrote in 1952 and published in May of 1955, in the first issue of the magazine *Bizarre*.

"Am-ster-dam" has as its hero a romantic figure whom its author compares to Gérard de Nerval. It is divided into five episodes. The first shows the hero drowning himself in a pond, from which his body promptly emerges again like a jumping fish, before returning to the water. With bait that is an eye hooked from his own head, deep in the water, the main character succeeds in catching a large fish. He has to use physical force to overcome his catch, which merely feigns exhaustion so as to be able to escape back to the pond, where it swims off again, in rhythm to a song it is singing.

After this "first attempt" at suicide, which he "considers a failure," the hero decides to shoot himself in the head:

> In the foreground his hand, holding a revolver, his head, in close up, his temple.
>
> Between the foreground and the lens a transparent glass on which, at the moment of the shot (muffled and long drawn out, brutal and raspy) a mass of thick red liquid spurts, mixed with pus and glair: blood and brains.

With a hole in his head and a blood-stained face, the hero wipes the glass clean "as though he wished to remove all trace of his act," collecting everything he removes in a bowl, prior to examining it under a microscope, which reveals "a terrible battle between monsters!" Stripping off his clothes, he watches the battle until his hair turns white and his microscope catches fire.

Throughout his scenario, Storck evidences sensitivity to the cinema's capacity to communicate the immediacy of physical impressions. In the third episode, for instance, it is the "marvelous sensation of liberation" and the "intoxication of speed" that he wishes to have stressed in a scene showing his hero standing on the front of a moving locomotive. A moment later, when the man has stretched out "nobly" across the tracks, the locomotive advances "softly, inexorably, and quietly runs over him." Storck notes, "He sees the immense wheel coming close to his face [. . .]. All this in slow motion, to give a terrifying impression." The realistic effect here contrasts strongly with what follows: "As the locomotive goes by, the body flames and burns. From the smokestack escapes steam in delightful shapes, to the sound of distant poetic music (Couperin). A ballet of smoke and clouds (a mixture of speed-up and slow motion), while the train continues its course."

Mingling of realistic detail with the fanciful is the hallmark of Storck's scenario. In its fourth episode, for example, the hero hangs himself from a gas bracket in an alley (just like Nerval), and then passes through a manhole in the street. Underground, he sees a number of red-headed women in bathing suits, lying on beds with red blankets. Following the lead of one of their number, each woman presses a breast, showering the hero with milk: "The jets of milk form gracious arabesques, it resembles a ballet like the fountains on the Place de la Concorde." Soon covered with thick oily milk, the hero is said to look like "a statue of lard or of snow." These realistic comparisons set off another image: "curious sea monsters, fantastic and horrible" playing the accordion and 'cello around the fishing boat in which the hero is trying once again to hang himself.

Emerging from a urinal, in the fifth episode, the hero meets a woman as attractive as a pin-up. When he kisses her under a tree, she changes into an ugly old hag. Describing the man as consequently "uneasy," Storck gives the keynote to the last section of his scenario, where one of the main visual effects is described as follows:

> The spectator observes a strange phenomenon, obtained by trick photography. The top of the character's body is de-

tached from the bottom. While the trunk slips by among pedestrians who are fairly indifferent, the legs go walking on their own. Deciding that this absurd game has gone on long enough, the trunk whistles to the legs, which come rushing up like a dog, but without enthusiasm. After making a show of refusing to rejoin the trunk, and trying to run away, the legs position themselves under the trunk, but obey in the end only before the master's anger.

The adjectives here speak for themselves. Meanwhile Storck takes care to obviate dismissal of this scene as one of comic relief. The preceding paragraph ended with the word "uneasy," and the succeeding one will begin, "Still uneasy, our character goes home, and enters a very modern bathroom." Here he lies fully clothed in his tub, whistling "as a snake charmer would." In consequence, a drop of purplish-blue poison drips from one faucet. Seeking to neutralize this, he turns on the other faucet. The water assumes a purple hue as it fills the bath. The character receives a jet of green and purple liquid from the shower nozzle.

Enclosed in an enormous green poison bottle, the man is buried in a graveyard where skeletons subsequently hold a party. "Suddenly, in the most unexpected fashion, like a bore, enormous waves sweep away the skeletons and the cemetery. The tombs float on the sea, with a marvelous rocking motion, to the sound of a majestic theme by Palestrina." The scenario is brought to a close on an inexplicable image:

> The poison bottle containing the hero's body floats in the hollow of the waves. It is caught in the hair of a woman floating in the water and rolling at the whim of the waves. But the sea is stilled, the hair is paralyzed, everything becomes strangely immobile. Anguish is expressed through a single muted note quietly introduced and then progressively amplified until it is as loud as we can bear.

Storck's awareness of the contribution color and sound can make to the enrichment of visual effect, without concession to reasonable demands, makes of his scenarios serious proposals for surrealist films. Only economic considerations stand in the way of their adaptation to the screen. Unfortunately, these considerations have presented an obstacle which most surrealists are resigned to regarding as insurmountable. This being so, it is worth while to consider the reaction of Jean Ferry.

Ferry's dedication to the surrealist cause is beyond question. Author of a notable study on Raymond Roussel and of a volume of short stories called *Le Mécanicien et autres Contes,* Ferry was the co-author with Buñuel of the screen play for the latter's *Cela s'appelle l'Aurore.*[18] Meanwhile, there is no doubting his professional competence to write for the screen, as he has done in the screen-play of Clouzot's *Manon* and *Quai des Orfèvres.* One may look to his scenario "Fidélité," written between 1947 and 1953, as a surrealist script by an author fully alert to the cinema's capacity for expressing the surrealist viewpoint. This is all the more reason, therefore, to feel disappointment at the results obtained.

"Fidélité" tells of Frank's search for a rugby ball, stolen during a game in which he participates one day when he leaves his office to captain a team. The search extends over twenty years, leading Frank among other things to the discovery of his real name, Frank Einstein. He possesses, then, the power to bring a monster back to life. This is "Dr. Schweik's Friend," immobilized in a coffin for reasons which Schweik cannot tell, because "That happened in another film . . . It would take too long to explain." The first scene, showing Frank at home, is interesting. Some kind of creature (later we wonder if it is human) lives under the dining table, concealed by a table cloth. Apparently, there is a two-headed baby occupying a crib in the middle of the room (a baby who, by the time the film is over, has attended four major schools at once, before dying of double meningitis). But we are not permitted to see these freaks. Nor do we see the invisible creatures which terrify the maid and at the end seem to have eaten her up for venturing into the garden.

All in all, we find nothing here that is distinctively cinematographic, nothing that could not be transposed without difficulty to the stage. Kyrou's admiration for "Fidélité" notwithstanding, Ferry's script has nothing more to teach than we have learned already about surrealism's influence upon script writing.[19] The significance of his text lies elsewhere.

The author evinces no false optimism about the commercial possibilities of his script. After an embarrassed letter preface in which Clouzot talks uncomfortably of the ability of the text to speak for itself (while yet alluding vaguely to its "ambiguity"), in an introductory note Ferry appears to pride himself on the unlikelihood of finding a producer for his film. He asserts that it could never be shown commercially. Far from expressing despair at his script's limited prospects, he provides "a note on the imaginary carrying-out" of his plans. He assigns roles to well-known actors (these include Pierre Fresnay as Frank and Erich von Stroheim as Dr. Schweik). He selects music—from a Laurel and Hardy movie. And he chooses

Charles Addams as an ideal set designer. No director is named, because the author believes none would consent to meet his requirement that screen adaptation be entirely faithful to his wishes.

Knowing his script would never be made into a film, Ferry was completely free to make of it what he wished. In the end, it reads more like a play by Raymond Roussel (Ferry's use of beneficent chance is very similar to Roussel's in *L'Étoile au Front* [1924]) than like a film. However, this resemblance is by the way. The important thing is that Ferry is a surrealist undeterred by the impracticality of his plans for a movie. Knowledge that he is not writing directly for the screen only strengthens his determination to address himself to a select few.

The key sentence in Ferry's introductory note to "Fidélité" is the one in which he names the actors and actresses whom he would use in ideal conditions for his movie. Here he invites his readers to engage in a *"matérialisation intime,"* by projecting his characters and their actions on an inner screen. Despite his professional manner of presentation, Ferry does not delude himself. He does not pretend to be providing in "Fidélité" the scenario of a film we can expect to see one day in a movie house. This is a movie for the imagination, not for commercial exploitation. In this sense, it marks a transition between scenarios which the writer hopes may eventually benefit from screen adaptation, and texts sufficiently different in origin to merit separate examination. The latter are indicative of another approach, evidenced among a number of writers of surrealist persuasion.

These are not writers like Soupault, who lack skill in utilizing the cinema to surrealist advantage. Nor are they, like Péret, content to take from the cinema whatever they can use in creative writing that betrays no serious desire to compete with movies. In some cases their viewpoint may be traced directly to the economic disability under which every film script of surrealist inspiration must suffer: the chance is remote that a movie will ever be made from it. In other cases, we have to entertain the possibility that more favorable economic conditions would not alter the writer's attitude materially. Yet, whatever the reasons making their influence felt, the result is very similar. These writers have not merely given up the hope of seeing their scenarios inspire movies but, looking upon such a hope with something close to scorn, take measures to dispose of it entirely.

It might seem fitting to treat the attitude of which we are speaking as a sign of despair, precipitated by frustration and disillusion only after a period of trial and error extended enough to convince certain surrealists they had no prospect of making their way in the cinema. Yet this plausible hypothesis is not supported by the facts. Indeed, it is noticeable as early as the twenties that a few surrealists cared little about reaching agreement between their demands upon the cinema and the practical requirements of the medium.

In 1928, B. Fondane published *Trois Scénarii,* "Barre fixe," "Paupières mûres," and "Mtasipoj." Prefacing his volume,[20] he opened with a declaration no surrealist would disavow: "It is not, consequently, to correct the cinema, to make it better *(let it not become an art;* that is all we ask of it) that we propose in our turn this mortar destined to ruin a certain form of the cinema in people's minds, to bring another into the world." However, Fondane soon advanced to a position some surrealists would be reluctant to occupy with him. "Let us open," he appealed, "the period of unperformable scenarios."

Had Fondane's appeal been answered already, and by more than one surrealist? We might think so, listening to Georges Neveux recall, "But the poets of that period were not content to love the (often involuntary) poetry of silent films, they wrote scenarios themselves, most of the time scenarios that could not be filmed [*des scénarios intournables*], oneiric confessions projected on an imaginary screen [. . .]."[21] There is a difference, however, between Fondane's *scénarii injouables* and Neveux's *scénarios intournables.* Unlike the latter—awkward, unpolished imitations of the movies— the former were conceived in disregard for cinematographic usage, and so betokened a distinctive conception of the scenario.

Fondane deliberately rejects the technical limitations and practical requirements of movie-making, knowingly following a direction of thought in which the projection of the "film" becomes conceivable only on the screen of the imagination. It is not a matter of ignorance or the technical limitations imposed by budgetary considerations. His is a form of film scenario that actively resists adaptation to the cinema. This calls for special stress because the phenomenon under consideration manifests itself in the theatre, as well as in the cinema. Among surrealist writers for whom the stage holds an appeal, Robert Benayoun and Jean-Claude Barbé are two who have distinguished themselves by qualifying certain of their own plays as "unperformable."[22] Placed next to the *pièce injouable* the *scenario injouable* takes on its true value. It can be seen as less a confession of failure than the expression of a wish to go beyond the technical restrictions of the film as form, in the direction of enlarged imaginative freedom.

The approach exemplified in what Fondane called the *ciné-poème* makes surrealism's relationship with the cinema a marriage of convenience, in which all the benefits fall to the former. "D'Or et de Sable," written by Paul Nougé in 1927, illustrates the kind of results such an approach produces:

> Buster Keaton leaves the auditorium to take a hand in what is happening on the screen, and suddenly looks at it. He picks a quarrel with the suitor who is also the detective, he slaps him in the face, but his fist gets lost in a fountain. Then the park seems pleasant to him, he walks around, he rests in the shade of an apple tree. He wants to pick an apple and it is the nose of an old lady that he pinches disrespectfully, in the middle of a crowd. He runs off, he escapes his pursuers with difficulty, a door opens, he climbs a staircase, another door (which closes behind him), there is an armchair, oops! he falls in a sitting position into a fishing bark lost in the middle of a deserted sea. The bark is empty, no oars, no supplies. He bends forward to search its smallest corners. There, a scent-bottle! He straightens and hands to the elegant lady the bracelet which she is awaiting, smiling. Delighted, Buster Keaton smiles also but at a blind man waiting for charity. Buster Keaton leaves the screen to enter the auditorium once again.
>
> A man explains to him that what affects him in the world is that, transported to Mars, a person weighing 154 pounds would weigh only 63 and that on Jupiter he would weigh 285. [. . .]
>
> But as this man is speaking a language that is not his, Buster Keaton does not understand. He goes to sit down and looks.[23]

Like all texts of surrealist inspiration, Nougé's raises certain problems for the rational mind. All attempts to handle these in the context of "D'Or et de Sable" will be frustrating and unproductive, unless attention is given to clues provided in the second and third paragraphs for elucidating the first. Here, after a succession of disconcerting elements in which visual effects pass unaccompanied by reported dialogue, an explanation is introduced. It is an irrelevant one; but that matters not at all. What counts is that scientific truths prove incomprehensible to Nougé's Buster Keaton. He speaks another language, and prefers watching to explaining.

Nougé's stress on looking rather than understanding indicates we have not left behind the characteristic stress upon images so noticeable in the scenarios of Artaud and in the theory underlying them. In Nougé's text, sound does not make sense of the image, any more than in "La Révolte du Boucher." And it is plain that here, just as in "La Coquille et le Clergyman," and "La Rue" too, the governing principle controlling the arrangement of images is neither aesthetic nor reasonable. Nougé's opposition to facile symbolism is as firm as Artaud's or Storck's, leading him in three paragraphs devoid of psychological underpinning to favor gratuitousness at the expense of rational, logical sequence.

Surrealists approach the cinema with the assumption that audiences can believe what they see in the movies, even if they are shown things on film that reason cautions them to doubt. This is why surrealists treat the scenario as preeminently subversive in function. And this is why the appeal a script has for their imagination may be enhanced on occasion, rather than reduced, by its author's lack of respect for the technical limitations of the film medium.

All the same, it would be naïve to conclude that, when a surrealist like Nougé grants his film hero unlikely privileges (like being able to watch a movie from the auditorium and to take part in it at the same time), this is out of ignorance about how a movie ought to be put together. It would be just as inaccurate to conclude that, to surrealists, the ideal cinematic form is identifiable with the film script which defies adaptation to the screen. When a screen-play can be placed in that category which surrealists pejoratively call literature, when writing one can be interpreted as a mere exercise in literary form, it ceases to have value or to attract attention. And it loses relevance for surrealism's plans for the cinema. A script can remain interesting and instructive only so long as it promises to draw us as far as possible in the direction of liberation. This is the direction Artaud, Desnos, and Storck have taken, in trying to help transform man's awareness of reality by illustrating that the real is subject to no more limits than we consent to impose upon it: the direction followed from the very beginning by those deserving the title of surrealist film-makers.

Surrealist Film-Makers

Original Barbarity

Attacking Wildean aestheticism and the "baneful confusion" created by film-makers who fall under its influence, Robert Desnos declared in an article on "Cinéma d'Avant-Garde," published in the seventh number of *Documents* in 1929:

> Please understand me. When René Clair and Picabia made *Entr'acte*, Man Ray *L'Étoile de Mer* and Buñuel his admirable *Chien andalou*, it was not a matter of creating a work of art or of a new aesthetic but of obeying profound, original impulses, in consequence necessitating a new form.

Desnos neglected to mention Dali, in connection with *Un Chien andalou*, just as he omitted to say what he himself had to do with *L'Étoile de Mer*. But he still made his essential point clear.

An instinct for revolt and renewal made the first surrealists attentive to the potential of the cinema as revealed in *Entr'acte* (1924). Delighting in the "marvelous barbarity" of the cinema and confessing, "I could easily resign myself today to admitting in the world of images neither rules nor logic,"[1] René Clair welcomed the opportunity to collaborate with Francis Picabia, who furnished the scenario for *Entr'acte*. Centered on complete disregard for habitual logic, and displaying the most violent humor, *Entr'acte* offered a succession of apparently unrelated images of scandalous gratuitousness, culminating in a scene showing a funeral procession, led by a hearse bedecked with publicity posters and drawn by a camel, passing through a Parisian amusement park. The grotesque effect was heightened by appropriate (that is, calculatedly inappropriate) use of slow-motion and speed-up, preparing for the final effect: bursting

77

from his coffin, the corpse waves a wand which makes all his friends and relations disappear. Here the iconoclastic potentialities of the movies are dramatically revealed. As Picabia wrote in the special number of *La Danse* devoted to the Swedish Ballet, *"Entr'acte* doesn't believe in much, in the pleasure of living perhaps; it respects nothing unless it be the desire to burst out laughing."[2]

Picabia was a dadaist, dedicated to devaluating and ultimately destroying all consecrated forms of art. His dadaist viewpoint had been shared by several of those who declared themselves surrealists, rallying to the call of the first *Manifeste du Surréalisme*, by the former dadaist Breton. Although they had tired of mere negativism by 1924 and were looking for more positive ambitions, they recognized without hesitation that the Clair-Picabia movie had noteworthy qualities. To the extent that *Entr'acte* wilfully departed from the conventional, and demonstrated the role technique may play in undermining convention, it stood as an invitation to film-makers to explore in new directions. Proposing to "translate the non-materialized dreams which take place in our brains," Picabia called upon Clair's knowledge of film technique to effect this translation, as he asked the fundamental question, "Why relate what everyone sees or can see every day?" This is the very question Artaud would soon have in mind when writing his scenario "La Coquille et le Clergyman."

It is just as well that Artaud did explain the motive underlying "La Coquille et le Clergyman." For when adapting his scenario to the screen in 1927, Germaine Dulac included among the credits the words "a dream of Antonin Artaud's." This reference to Artaud's text was made in violation of contract. More than this, it amounted to distortion of the script's nature and purpose. When the film Mme Dulac had made from his scenario was being shown at the Studio des Ursulines, Artaud asked the surrealist group to undertake a "punitive expedition" against the movie and its director. During the première performance, he led a protest from the auditorium. Georges Sadoul, who alludes to this incident as one in which Mme Dulac was found guilty of having "deformed and betrayed" a surrealist script,[3] confirms that the reasons for the surrealists' attack on the film *La Coquille et le Clergyman* are those noted by Artaud's publisher:

> Antonin Artaud had hoped to participate in making the film,[4] but it seems that Germaine Dulac did not want his participation. Later, Antonin Artaud disavowed Germaine Dulac's adaptation, which he accused of being a solely oneiric interpretation of his scenario.[5]

Artaud explained the purpose of his script in *La Nouvelle Revue Française*, when stressing that he was searching for a type of film with "purely visual situations." Instead of being the adaptation in visual terms of a given text, the action of a film should come, he asserted, from "a shock to the eye, drawn so to speak from the very substance of the eye." Declaring that he had tried in his scenario to transpose action to a plane on which it makes its effect "almost intuitively on the mind," he warned, "I will not seek to find excuse for its apparent incoherence through the facile loophole of the dream." Interpreted as nothing more than the record of a dream experience ("rêve de Antonin Artaud," Mme Dulac insisted), *La Coquille et le Clergyman* lost its revolutionary force. Presenting Artaud's material as merely a nocturnal vision, Germaine Dulac was inexcusably unfaithful to his intentions, as he himself has summarized them: to display the motives of our actions "in their original and profound barbarity," and to transmit them visually.

Artaud's use of the same word as Clair, "barbarity," testifies to the nature of the appeal movies held for both of them. In addition, it makes clear that both were determined to resist any attempt to assimilate their work with reassuringly familiar trends in cinematographic expression. In *Le Monde illustré* for October 1927, Artaud commented:

> *La Coquille et le Clergyman* plays with created nature and tries its hand at making it render up a little mysterious something from its most secret combinations. One must not look in it for a logic and a sequence which do not exist in things, but rather interpret the images that unfold in the sense of their essential, private signification, an internal signification that moves inward from outside. *La Coquille et le Clergyman* does not tell a story but develops a succession of states of mind.

It was more than pique that prompted Artaud to disrupt the first performance of Mme Dulac's film by loudly engaging Desnos in an offensive conversation about her. Germaine Dulac had called his script "mad." Now he countered, calling her "a cow" for not seeing that his scenario's madness resulted from an innovatory conception of the cinema about which he was to make the following observation: "The cinema implies a total inversion of values, a complete upheaval of optics, of perspective and logic. It is more exciting than phosphorus, more captivating than love."[6]

In her version of *La Coquille et le Clergyman*, Germaine Dulac achieved a remarkably fluid cinematographic movement, sure to find favor with contemporary exponents of vanguard technique.

In doing so she betrayed her total incomprehension of the surrealist viewpoint on film. Yet although she made a determined effort to control its "madness," she did not succeed altogether in emptying Artaud's scenario of surrealist content. For this reason alone, her *Coquille et le Clergyman* deserves mention among the first surrealist films, even though the form of her movie is quite unsatisfactory to those who, like Brunius (p. 55), saw much less to admire there than in *Entr'acte*, an essentially discontinuous movie in which they found supporting evidence for their conviction that too much attention to rhythm can lead only to neglect of content in film.

Among the most noteworthy surrealist experiments in film during the years immediately following *La Coquille et le Clergyman* stands Man Ray's cinematographic interpretation of a poem by Robert Desnos, called *L'Étoile de Mer* (1928).

Man Ray has spoken openly of the method from which his movie resulted, explaining, "All the films I made were improvisations. I wrote no script. It was automatic cinema. I worked alone. My intention was to set in movement the compositions I made in photography."[7] His distinction as a still photographer rules out the possibility that ineptitude made him neglectful of composition, when working as a film cameraman. Rather, a certain impatience to which he has confessed protected his film experiments from the temptations of aestheticism. By his own admission, *Emak Bakia* (1927), described in his autobiography as "a hodge-podge of realistic shots and sparkling crystals and abstracts forms" obtained by using deforming mirrors, was intended to be "a satire on the movies."[8] This film includes a comparatively extended sequence, introduced, Man Ray says, as "some sort of climax, so that the spectators would not think I was being too arty." It shows Jacques Rigaut taking a dozen stiff white collars from a suitcase, tearing them in two and dropping them on the floor. By having a reverse print made of the falling collars, Man Ray was able to show them jumping up to engage in a rhythmic dance, animated by revolving deforming mirrors. Running from Rigaut's arrival by taxi to his departure, the scene is preceded by the film's only subtitle, "The Reason for this Extravagance." This subtitle, the director informs us ironically (p. 272), was inserted to "reassure the spectator," like the title of his first short film, *Retour à la Raison* [*Return to Reason* (1923)], made for a dada manifestation in Paris. Needless to say, Man Ray intended to be anything but reassuring. He included his subtitle more to disconcert the spectator than to give him confidence: "to let him think there would be an explanation of the previous disconnected images." Supplying an ex-

planation which patently was no explanation at all, Man Ray highlighted the discontinuous nature of the material assembled in his
film. Meanwhile his blatant disregard for compositional concerns
showed he had no wish to satisfy the aesthetic appetite of the devo-
tee of vanguardism any more than to please those who hoped simply
to see a movie "make sense" before it came to an end. Not until the
close of *Emak Bakia* does Man Ray address himself to his audience
without irony. A close-up of his favorite model, Kiki, demands a new
visual responsiveness, as we are shown artificial eyes painted on her
eyelids which disappear when she really opens her eyes.

At the end of *Emak Bakia,* surprise confronts us with the necessity to turn upon reality a glance that is neither false nor imitative.
L'Étoile de Mer (The Star of the Sea or *The Star-Fish)* shows what
Man Ray expects us to do with our eyes. Hearing Desnos read a
poem of his one evening, Man Ray was impressed by its resemblance
to a scenario for a film, each line seeming to present a clear, detached image:

> A woman is selling newspapers in the street. On a small stand
> beside her is the pile of papers, held down with a glass jar
> containing a starfish. A man appears, he picks up the jar, she
> her pile of papers; they leave together. Entering a house, they
> go up a flight of stairs and into a room. A cot stands in a
> corner. Dropping her papers, the woman undresses in front of
> the man, lies down on the cot completely nude. He watches
> her, then rises from his chair, takes her hand and kisses it,
> saying adieu—farewell—and leaves taking the starfish with
> him. At home he examines the jar with its contents, carefully.
> There follow images of a train in movement, a steamer dock-
> ing, a prison wall, a river flowing under a bridge. There are
> images of the woman stretching out on the couch, nude, with
> a glass of wine in her hand, of her hands caressing a man's
> head in her lap, of her walking up the stairs with a dagger in
> her hand, of her standing wrapped in a sheet with a Phrygian
> bonnet on her head—symbol of liberty, an image of the
> woman sitting in front of a fireplace, suppressing a yawn. A
> phrase keeps recurring: *she is beautiful, she is beautiful.*
> Other phrases, irrelevant, as, *If only flowers were made of*
> *glass,* and, *One must beat the dead while they are cold,*
> appear in the poem. In one line the man picks up a news-
> paper lying in the street and scans a political headline. The
> poem ends with the man and woman meeting again in an
> alley. A newcomer appears, taking the woman by the arm

and leads her away, leaving the first man standing in be-
wilderment. The woman's face appears again, alone, in front
of a mirror, which cracks suddenly, and on which appears the
word: *beautiful.* (pp. 275–276)

If Desnos' poem was indeed only fifteen or twenty lines long as Man
Ray tells us, it must have been a masterpiece of compression. As he
recalls it here, Man Ray evidently is evoking all it suggested to him.
"I saw it clearly as a film—a Surrealist film," he comments, "and
told Desnos that when he returned [from an assignment as journalist
in the West Indies] I'd have made a film with his poem." So it is as
a summary of the content of Man Ray's film rather than of Desnos'
poem that the passage reproduced above interests us.

As Desnos himself had indicated more than once, the art of
acting was based too firmly on the needs of the theatre to serve the
purposes of the surrealist cinema. It did not concern Man Ray, who
saw no reason to account for his characters' conduct in terms of
psychological motivation. He saw all three as "mere puppets," who
could be played by Kiki, by one of Desnos' neighbors, and by Desnos
himself as the second man. As for technical matters, they were given
focus not by aesthetic preoccupation but by practical considerations.
Instead of utilizing soft-focus or artistic silhouette effects, Man Ray
prepared some pieces of gelatine by soaking them, so obtaining "a
mottled or cathedral-glass effect through which the photography
would look like sketchy drawing or painting" (p. 277)—all with the
purpose of persuading the censors to pass a film in which he refused
to resort to the usual devices by which nudity was made acceptable.
The desired result was obtained. Indeed, as Man Ray reports events,
those to whom the film was submitted for visa approval found "its
apparent incoherence" more upsetting than its nudity. The film was
passed, subject to elimination of a shot showing the woman undress-
ing and of a subtitle which has a familiar ring for someone more
acquainted with surrealist verse than the board of censors were:
"One must beat the dead while they are cold."[9]

In his *Self Portrait* Man Ray declares categorically that he
was not interested in the art of the cinema, having no desire to be a
successful director (p. 278). After *L'Étoile de Mer*, only unlimited
funds would tempt him to make another movie. Temptation came
quite soon, in the form of an invitation from the Vicomte de Noailles.
Noailles was so "infected with the movie bug" (p. 284) that a little
later he was to sponsor two films which violently contradicted one
another: Buñuel's *L'Age d'Or* (1930) and Jean Cocteau's *Le Sang
d'un Poète* (1932). In 1929 he invited Man Ray to come to his house
in the south of France to film his home. Assured of complete free-

dom in the form of his movie, Man Ray accepted, making *Le Mystère du Château de Dés (The Mystery of the Château of the Dice).* Its actors, all Noailles's guests, wore stockings over their faces. Deliberately undercutting the dramatic possibilities of a dive in the private swimming pool after which Noailles failed to surface promptly, in one scene Man Ray used a reverse print. But by doing so he merely repeated an effect utilized before, in *Emak Bakia.* All in all, in this film, his last, Man Ray failed to take full advantage of Noailles's generosity as Buñuel was to do in *L'Age d'Or.*

The fact is that while Buñuel is by instinct a man of the cinema, Man Ray is not. The relative success of *L'Étoile de Mer* comes from felicitous blending of the language of the cinema with the verbal poem which inspired an attempt to parallel its effects in the medium of the film. As his film complements the scenario, so, going much further than simply illustrating it, Man Ray enlarges and enriches the text's content for the audience. The latter are invited to respond at one and at the same time to the images they see and to the subtitles they read.

A few years later, at the summer home of Lise Deharme, Man Ray began work on another film for which Breton and Éluard prepared a scenario. However, he was unable to carry the project through. All that remain are a number of stills which include a shot of Breton, reading at a window, a large dragonfly poised on his forehead.[10] The character of these stills indicates that the first reason Man Ray gives in *Self Portrait* for abandoning the cinema was not really a compelling one: "My curiosity had been satisfied—surfeited" (p. 286). His later confession comes closer to the mark: "I prefer the permanent immobility of a static work which allows me to make my deductions at my leisure, without being distracted by attendant circumstances" (p. 287). The most persuasive clue is one provided in the stills salvaged from the film he was not able to finish. Man Ray, who began to film because he was curious to see how a succession of pictures would look, fell back at last upon still photography as the form of picture-making most suited to his temperament. Breton's tribute "But here is Man Ray, Here is THE MAN WITH THE MAGIC-LANTERN HEAD"[11] highlights the important fact that, in the last analysis, the frame draws and holds Man Ray's attention in isolation, not in sequence. It is when he concentrates on the static image, such as he offers in his Rayograms and by use of the technique of solarization, which he invented, that he feels he can best provoke the spectator to adopt a new perspective upon reality. When Hans Richter invited his collaboration on the film *Dreams That Money Can Buy* (1944) Man Ray prepared a scenario, but declined to involve himself in the process of filming. The terms in which he expresses pleasure with the results Richter obtained are revelatory: "It was a miracle to see many concrete images formed out of a few words, without any fuss on my part over technical details" (p. 361). Since the forties, the man who no longer has the patience to wrestle with technical details in the production of concrete images in the cinema waits for a film that will show him something he has never seen and that he does not understand.[12]

Man Ray's experiments with film were never intended to do anything more than express dissatisfaction with the cinema as an art form and curiosity to see how difficult it might be to resist the influence of art on movies. Having presented his testimony, Man Ray has seen no reason to try to go further. He has even declined offers of financial assistance which would have permitted him to continue experimenting. His connections with the surrealist group were never so close that he felt under an obligation to surrealism to pursue his inquiry into the potential of the cinema. In any case, he could argue with clear conscience, he was free to withdraw from a campaign in which he had acquitted himself honorably. He could be confident that the surrealist campaign in the cinema had found in Luis Buñuel, whose *Un Chien andalou* (1928) was made the same year as his own *L'Étoile de Mer,* a general of incomparable ability.

In Paris since 1925, Luis Buñuel had worked as assistant director on three films, two of them made by avant-garde director Jean Epstein. He had read the surrealist publications circulating since that date, but made his first film independently of the surrealist group, from a script written in collaboration with another young Spaniard, Salvador Dali, no better known than he to Breton and his associates. When it was announced that a "surrealist film" called *Un Chien andalou (An Andalusian Dog)* would be shown at the Studio 28, which specialized in avant-garde movies, the surrealists were as suspicious as might be expected. However, after Breton had viewed Buñuel's movie at a private showing, *Un Chien andalou* was granted full approval by the surrealist group, and for good reason.

Like Man Ray in *L'Étoile de Mer,* Buñuel and Dali revealed in the scenario of *Un Chien andalou* their firm rejection of aestheticism. It opens with a prologue:

Once upon a time . . .
    A balcony at night. A man is sharpening his razor near the balcony. The man looks at the sky through window panes and sees . . .

A light cloud advancing toward a full moon.
Then a young woman's head, with eyes wide open. Toward
one of the eyes a razor blade advances.
The light cloud passes now in front of the moon.
The razor blade moves across the young woman's eye cut-
ting it open.

One limits the purpose and scope of *Un Chien andalou* in saying, as
an American critic has done, that it aims simply to horrify and
shock its audience.[13] Dali and Buñuel, who wields the open razor in
the first sequence, wanted to go beyond this. Knowing only too well
that the vanguard cinema was, as Buñuel has put it, directed exclusively to "the artistic sensibility and to the reason of the spectators,"[14] they were determined from the start to undermine the
avant-garde's appeal. They began doing so by alluding ironically to
the techniques characteristic of vanguard trends.

The movement of the cloud as it approaches the moon parallels that of the razor brought close to the eye. However, since the
cloud obscuring the moon is anything but the equivalent of an open
razor slicing an eyeball, this movement is not limited in value to
creating a simple formalistic equation. The elementary aesthetic
pleasure which seems to be promised by the parallelism of similar
forms and movements is exploded. A movement introducing one of
the commonplaces of the cinema (clouds shutting out moonlight)
liberates physical revulsion, as the razor suppresses sight, producing
results so unpleasant that Buñuel himself was physically ill, after
he had cut through the eyeball of a dead animal to create a realistic
effect.

The prologue is followed by a scene which takes place eight
years later, involving a male character clearly different from the one
played by Buñuel earlier. The absence of a consecutive plot sets off
the film's initial brutal gesture as offensively gratuitous. The script-
writers' refusal to explain how their prologue relates to what comes
after makes their first sequence stand out from the film, instead of
being absorbed or justified through the action that comes later.

Frédéric Grange has noted that "a systematic analysis of the
film's content would remain vague and imprecise."[15] But he has not
noticed that this is because a systematic analysis is impossible. He is
like the majority of commentators, giving away his unwillingness to
acknowledge Buñuel's method in *Un Chien andalou* for what it is:
an attack upon systematization in film commentary. Typically,
Grange prefers to attribute the lack of "internal coherence" in *Un
Chien andalou* to conflict within Buñuel who "seems not to have

been able to accept this incoherence" (p. 10). He would have done better to confine himself to confessing what he himself cannot accept. Nothing in Buñuel's adaptation of the script or his subsequent comments on his first film entitles us to conclude that *Un Chien andalou* says anything less than it was designed to say.

Another critic, Martine Mabire, is just as misleading. Making a commendable if misplaced effort to grant Buñuel a respectability which could have no appeal for him, she speaks of "obsessional images" and "exterior elements" in his movie as being "interpreted" by the "heroes" of *Un Chien andalou*. These images and elements, she suggests, "punctuate the dramatic construction." It would appear that whatever Buñuel has done, it is thus "justified" by something Mlle Mabire calls his "conception of art."[16] Failure to adduce a definition of this conception of art is an especially noteworthy feature of Martine Mabire's essay. Just as noteworthy is her inconsistent admission, at the end; "We see laid before our eyes with the persuasive force of the cinema that which we try to reject from our consciousness."

Turning from unconvincing interpretations of this nature, we discover that Dali and Buñuel, in order to place their intentions beyond doubt, planned their film so as to demonstrate their lack of concern for plot structure. To stress this feature of the movie, they included several disparaging allusions to the conventions of the silent movie drama, ridiculing its pantomine of passion and stylized gesture. The scenario notes the "angry rancorous gesture" of the young woman who, "eight years later," has just watched from her window as a man passing in the street below fell from his bicycle into the mud of the gutter; her "frenzied" kisses on his mouth, eyes, and nose, when she has rushed down to his aid; the "anguished attention" with which later, in her room, the man stares at his right hand, overrun with ants; a second woman's display of "extraordinary emotion" when a policeman, picking up a stick which is really a severed hand with painted finger nails, gives it to her, after wrapping it up and putting it in the mysterious box the cyclist was wearing when we first saw him; communication of the same emotion to the cyclist and to the first woman, who have been observing the second from upstairs; mutilation of the woman in the street by a passing car. In each case the scenario places emphasis upon the theatrical character of emotion and gesture. And appropriate stress is given in the film itself.

In the order noted, this unrelated succession of incidents and responses is followed by a major scene showing the man attacking the first woman. The tone of the scenario and the mood of the film remain unchanged even here. As the man palpates the woman's breasts and thighs, we are to notice "the terrible expression of anguish" on his face. In a dramatic film, the shot bringing his expression to our attention would be a prelude to the moment of greatest tension. In *Un Chien andalou*, however, this shot introduces some deliberately humorous effects for which Dali and Buñuel have been given less than full credit. Not until the man's mouth has released a dribble of blood that falls on her bare breast, not until his expression has changed (his eyes now shining "evil" and "lustful"), not until he has chased her across the room, his mouth closed "as though drawn in by a sphincter," does the scenario note, ironically, "She realizes that a disagreeable or violent scene is about to begin." As she hides behind a little table, the man "gestures like the villain of a melodrama," and looks about him, "seeking something." Now his hands grasp two ropes which he strains to draw with him, as he advances toward her.

At this point certain spectators, whom a feeling of disorientation earlier in the film has left ill at ease, regain confidence. At last, they judge, a scene straight out of Freud ("rêve de Buñuel et de Dali, presumably)! The scenario lists elements which the film faithfully places before our eyes:

> We see passing by first a cork, then a melon, two Brothers from a parochial school and last two magnificent grand pianos. The pianos are filled with the rotting corpses of donkeys whose hooves, tails, rumps and excrement overflow. When one of the pianos passes the camera we see a big donkey head resting on the keyboard.

As we watch the man straining "desperately" to reach the woman, slowed down by his grotesque burden, are we not being offered images of inhibitive influences which hold him back, when he attempts to rape her? This interpretation is permissible, no doubt. But those who defend it exclusively betray two weaknesses of which no surrealist would be guilty. They testify to their need to view *Un Chien andalou* in such a manner as to account for what it presents in terms and on a level that seem to them reasonably acceptable. On top of this, their need for a reasonable explanation causes them to ignore the specifically subversive form of surrealist humor which is one of the most distinctive features of a film called, irrelevantly, *An Andalusian Dog*. In so doing, they restrict the scope of the scene they are analyzing so earnestly. They neglect to notice that its humor contributes to mounting an attack upon good taste, which Dali has condemned as "one of the principal causes of the growing sterility of the French mind."

It was Dali who "made up" the donkeys, pouring pots of glue over them, enlarging their eye sockets with scissors, and cutting their mouths open "to make the white row of teeth show to better advantage." Reporting these details,[17] Dali helps us see the predicament into which *Un Chien andalou* maliciously precipitates the film-goer whose taste has been developed by aestheticism. The white teeth of the rotting donkey pick up, visually, the white keys of the piano. Yet disgust makes us reluctant to accept the parallel.

Elsewhere Buñuel and Dali use the same mocking approach, in order to provoke us to caution in our well-educated response to avant-garde techniques. A close-up of the striped box strapped to the cyclist's chest is easily identified with the falling rain of the first scene after the prologue. Indeed, the scenario draws attention to this: "A fade-in with the box whose oblique stripes are superimposed on the streaks of the rain." When hands holding a little key open the box and take from it an object wrapped in tissue paper, the script specifies that only thickness of line distinguishes the falling rain, the stripes on the box, the tissue paper, and the pattern on the object taken from the box, a striped tie. Visual association of the kind to which the avant-garde cinema had accustomed its audience makes it impossible for the viewer of *Un Chien andalou* to ignore a flagrant sexual symbol, which the woman soon after lays out on her bed.

To escape from her attacker, the woman takes refuge in an adjacent room, identical with the one she has left. On "the same bed" lies her pursuer whose hand is "still" caught in the crack in the door where she has imprisoned it. He is now dressed as he was when cycling, and wears, we are told in the script, "a superstitious expression that seems to say: 'At this moment something really extraordinary is going to happen'." The arrival of a second man promises to heighten the suspense, and precipitates a scene of melodrama. The man on the bed "trembles." The other "imperiously" orders him to get up, and divests him of his strange cycling uniform as well as of the striped box. Inexplicably (the plot thickens!), the second man is shown full face, in slow motion, and appears to be a younger version of the first.

Made to stand in the corner like a disobedient schoolboy, and obliged to balance school books on each hand, the first man now has "a bitter treacherous expression." As the books change mysteriously into revolvers, amateur psychoanalysts in the audience bestir themselves, while those who delight in high drama also become particularly attentive, as they see the tables turned. The first man, "threatening the other with his weapons, forces him to 'put 'em up!'," then mortally wounds him, despite his compliance. Spectators of every persuasion are allowed plenty of time to interpret the climax to this sequence in their own way, while the fall of the wounded man's body is shown in very slow motion. Then they are obliged to reconsider their conclusion, as they discover that, by the time he has finished falling, the man is no longer in the room where he was shot. He is in the park, where his last gesture is to attempt to caress the bare shoulders of a woman seated beside him.

Throughout *Un Chien andalou* the pattern is the same. Dramatic interest is generated as readily as the impulse to psychoanalyze is stimulated. Yet every time humor intervenes, to dissipate effects it appeared at first the director's wish to create. Everything conspires to disorient the audience and undermine confidence in their ability to handle the material this movie assembles. No preconceptions are valid any longer, no preconditioning is proof against the force of humorous surprise.

When the cyclist raises his hand to his face, the woman looks at him "disdainfully." Removal of his hand reveals his mouth has disappeared. "The young woman seems to say to him, 'Well. So what?'" and applies lipstick to her own mouth. It takes the discovery that the man's mouth has been replaced by sprouting hairs to provoke a reaction in her. Some instinct causes her to look at her own armpit which appears hairless. Next she "contemptuously" sticks her tongue out at him and, opening "a connecting door," walks into another room. This room we confidently expect to be the identical one from which she came earlier. But now it is "a wide sea shore," where the waves cast up the cyclist's box and uniform (thrown out of the window by the *alter ego* who tore them off him, earlier), and his bicycle too. The story which began "once upon a time" ends "in the spring time," with a desert in which the two main characters appear blind, buried to the chest in sand, their clothes torn and their bodies covered with insects.

In his notes on the making of *Un Chien andalou*, Buñuel assures us that, when working out the sequence of scenes, he and Dali rejected as "irrelevant" every idea of a rational, aesthetic, or technical nature. But this is not, as it may seem at first, tantamount to a confession that only the irrelevant appeared admissible during the creation of a movie Buñuel qualifies as "deliberately anti-plastic, anti-artistic." In *Un Chien andalou*, ends take precedence over means. The script-writers did not fail to turn to their own advantage techniques borrowed from the modes of cinematic expression they wished to depose. Buñuel reports, for example, that although he and Dali refused to merely transcribe dream experience in their movie, they found in dreams "a fruitful analogy." To the extent that the story line—to utilize a conventional term hardly applicable here—is the consequence of "a CONSCIOUS psychic automatism," it does not attempt to reconstruct a dream, Buñuel affirms. But it "profits from a mechanism analogous to that of dreams."

Buñuel explains further that the principle of free association was intentionally applied in *Un Chien andalou:* when an image suggested itself it was "immediately discarded," if it had "a conscious association with an earlier idea." He has confided to François Truffaut, who cites him in the magazine *Arts* on July 22, 1955, "Dali and I would choose gags and objects that came to our minds and we would reject without pity anything that could signify something." Far from denying significance, then, Dali and Buñuel simply rejected as unworthy of interest meanings dictated by rational associations and sequence. Irrational associations, on the other hand, are not only admitted in their film but—as those who would like to impress us with their skill in interpreting them neglect to point out[18]—openly invited.

Like the film Artaud imagined under the title "La Coquille et le Clergyman," like Man Ray's *L'Étoile de Mer,* Buñuel's first movie stands as a statement of faith in irrational imagery as more promising than rational imagery for those who wish to see the cinema return to its original barbarity, and who judge its originality by the film's capacity to explore the unknown.

The Moral Path

Results in which surrealists find every justification for Buñuel's use of the cinema as a mode of inquiry into the nature of the surreal were obtained at some risk, in *Un Chien andalou.* The care taken to leave this film open to interpretation by a magnetizing imaginative attraction, exercised by surrealist aspiration, leaves it open also to misinterpretation, thanks to the pull of forces quite independent of surrealist thought and feelings.

To a surrealist, the intangible mystery of *Un Chien andalou* lies in the magic which has transformed a movie that mimics film melodrama while mocking it mercilessly into a disturbing drama about human life. It is played out by characters whose actions immerse us in violence, even as humorous presentation of their conduct reduces them to pasteboard creatures posturing wildly, and acting largely in contempt of psychological motivation. Yet how many of those who saw it in 1928 were sensitive to the nature of the transformation of elements wrought in Buñuel's movie? Very few, if we are to believe the director himself. Publishing the scenario in the twelfth and final issue of the first surrealist magazine, *La Révolution surréaliste* (December 15, 1929), he added the following statement:

> The publication of this scenario in *La Révolution surréaliste* is the only one I authorize. It expresses without any sort of reserve my complete adherence to surrealist thought and activity. *An Andalusian Dog* would not exist, if surrealism did not exist.
>
> A *successful film*, that is what the majority of the people who have seen it think. But what can I do against the devotees of all forms of novelty, even if the novelty outrages their deepest convictions, against a press that has been bribed or is insincere, against the imbecile crowd that found *beautiful* or *poetic* something which was, basically, but a desperate, passionate call to murder?

Buñuel perceived, now, that *Un Chien andalou* was too closely patterned after the dream to avoid the dangers foreseen by Artaud when publishing "La Coquille et le Clergyman." He had been able to take full advantage of the freedom with which the oneiric state permits images to present themselves, in the absence of an order prescribed by reason. But Buñuel had not succeeded in preventing those viewers who wished to do so from treating his film as simply an attempt to communicate the illogicality of dreaming. He left them free to see *Un Chien andalou* as a succession of disparate incidents, bearing no necessary relationship to everyday living. It took the response of his public to prove he and Dali had not been as alert as circumstances warranted to the need for making clear to everyone that *Un Chien andalou* was far from being just another technical exercise in cinematographic form.

Of course, a first important step had been taken already. *Un Chien andalou* had fought the commercial and vanguard cinematic modes on their own terms. While it had seemed essential to begin by doing this, it was imperative, next, to make sure to erase from the public's thoughts misconceptions about surrealism's reasons for treating the movies as it elected to do. Realizing this, and appreciating too that he had only himself to blame for not safeguarding against misrepresentation of his call to murder. Buñuel could see that he had not yet gone far enough. At this stage he needed an opportunity to remedy matters, the chance to establish his position beyond a shadow of doubt. Sooner than he might have expected, the opportunity did come. The Vicomte de Noailles offered to sponsor a film which Buñuel would be free to make in his own way. Drawing up the following scenario, Buñuel called it *L'Age d'Or (The Golden Age)*:

> Scorpions live in the rocks. Climbing on one of these rocks, a bandit catches sight of a group of archbishops who are singing seated in a mineral countryside. The bandit runs to announce to his friends the presence close by of the men from Majorca (these are the archbishops). Having reached his hut, he finds his friends in a strange state of weakness and depression. They pick up their arms and all leave except the youngest who can no longer even get up. They set off through the rocks; but one after the other, giving up, they fall to the ground. Then the bandit chief collapses hopelessly. From where he is, he hears the sound of the sea and perceives the men from Majorca who, now, are in the state of skeletons strewn among the stones.
>
> An enormous convoy reaches the coast at this precipitous, desolate spot. The convoy is made up of priests, soldiers, nuns, ministers, and various people in civilian clothes. All head for the spot where the remains of the men from Majorca lie. Imitating those in authority who lead the convoy, the crowds bare their heads.
>
> They are engaged in founding Imperial Rome. Its first stone is being laid when piercing cries distract everyone's attention. In the mud, a few feet away, a man and a woman struggle amorously. They are separated. The man is beaten and the police drag him off.
>
> This man and woman will be the protagonists of the film. The man, thanks to a document which reveals his high estate and the importance of the humanitarian and patriotic mission with which the government has entrusted him, is soon set free again. From then on, all his activity is directed toward Love. In the course of a scene of unfulfilled love, presided over by the violence of acts that accomplish nothing, the protagonist is called to the phone by the high personage who has charged him with responsibility for the humanitarian mission in question. This minister accuses him. Because he has abandoned his task, thousands of old men and innocent children have perished. The protagonist of the film receives this accusation with insults and, without hearing any more of

it, returns to the side of the woman he loves at the moment when a very inexplicable chance occurrence succeeds, more finally than before, in separating her from him. Subsequently, one sees him throwing out of the window a burning pine tree, an enormous piece of agricultural machinery, an archbishop, a giraffe, feathers. All this at the precise instant when the survivors of the Castle of Selligny cross its snow-covered drawbridge. The Count of Blangis is evidently Jesus Christ. This final episode is accompanied by a paso doble.

Despite the interpolation of disconcerting elements, the scenario of *L'Age d'Or*, sketchy though it is, allows us to anticipate a film far more conventionally put together than *Un Chien andalou*. At first sight, the initial section, devoted to scorpions, appears dispensable. And since only a minority among film audiences will identify the closing sequence as an illusion to the Marquis de Sade's *Les 120 Journées de Sodome (The 120 Days of Sodom)*, it seems, for the time being, that we can ignore this part, too. Thus we are left with a plot outline which looks fairly unified and coherent. It is true there is still evidence of lack of proportion: the two main characters are not introduced until the last paragraph. All the same, one has confidence, more than with the previous film Buñuel directed, that this one will have a theme and a sense of purpose.

Commenting on that purpose, Frédéric Grange has remarked, "Now Buñuel wants to establish in *L'Age d'Or* a total critique of the world and of its history. Hence he can do nothing other than be in contradiction with the surrealist group."[19] However, Buñuel himself supplied proof that Grange's interpretation is totally erroneous, when declaring, "It was surrealism which revealed to me that, in life, there is a moral path man cannot refuse to take. Through surrealism I discovered for the first time that man isn't free."[20] Far from discouraging him, surrealism impelled him to uncover the weakness of contemporary society in *L'Age d'Or*.

By the time Buñuel made his film, in 1930, the first surrealist magazine had been replaced by a second, *Le Surréalisme au service de la Révolution* [*Surrealism in the Service of Revolution* (1930–33)]. The trend to which the new title pointed anticipated in Breton's *Second Manifeste du Surréalisme*, evidenced keen social awareness among all surrealists in France. By now, their conception of revolt and freedom was colored by a growing sense of increasing social estrangement and by appreciation of the critical need to direct their activity against society. The surrealist group's struggle against oppressive social forces, which seemed intent upon stifling their call for individual freedom of action and moral courage, provided a background against which *L'Age d'Or* stands in clear definition.

Although the scenario of *L'Age d'Or* delays mention of its central characters, it leaves no doubt on one score. Kyrou cannot be found guilty of falsifying the evidence it supplies for writing, "There are two camps: the lovers and the others. By the very structure of rotting society, they cannot but find themselves face to face, and society, outraged and terrified by love, will set in motion all its poison-spilling machines: government officials, priests, families, fine words, police, members of high society."[21] Speaking from the surrealist standpoint, Kyrou is simply paraphrasing in 1950 the declaration made by the surrealist group in Paris, when *L'Age d'Or* was first shown twenty years before—"In a period of 'prosperity,' the social values accepted in *The Golden Age* must be established by satisfying a need in the oppressed to destroy. [. . .] Despite all threats to stifle it, this film will serve very usefully, we think, to pierce heavens that are always less beautiful than those it shows us in a mirror."[22]

The end of the declaration just quoted remains cryptic so long as we confine our acquaintance with *L'Age d'Or* to what the scenario tells us about the film. The significance of what the surrealist group had to say emerges much more clearly from examination of the movie by way of the detailed shooting script, in which Buñuel elaborated on the virtualities of the original sketch.

Taking the sequence involving the mirror as our starting point, we find its content to be somewhat confusing, on first contact, after the impression we have gathered from the scenario, with the help of Buñuel's comments on his film, and of the surrealists' remarks about it:

> 92. Close-up of the dressing-table taken at an angle so one does not see the image reflected in the mirror. Young woman arrives and sits facing it. Her face reflects great serenity, although her eyes, as if wrapt in a vague dream, indicate she is contemplating a cherished image within. She looks absent-mindedly at the mirror, almost automatically, she takes the buff in her hands. (These scenes very slow.)
>
> 93. Very close shot. Link up with the young woman seated facing her dressing-table, front view. She begins to polish her nails with a mechanical movement using the buff, but not continuously, but rather without watching and keeping each movement distinct. After polishing for a while, she puts it

down on the table. She looks at her fingers without seeing them: then she turns her eyes to the mirror. Her eyes almost covered with tears. Her crossed hands have been laid on her chest, near her heart, but still automatically, thus nullifying the theatrical side the gesture can have. (Rapid fade) (94.) The woman continues her dream of love, her head swaying gently, her brow furrowed, with tears spilling from her eyes. Hearing the barking of a dog she will give a start and her emotion will be increased. She bites her lips to link with the movement made by the character in 95.

94. Fade-in. Shot taken from behind a garden railing. In the foreground leaning against it a dog is barking at someone who must be coming along the sidewalk. The arrested man and the policeman appear walking on the sidewalk behind the railing. The man's expression is similar to the woman's, that is to say his eyes are also almost covered with tears and his hands with the handcuffs like those of the woman, on his heart. The prisoner tries to stop, looking at the dog with great tenderness (93).

95. Insert of the prisoner in the attitude described. He bites his lips a little to link with the gesture of the woman in 93.

96. Insert of the young woman in the state described, looking at herself absent-mindedly in the mirror (97). Her hair and her clothes begin to ripple under the gust of wind coming from the mirror. (End 97.)

97. Close-up of the mirror that reflects neither the woman nor the room, but a beautiful sky with oval clouds, lazily drifting by in the sunset. In the foreground, the dry silhouette of a tree shaken by the wind.

98. C-U side-face of the young woman and the mirror, but in such a way that one sees what the latter reflects. The woman with her hair still tossed by the wind resting her face on her hands, lays her forehead against the mirror.

(Slow fade-out. After, keep the screen dark for a few feet.)

Are we not to conclude we have just read in summary an episode destined to provide, at best, only temporary relief from suffering, through a dream of evasion? And are we not, in consequence, on the brink of accepting *L'Age d'Or* as a film that takes the route of evasion? Do we conclude that it uses love not as a challenge to the world we know, but as a satisfying means of escaping its pressures and demands, albeit to a limited extent? No firm answers to these questions can be reached unless the opening section of the film, the one dealing with scorpions, is taken into account.

Looking over the original plan, we discover Buñuel has decided to use sound in his movie. A reference to the archbishops singing may not seem very persuasive proof of this, since the audience could well be made to understand what the clerics are doing without actually hearing them. However, the sense of one notation regarding the bandit chief ("From where he is, he hears the sound of the sea") would be very difficult to communicate without a sound track. Later, too, one would expect "piercing cries" from the lovers to be heard. And we can be sure the concluding episode would not make its full effect unless the accompanying paso doble were audible. In view of other surrealists' mistrust of sound in films, then, Buñuel's intention to use it for *L'Age d'Or* is of major significance, calling for consideration of the advantages he felt it could bring in a movie designed to express the surrealist viewpoint on life and love.

Although the original scenario anticipates the use of sounds, it gives only the haziest impression of the function reserved for them, neglecting to stress every point at which sound will be used. One important omission is noticeable at once, if we watch the film with the scenario to hand. The opening sequence about scorpions is accompanied by featureless music of the variety favored by directors of documentary films. Here the music serves to insist upon the documentary nature of the first episode, which treats us to subtitles like this one: "The scorpion is a genus of Arachnida that lives generally under rocks." The ironic tone of *Un Chien andalou* is present once again. But its adoption in *L'Age d'Or* cannot be taken to signify the director is merely trying to be humorous, this time. Buñuel's next film, the short subject called *Las Hurdes* (1932) will show he does not scorn the documentary. In fact, the existence of his third movie, made so soon after *L'Age d'Or*, bids one think twice before dismissing the sequence about scorpions as being without organic relationship to what follows in *L'Age d'Or*.

Addressing himself to those who elected to believe *Un Chien andalou* was a filmed dream, Buñuel uses sound to insist that they have no right to relegate his new film to the category of cinematographic experiments extraneous to life. The documentary section upon which *L'Age d'Or* opens characterizes this as neither an evasive nor a fanciful movie. The audience's attention is held by subtitles which instruct. Meanwhile background music encourages them to give the film director no less trust than they are in the habit of according the makers of documentaries, with no less confidence in the scientific accuracy of the material he puts before them. *L'Age d'Or* begins as an object lesson. Only those determined to ignore its message should be able to come away from this film having learned nothing.

Sound helps place emphasis where Buñuel feels it necessary, conditioning audience response to what follows the opening sequence. After his first, the contrast offered by Buñuel's second film is thus sharply defined. The director's purpose in *Un Chien andalou* was to sever consciously perceived connections between succeeding images and sequences. It is much more characteristic of his method in *L'Age d'Or*, though, that sequences and individual shots are connected in such a way as to oblige the spectator to draw conclusions which will influence his view of life. Buñuel intends to control viewer reaction here far more directly than in *Un Chien andalou*. His intention is evidenced in his shooting script by the prominence given effects plainly designed to elicit anticipated responses, no less by use of sound than by arrangement of images.

As we turn again to the mirror episode, it is as well to remember it follows a scene in which the hero was arrested, because he and the young woman had interrupted an official ceremony with their love-making. Durgnat's naive comment that arrest comes as a result of some misunderstanding[23] shows that he, for one, misses the point: society, Buñuel wants to demonstrate, deprecates love, turning lovers into outlaw figures and separating them. While the hero is being led through the streets, billboards displaying beautiful women give him the chance to pursue an erotic daydream, the young woman being substituted in his thoughts for the film-star types represented. As substitution occurs, we see the young woman reclining in the attitude adopted by the model on the bill-board, and Buñuel insists that the man's dream coincides with the woman's. The effect carefully introduced at this stage closely parallels that of the shared dream in Hathaway's *Peter Ibbetson*. But Buñuel goes further; using the woman's "libidinous trembling" to give focus to several earlier hints at onanistic activity.

During the mirror episode, the onanistic motif is merely suggested, as the woman absent-mindedly buffs her finger nails. However, Buñuel stresses the freedom she and her lover enjoy to be together, despite their separation and regardless of the handcuffs the man wears as his captors lead him away. Without consciously knowing what she is doing, the woman lays her hands on her chest, so establishing a visible link with her lover, who bites his lips, without knowing she is biting hers. Visual parallelism, here, places before us evidence of unity between two people in love, as impermeable to the efforts of those determined to separate them as it is rationally inexplicable in its manifestations.

When the young woman hears a dog bark, the noise does not wake her from her daydream. On the contrary, although she "will give a start," the shooting script specifies that her emotion will be *increased*. The reason for this is made apparent without delay. The dog she hears is not outside the house where she sits before her mirror, but in the street along which her lover is walking, in another part of the town. Through juxtapositions of this sort Buñuel illustrates the interrelation of dream and reality Breton will discuss at length in his *Les Vases communicants* [*The Communicating Vessels* (1932)], by making use of evidence inadmissible to reason. As the heroine of *L'Age d'Or* hears a sound too far away to be audible, reality breaks in, not to terminate her dream but to prolong it and confirm its validity, as spatial barriers between her and the man she loves are overthrown by the passion uniting them.

Sound gives another dimension to the revolt of lovers who deny the conventional obligations society imposes, and assert their freedom to go their own way. While society invokes moral pressures in its attempt to cripple love, love offers the prospect of release from all restraint. Hence the care taken in the shooting script of *L'Age d'Or* to ensure that the image appearing in the young woman's mirror will remain concealed from the audience until they have had time to understand *why* it does not reflect either the woman herself or the everyday reality of the room where she sits. The mirror images desire; it presents a picture of what the woman's daydream projects with such force that the conventionally realistic reflection of reality is displaced by an ideal vision, born of love.

The barking of a dog is not the only sound to be heard in the mirror episode. Two other important auditive impressions claim the audience's attention. The first supplies a definite link with the previous sequence, during which the heroine entered her bedroom and found a cow on her bed.

Providing the spectacle of a cow lying on her bed, Buñuel translated into visual terms the familiar identification in colloquial French between "cow" *(vache)* and "cop" *(vache)*. The young woman in *Un Chien andalou*, we remember, laid out the necktie-penis on her bed. It is not difficult therefore to account for the presence of the unwelcome bovine creature on the bed of the heroine of *L'Age d'Or*, whose lover has been taken from her by the police. And we have no trouble understanding why the young woman wished to rid herself of her unwelcome guest. However, although she has with comparative ease persuaded the cow to leave, the sound of the bell hanging from the animal's neck is still to be heard, after the door has closed behind it.

The clang of the cow-bell persists, when Buñuel cuts to the lover, shown walking between two *vaches*. In this way sound explains the pun the director has just made, as it connects the two sequences, in a manner making intelligible to the spectator the addition of the noise of baying hounds—to emphasize the man's role as quarry, tracked down by social and moral prejudice. The effect introduced through these two sequences is cumulative, leading into the mirror episode, throughout which the cow-bell and the baying of the pack can be heard in the background.

Now a third sound is introduced, coming from the gust of wind emanating from the mirror to ruffle the woman's hair and clothes, as she gazes at the scene visible in the glass. We hear the wind, just as we see its effect, before we know where it comes from and discover that the vision revealed in the mirror is not imprisoned behind glass. Sight and sound have combined to present proof to two of the senses by which we make contact with reality that the dream can exert an influence in the world we all know.

Throughout the sequence taking place before the mirror— truly typifying the mirror of the marvelous, about which Pierre Mabille has written a book-length study[24]—the liberating dream conjured up by love intrudes visibly and audibly upon conventional reality, as space surrenders its power to separate those whom love brings together, and as all efforts to police emotion come to nothing.

No sooner has this scene presented its testimony to the capacity of love to surmount all obstacles than the hero produces proof of political immunity. This is a document proving the respectability of his official role and his acceptability, from both the social and moral standpoints. However, as the scenario promised, he will use his freedom to pursue a course of action dictated by love, at the expense of all other commitments. Production of the document that has earned him liberty is revealed to be an act of political opportunism, in defiance of the obligations to which he seemed to be submitting. In dealing with the oppressive forces of society, we discover, the individual is entitled to use all means available to gain and to defend his liberty. Hence the "moral path man cannot refuse to take" exemplifies repudiation of the moral values by which society seeks to confine his freedom of action.

From now on the hero's conduct offers no surprise to someone who remembers that he and the woman he loves committed the scandalous act of protesting against the status quo at the very moment when society was organizing itself into a political structure based upon the Church (the allusion to building Rome on a rock is transparent). Their erotic cries in the mud draw attention to the subversive role of *l'amour fou*, which society must try to control and if possible eradicate. Once he has been released again, the hero confounds society's plans to curb love. He has been swept along by what Breton termed "the wind of perdition" which is—as the mirror sequence has amply shown—the liberating wind of desire. Now he will combat all that stigmatizes the cause of love. Embarking on the "anxious headlong life" to which Desnos promised that eroticism introduces us, he strives to attain "absolute liberty."

In the scenario of *L'Age d'Or* a brief footnote declares, "You see also in this film, among other details, a blind man ill-treated, a dog run over, a son almost killed for no reason at all by his father, an old lady slapped, etc." In accordance with this specification, Buñuel's tale of iconoclasm and anti-conformity is presented in an atmosphere of violence far less ambiguous than in *Un Chien andalou*. As the hero is beaten and dragged away, he kicks a dog and crushes an insect. These apparently insignificant details are highlighted by the documentary sequence devoted to the poisonous scorpions, shown killing a rat. A second documentary passage places identification of Rome with the Church beyond question, through a succession of shots of the Vatican (all of them, the shooting script stresses, "anodyne"). These picture-postcards views are followed by a sequence showing a respectable gentleman kicking a violin along the sidewalk.

Like the presence of a cow on a bed a little later on, the conduct of this man, whom we do not see again, would seem pointless and distractingly ludicrous, without its contribution to the undercurrent of violence that Buñuel takes care to sustain even in his second documentary section. As *L'Age d'Or* progresses, Buñuel's camera interrupts its exploration of the Vatican to capture proof of the intrusive character of violence. Very shortly afterward, the hero is roughly treated by those escorting him through the streets. When he pauses to look at a billboard the shooting script specifies, "'Quite brutally, striking him, they tear their prisoner from this sight."

Forcibly denied fulfillment of his desire, the hero protests by resorting to violence. After his release, his first action is to knock down a blind man. Not long after, when his mistress' mother drops a little wine on his suit, he slaps her face. The daughter is delighted, for she too recognizes the part violence must play in the rejection of society's usages. Meanwhile, no one betrays sympathy when a servant girl is burned by a fire in the kitchen. And there is hardly any more show of concern when a gamekeeper shoots his son for spoiling a cigarette he is rolling. The hero's callous indifference to duty leaves the minister by whom he has been entrusted with his mission no alternative but to commit suicide.

Throughout *L'Age d'Or*—a contemporary Spaniard's ironic *Siglo de Oro*—violence provides the counterpoint to frustration, placing emphasis upon the ethical posture to which surrealist convictions destine man. While the mirror episode serves to call upon the audience to look beneath the surface appearance of things and to penetrate their meaning, as surrealism reveals it, onanism in *L'Age d'Or* represents protest against contingent circumstance. Reaffirming something "Hands Off Love" declared three years before, Buñuel's film depicts love as *l'amour fou*, a disruptive agent of the first order. But it depicts also the "torment" which according to Desnos is the characteristic state of those in love. In a society where sexual relations are relegated to the level of animal contact, love is in constant danger of being crushed out. As Buñuel's lovers come together once more, during a concert in the garden, circumstances combine to make love difficult for them. Called to the phone to answer to his superior, the hero leaves the heroine consoling herself by sucking the toe of the statue beside which they have been sitting. Upon his return, they attempt to resume their love-making, but without visible success.

At the crucial stage where society appears to have defeated love, Buñuel makes use of sound to communicate a message of protest no less impervious to rational objection than that of the mirror episode. Inhibition and prejudice may still stand in the way of love. But it cannot limit the lovers' enjoyment of one another. Although their lips remain motionless, they carry on a conversation —the *monologue intérieur*, as the French call stream of consciousness in fiction, being replaced by a *dialogue intérieur* during which the lovers are entirely free from the restraints paralyzing them. Their exchange culminates triumphantly in the repeated phrase "Mon amour," even though what appears on the screen—a gush of blood from the hero's mouth, for example—testifies to anguish, not happiness. Space was no obstacle earlier. Now physical conditions are just as powerless to prevent man and woman from enjoying one another. And even time counts for nothing. We see the woman age, yet the amorous conversation continues, undiminished in its passion, despite the visible ravages of time.

While love is consummated in another place, conventional ties take their toll in the garden. The woman leaves her lover to join the orchestra leader, who arrives holding his hands to his temples in a gesture reminiscent of the suicide of the minister, who has blown his brains out. Enraged at seeing love sacrificed in this way, the hero carries out the violently destructive act foreshadowed in the scenario. Tearing pillows to pieces in an ornate bedroom, he throws feathers and a variety of objects, predominantly of phallic shape, out of the window.

Love has been defeated, but by inhibition, not by social and political pressure. Hence the rage displayed by the lover. He has denied all obligations so as to give himself over to his passion, but finds the woman he adores is not as free as he. Hence, too, the final section of Buñuel's film, where the invocation of the name of Sade introduces a sequence that is anything but redundant.

The shooting script is firm in its stress upon the connection to be established between the last section and the hero's act of destruction: "At the precise instant when these feathers torn by his furious hands were covering the ground at the foot of the window, at that very instant, we say, but very far from there, the survivors of the Castle of Selligny were coming out, back home in Paris." Buñuel's insistence provides the needed key to the function of the concluding passage which Kyrou confesses in his *Le Surréalisme au Cinéma* (p. 214) to finding "the most enigmatic" in *L'Age d'Or*. The hero has been shown repudiating his prescribed role in society, in order to devote himself exclusively to love. Socially undesirable, he has become an outcast, ostracized by those who no longer regard him as fit for their company. Condemned to frustration, he has been only partly successful in freeing himself from its consequences. And yet the feathers he scatters during his final outburst of revolt are to be considered an appropriate link between his rejection of society and the one represented in Sade's *Les 120 Journées de Sodome*.

The surrealists' admiration for the Marquis de Sade is beyond doubt, and so closely linked with their outlook upon life that there is no question of Buñuel's not sharing it. All the same, Kyrou takes the orthodoxy of Buñuel's thinking about Sade too much for granted. He fails to notice how originally Buñuel treats material for which he is plainly indebted to the writer revered by all surrealists as the Divine Marquis. To measure the extent of his originality we need to begin with the passage in the shooting script of *L'Age d'Or* where Buñuel makes his first reference to Sade's most revolutionary novel:

> To celebrate the most bestial of orgies, one hundred twenty days earlier four self-confessed deep-died scoundrels had shut themselves up in this impregnable castle. They have for God only their lubricity, for law only their depravity, for brake on their actions only their debauchery, being Godless roués,

without principle, without religion. The least criminal among them is soiled by more infamy than you can recount. In his eyes the life of a woman—what am I saying, of a woman—of all women on the globe is as indifferent as the destruction of a fly.

They had introduced with them into the castle, solely to serve their disgusting ends eight marvelous, eight splendid adolescent girls. So that their imagination, already corrupted in the extreme, should be continually excited, they had also brought with them four depraved women who incessantly kept the criminal voluptuousness of the four monsters alive with their stories. Here now is the departure from the Castle of Selligny of the survivors of the criminal orgies.

The four organisers and leaders. The Duke of Blangy [*sic*].

In Buñuel's summary of the plot of Sade's novel, the characters and their behavior are presented as monstrously repulsive and disgusting. Buñuel underscores all that is horrible in their outlook and terrifying in their conduct. There is not the slightest hint of the reasons for which the surrealists have always felt drawn to Sade as one of the greatest revolutionary thinkers of all time. In fact Buñuel's account might well have been written by someone to whom the name and work of Sade are totally abhorrent. Nothing he tells us highlights the special viewpoint that is Sade's. Nothing reminds those who know—and, more important, tells those who do not know—that Sade depicts all his monstrous heroes as products of nature. Instead, Buñuel speaks of those whom Blangis leads as having turned against nature. Every one of the key adjectives in the extract from his shooting script reproduced above stresses the perversion of natural instinct. Each points to the deviated form taken by desire, behind the "door which opens slowly as if the rust on its hinges prevented it from opening," when we first see Blangis and his companions, at the end of *L'Age d'Or*. Furthermore, the prominence given Blangis in both scenario and script strengthens, not weakens, the impression with which Buñuel leaves us.

Of the four leaders, the Duke of Blangis is not the least but the most criminal. Sade describes him in the following terms: "Born deceitful, hard-hearted, imperious, barbarous, selfish, equally prodigal in his pleasures and parsimonious when it came to being useful, a liar, glutton, drunkard, poltroon, sodomite, an incestuous man, a murderer, incendiary, thief, [. . .]." Noting that not a single virtue made up for all Blangis's vices, Sade adds:

What am I saying? not only did he not revere a single one, but they all inspired horror in him, and one would often hear him say that a man, to be truly happy in this world, should not only give himself over to all the vices, but never allow himself to have one virtue, and that it was not only a question of always doing evil, but that it was even a matter of never doing good.[25]

This is the man whose resemblance to the Christ the scenario promises to make evident to the audience.

Sade, who left *Les 120 Journées de Sodome* unfinished, providing not a single reference among his working notes to the circumstances in which his characters eventually would leave the Castle of Silling.[26] Since Buñuel found no authority in Sade's novel for the final sequence of *L'Age d'Or*, showing the main characters coming out through the doorway of the castle, what does he want to accomplish as he brings his film to a close?

The scenario announces the following. A little girl about thirteen years old appears on the threshold, a blood stain on her clothing at the height of one breast. She falls, exhausted, and is carried back into the castle. The script notes: "A pause during which nothing abnormal occurs, except a dreadful cry that comes from within." After a few moments the man who took her back inside reappears, without her. As all this is of Buñuel's own invention, he is entirely free to make a highly significant change, during the shooting of the scene. His script calls for the final act of murder to be carried out by one of Blangis's companions, the one dressed in the garb of a sixteenth-century bishop. But in the film the child is immolated by Blangis himself.

In view of Buñuel's original statement "The Count [*sic*] of Blangis is evidently Jesus Christ," it is significant that nothing in Sade's text authorizes identification in terms of physical resemblance. In fact, his portrait in *Les 120 Journées de Sodome* precludes such identification: "The Duke of Blangis, fifty, built like a satyr, endowed with a monstrous member and prodigious strength. One may regard him as the receptacle of all vices and of all crimes. He has killed his mother, his sister and three of his wives" (p. 62). Clearly, the physical similarity of the bearded Blangis in Buñuel's movie to the conventional Christ image is meant to prompt the audience to perceive resemblances of another order. As we detect these, we identify what is original in Buñuel's treatment and come to appreciate that he did not seek originality at the price of infidelity to Sade.

When characterizing his monstrous hero, Sade inverted the image of virtue depicted in Jesus' teachings: virtue was to inspire horror in Blangis, while he would dedicate himself exclusively to the pursuit of anti-Christian ideals. This "receptacle of all vices" was Sade's answer to New Testament teaching. Beyond doubt, Buñuel heartily approved of this. Refining his script right up to the moment when he filmed it, he offered an entirely consistent portrait of Blangis as the inversion of the Christ. Thus it is superfluous to let the audience hear the words "Suffer little children to come unto me . . . " as Blangis commits his final act of horror to the hideous accompaniment of a paso doble, within earshot if not before our eyes.

Only on the surface does Buñuel seem to contradict Sade, when he evidences disgust for all that Blangis represents. Sade's hero is spared censure because he is a product of nature. Buñuel's Blangis brings condemnation down upon himself because, as a Christ-figure, he represents denial and perversion of natural impulse. If Sade's Blangis is an Antichrist, Buñuel's is an unnatural Christ whose criminal success is contrasted with the defeat of natural passion which society attempts to stamp out, supporting and supported by the Church.

As Buñuel links the Savior with Sade's arch-criminal, on the basis of the inversion of values for which surrealists blame Christianity, the audience find themselves implicated. As they are called upon to condemn the brutal cruelty of Blangis-Christ, they are invited to condone the violent rebellion of Buñuel's hero against society and its ways. Caught between conflicting emotions, they cannot help feeling disturbed. Shown for the first time on October 28, 1930, *L'Age d'Or* provoked a riot in the Studio 28, on December 3. On December 8 the Préfecture de Police demanded the suppression from the film program of the phrase "The Count of Blangis is evidently Jesus Christ." On December 11 the movie was officially banned, all prints being confiscated by the police, as though suppression of material evidence of surrealist revolt could erase from everyone's mind the final shot of a snow-covered cross "draped in woman's hair cruelly tossed by the wind and whitish with snow."

The Documentary

Tony Richardson has observed that, after *L'Age d'Or*, Buñuel "was to abandon surrealism completely" in his next film, *Las Hurdes* [*Land without Bread* (1932)].[27] Regrettably, Richardson does not say what basis he has for his claim. It is safe to assume, though, he would erect his argument on the fact that, in *Las Hurdes*, Buñuel confines himself to the documentary mode, suppressing all vestiges of plot, and allowing himself no incursions into the rationally unacceptable or inexplicable. Persuasive as this may be, at first sight, it is hardly sufficient evidence for concluding Buñuel turned his back on surrealism, with *L'Age d'Or* behind him. When Jacques Doniol-Valcroze and André Bazin asked, "How do you see the relation between surrealism and the documentary standpoint?" he replied unequivocally, in 1954, "I see an important relationship."

Like Frédéric Grange,[28] Richardson attempts to reduce surrealism to movie technique and use of film technique for the purpose of escaping or turning away from life. Buñuel, as it happens, is completely faithful to surrealist principles, seeing it as projecting an outlook on life that is anything but escapist. Provided the documentary approach can reflect that outlook, he and surrealists agree, it can be counted on to advance their ends. In *Las Hurdes* it does so admirably.

Kyrou's *Le Surréalisme au Cinéma* presents *Las Hurdes* as "the obvious prolongation of the two preceding films, an image of the world in which 'Imperial Rome' has finally triumphed" (p. 221). Without attaching *Las Hurdes* quite so rigidly to Buñuel's earlier work, we can still agree it marks a logical and indispensable step forward, fully prepared by *Un Chien andalou* and *L'Age d'Or*. Expanding his reply to Doniol-Valcroze and Bazin, Buñuel pointed out, "I made *Las Hurdes* because I had a surrealist way of looking at things and because I was interested in the problem of man. I saw reality in a way different from the way I would have seen it before surrealism."[29]

Returning home to Spain, Buñuel made *Las Hurdes* with funds won in a lottery. He was assisted by Éli Lotar and the surrealist Pierre Unik, who was already moving toward Communism. Like *L'Age d'Or*, *Les Hurdes* provoked a scandal. It was promptly banned by the Spanish republican government.

In *Las Hurdes* there are no actors, naturally. There is no scenario, either. Buñuel's material is life in the villages of a remote area of his homeland, where peasants live an incredibly miserable existence, dominated by abject poverty, disease, and death. As each picture appears before us—set agonizingly in isolation, since no effort is made to construct a narrative from successive shots—we are brought to a fuller realization of the function Buñuel habitually reserves for his camera.

No distracting technical experimentation is ever allowed to intrude, and the dominant impression communicated by the camera work is one of objective detachment. In reality, however, detachment is an illusory impression in *Las Hurdes*. Buñuel betrays no passion, it is true. But he does this so as to let the revolutionary testimony of his film take full effect. Thus the paradox of his method is this: like the use of Brahms's Fourth Symphony as background music in certain sequences, by establishing distance film technique stimulates us to involvement, not detachment; to horror not indifference. Just as the monstrous final sequence of *L'Age d'Or* is accentuated by the inhuman irrelevance of the paso doble, so the music of Brahms is scandalously out of place in the universe of suffering through which Buñuel's camera guides us without flinching or compromise. The detached voice of the commentator, whose even tones ought to be reassuring, heightens the shock of the visual imagery, as Unik's dispassionate commentary pursues us whenever we are tempted to close our eyes or to look away.

Buñuel is determined to spare his audience nothing. He compels us to witness the death of a donkey that has stumbled, spilling its load of hives. When these discharge hundreds of bees, by which the animal is stung to death, he makes us watch a dog feeding off the donkey's carcass. He and his camera crew refuse to help the poor beast, while we are powerless to do so—just as we are powerless to assist the cretins, of whom there are many in this part of the world, the commentator tells us in a toneless voice to the accompaniment of the languorous strains of romantic music.

The effect of the static camera, pitilessly immobile before cretinous children, is paralyzing in its horror. The role usually given the spectator during the projection of film documentaries is radically changed: Buñuel instructs by replacing enjoyment with suffering, as he provokes us to revolt against our passivity as mere onlookers. Where the documentary familiarly rests upon acceptance, the surrealist documentary of Buñuel is intended to solicit rejection. The revolt we come to feel wells up from emotion and from moral indignation at the plight of those we are obliged to watch live as the people of *Las Hurdes* do. *Las Hurdes* reveals the real to be no less unsettling than the irrational, and just as capable of disrupting our preconceptions about what *can* be. Surreality is born here of the conflict between, on one side, what we would prefer to believe reality is like and, on the other, what our ears and eyes show it to be. We see parents throwing away the bread given their children by the school teacher, because bread is a commodity they have never known in a world impermeable to Christian charity, where the only signs of wealth are to be found in the decoration inside churches.

The poetry of revolt translated through *Las Hurdes* testifies to the adaptability of the documentary mode to the expression of surrealism. Not surprisingly, *Las Hurdes* has been followed by a small but significant number of film documentaries directly inspired by surrealism. It seems appropriate, at first, to divide these into two categories.

The most easily identifiable category is that of the documentary film having the primary purpose of providing a photographic record of the work of a surrealist painter, with appropriate explanatory comment. The intention of documentary movies of this type is limited to introducing the audience sympathetically to the world evoked by the artist under examination. Raymond Borde's *Pierre Molinier* (1964) is an excellent example of these in their most successful form.

Publishing a selection of stills from *Pierre Molinier,* Borde observed, "This film is not a documentary related like a story. The preceding pictures therefore do not need editing. Kindly take them for what they are: breaking and entering into an oneiric world." Meanwhile the commentary, written by Breton, is no less to the point than Borde's note to the reader:

> Don't hang up, someone is speaking to you. Yes, something is welling up from the depths of a whirlwind to *become ecstatic* on the indefinitely troubled surface, whipped by thongs of water and troughed by hair spreading out in all directions.
>
> Pierre Molinier renews the pact with thunder. It is not surprising that the eye should be, in front of his canvases, called upon to divest itself first of all the habits and conventions which today preside over our way of seeing, increasingly blindly subject to fashion.[30]

Both Borde and Breton make clear their assumption that audiences are in need of assistance in learning to appreciate the magnificent painting of Molinier. This is why, between them, the former by his choice of canvases and the latter by his manner of introducing these offer a bridge into the world of magic eroticism Molinier made his own. They see their task as opening the marvelous window of the screen and keeping it open at all cost. For this reason their presentation of Molinier bears comparison with Jacques Brunius' best-known film, *Violons d'Ingres* (1939).

Asked to characterize the attraction surrealism held for him when he became a member of the group in 1936, Brunius replied, "It helped me to crystallize and formulate my conception of the world and my attitude to life. Their revolt was the same as mine, and that of my best friends. It was youth. It offered freedom of thought and development of individuality within the common intellectual and ethical self-discipline of a friendly group. It was, and still is, the only philosophy which embraced art, life, morals, politics, games, and integrated them into some sort of unity."[31] To put it simply, surrealism dictated both the subject and the treatment of *Violons d'Ingres*.

The representative documentary of realist intent informs its audience about aspects of the world which are strange in the degree that they lie outside common experience. It may be said, therefore, to have a utilitarian function, based on the didactic principle. As such, it represents a norm from which Brunius departs in *Violons d'Ingres*, without a trace of nostalgia. The title of his movie is a French colloquialism alluding to Ingres's insistence upon having visitors to his studio listen to his inferior violin-playing instead of looking at his superior canvases. By extension, it applies to any avocation claiming more time, concern, and energy than, by practical standards, a mere hobby should be granted. *Violons d'Ingres* is devoted exclusively to people who have refused to measure their lives by the utilitarian. These people have devoted themselves to the pursuit of ideals so private in significance that their behavior emerges from Brunius' film as a form or protest against society's custom of assessing effort by return, on a level to which these artists are patently indifferent.

Brunius introduces us to a number of individuals to whose lives society consents to attach little or no importance. Henri Rousseau, for example, in whom his contemporaries could see only a Customs official with a mania for painting; Ferdinand Cheval, who built a dream castle, stone by stone, from material gathered on the delivery route he followed day after day as a country mailman; Léon Corcuff, the Parisian taxi-driver in whom Brunius discovered "an inventor of useless devices" like aluminum shoes, extensible frames, and collapsible beds . . . Following Brunius' lead, nearly a quarter of a century later Giles Ehrmann was to photograph the work produced by marginal figures of this kind, whom he called *inspirés*.[32] Only one artist (Cheval) is represented both in Brunius' movie and Ehrmann's book. All the same, the comments made by Breton on the achievement of Ehrmann's *inspirés* apply just as well to those who claimed Brunius' attention. And these observations help disclose in what sense *Violons d'Ingres* is a documentary of surrealist significance.

Naturally, Breton insists upon the protest embodied in products by *inspirés* against society's tendency to identify as "reasonable" only activities it is prepared to acknowledge as *useful*. Of those whom Brunius presents only one (Rousseau) has left work to which society is prepared to attach value. The same is true of Ehrmann's selection of *inspirés:* only the work of the cobbler turned artist, Gaston Chaissac, has market value today. Now Rousseau and Chaissac had this in common: they were both painters; that is, they created objects to which a price tag could be affixed without undue difficulty. In contrast, an uninhabitable castle of stones covering almost three acres could hardly be said to be a salable product. As for a collapsible bed, what could its commerical potential possibly be?

Since we know he advocated giving form to dreams, through reproducing in the world of day-to-day experience objects revealed during nocturnal vision, it is not enough to note Breton's appreciation of an artistic work devoid of value on the market place. The effort of Ferdinand Cheval holds a particular attraction for him and his friends for another reason. Cheval has testified that, as he walked his mail route, he would dream, building in his imagination a fairy palace.[33] At the age of forty-three, he began to erect his castle; not in the air, but in the village of Hauterives, where it stands today, rising to a height of thirty feet. It took him twenty-five years to realize his dream and to render his desire concrete, so proving his own assertion, "From dream to reality, the distance is long," and validating his triumphant claim, "The word impossible does not exist. . . ."[34]

No less than the other artists of *Violons d'Ingres*, each of whom rode his hobby horse so impressively, Cheval (whose name means "horse" in French) may be seem, as Breton puts it, to be "at grips with the irresistible need to give form to some organization of phantasms dwelling within."[35] Objectifying his dream, the country mailman's creation asserts the superior value of the pleasure principle, in conflict with the reality principle. Like others to whom tribute is paid in *Violons d'Ingres*, he externalizes an inner world, so provoking what Breton calls enthusiastically "the spectacular explosion of desire which saves" (p. xvii). Accordingly, Brunius' care for the work of Cheval and of people like him questions the sense in which the phrase "violon d'Ingres" is generally used.

Brunius' attention goes to a variety of individuals whose ambitions alienate them from society, severing ties of dependence upon it. Sympathy leads him to assemble in his film evidence which will appear strange, he believes, in a more disturbing way than material gathered from remote corners of the earth can ever be. In this way, his documentary amounts to a critique of the values by which we judge success and useful activity. It presents real objects that are fantastic because they are the realization of fantasy, and which are real for that very reason. *Violons d'Ingres* calls upon us all to revise our preconceptions about what really ought to exist in our world. The didactic principle has become anti-utilitarian: we are shown desire made concrete, and become so real as to impose a new scale of values by which familiar standards are brought under re-examination.

It is primarily the materials used in *Violons d'Ingres* and *Pierre Molinier* that compel us to review our relationship with the world we call real. Intervention on the part of the film-maker is limited in these movies to holding up a mirror to an expression of desire he wishes to reflect without distortion. Borde's method resembles Brunius' in being restricted to discreet assemblage of documentary evidence that strikes the spectator as revolutionary in essence, when considered beside material usually found in documentary films. This is why it is permissible to place *Pierre Molinier* and *Violons d'Ingres* in the same category. In order to identify the other category of surrealist film documentaries, it is as well to look once again at *Las Hurdes*.

Despite its apparent formlessness, *Las Hurdes* is carefully enough structured to justify Ado Kyrou's reference in his *Le Surréalisme au Cinéma* to a "dramatic architecture," based, in his opinion, on the phrase "Yes, but . . . " (p. 222). Bread, we recall, is unknown; however, the school teacher sometimes gives his pupils slices; but the children's parents, fearing the unknown, throw these away: yes, there is hope; but, in the end, hopes are dashed. Buñuel's method is simple enough. The selection of examples attests the rule he sees underlying the mode of life of poor people hopelessly confined within a vicious circle of misery. Reality, he shows, only *seems* to be immutable; its appearance changes for us as we change our stance before it.

Response to *Las Hurdes* takes us through two discoveries. First, Buñuel is capable of making a telling point by careful selection in the glimpses he offers us of village life: a child dressed in rags writes on the school blackboard the admonishment, "Respect the property of others." Second, Buñuel edits his movie so as to suggest to his audience conclusions which adoption of detachment in the commentary precludes stating: as Unik tells us noncommittally, "The monks live like hermits surrounded by a few domestics," Buñuel's camera lingers over an attractive young girl.

Brunius helps show what is at issue here. Taking up the question of sound in the documentary, *En Marge du Cinéma français* notes that in the first documentaries use of commentary was generally inept. "Most of the time it taught you nothing useful that a subtitle could not have told you effectively," Brunius observes. He then points out where he feels the deficiency lay: either words were rendered redundant because, coming after the image they supposedly explained, they stated the obvious: or, by preceding the image, they undercut the surprise effect entrusted to it. In *Las Hurdes* Buñuel proved this need not always be the case. Judicious handling of sight and sound, he demonstrated, could provoke surprise of a kind unobtainable unless an appeal were directed at one and the same time to eye and ear.

Brunius reports, too, having glimpsed "an almost limitless field" which seems to open up, once one thinks of using images, words, background sounds, and music, all concurrently. "In sum," he recalls, "it was a matter of treating images and sounds as absolutely on an equal footing, giving first the one and then the other primacy over the rest" (p. 130). Reflecting upon the documentary's potential under these conditions, Brunius became convinced it was essential to dispense with the "ridiculous" term *commentary* as designating the function of words in the sort of film he had in mind. "The principle was that image and sound should be really *complementary*, even at the cost of a certain distance between them," he concluded. The *film de montage*, a movie in which the director impresses his intentions upon his audience by skillful editing, struck Brunius as the ideal form for experimenting with movies: "The experiment should be carried out, it seemed to me, with the greatest possible number of 'ready-made' elements: images taken from newsreels, sound from film libraries, music already recorded" (p. 131).

Noting in passing that Buñuel is not averse to making use of "ready-made" music in his films,[36] we may note at the same time that Brunius admits to having often spliced together pieces of unrelated film footage:

> there must still exist somewhere in some canister a scene in which one sees my assistant Georges Labrousse, at the dining table, devouring with signs of appetite and delectation what a surgeon, whose scalpel alone is visible, withdraws from a skull open like a boiled egg. (p. 126)

Brunius cites this brief scene of "cannibal orgy," as he cheerfully calls it, to indicate what can be done with the most realistic material. As he demonstrates how elements furnished by the real world may be so assembled as to undermine confidence in reality, he uncovers the "imposture," as he terms it, of those who purport to be making realistic films, documentary or otherwise. He then goes on to accuse directors who supposedly present a realistic impression of life of "dishonesty."

Honesty is not the prime issue for us, even though Brunius implies it is less deceitful to let spectators see how one is interfering with elements drawn from the objective world. He himself does this in his little cannibal feast, and Buñuel does too, when he suggests that the monks of *Las Hurdes* enjoy their servant girls (*bonnes à tout faire*, as the French say) as concubines. What counts is Brunius' conclusion: "In the cinema, a simple splice can replace the word *like*, the words *just as . . . so*, the word *à*, as Raymond Roussel used it" (pp. 127–128).[37]

Speaking this way of the potential of the cinema, Brunius puts us in mind of Breton's discussion of the surrealist image in verbal poetic practice. In his text of 1947 called "Signe ascendant," for instance, we find Breton asserting, "the most exciting word we dispose of is the word 'COMME' ['like']," whether this word is articulated or not. That is to say, Breton's article dots the i's on a statement made many years before, in his first surrealist manifesto of 1924:

> It is false, in my opinion, to claim "the mind has grasped the relationship" between two realities brought into contact with one another. To begin with, it has grasped nothing consciously. It is from the somewhat fortuitous proximity of the two terms that a particular light has flashed, *the light of the image*, to which we show ourselves infinitely sensitive. The value of the image depends on the beauty of the spark produced; it is, consequently, a function of the difference in potential of the two conductors. (p. 52)

Just as the word "like," used surrealistically, can link two realities which reasonable association would never bring together,[38] so the film splice can lend itself to producing comparable results. The spark is particularly impressive in Brunius' "cannibal orgy," where the operating room is made to provide a hungry man with an appetizer which, good taste notwithstanding, tastes good. The light of the image may flash less brightly in *Las Hurdes*. There the production of the generating spark does not benefit from the presence of the "rarefied gases" that, the first *Manifesto* tells us (p. 53), are produced in verbal poetry by the practice of automatic writing. All the same, no less than Brunius, Buñuel demonstrates how the splice can be made to help communicate a conception of the world quite unsubmissive to realist convention, even though apparently faithful to reality.

Under the ideal conditions projected by Brunius, the impression created by editing would be enriched by the freedom with which imagery would be allowed to suggest comment, and vice versa. Meanwhile, music would supply a "rhythmic mold" (p. 30), in passages where no words would be heard. He had to wait until 1936 before getting the opportunity to try his hand at film-making under conditions approximating those he had imagined. That year, Jean Renoir invited him to edit the first two reels of *La Vie est à Nous*. Brunius now had the chance to try associating words, thoughts, and cinematographic images rhythmically. The result was not unsatisfactory, to judge by the response of others involved. However, Brunius was hampered by having to work with a commentary imposed in advance. In his part of *La Vie est à Nous*, he could not implement his plan to modify the role of words in such a way as to render the term "commentary" fully obsolete. Nevertheless, he made an important discovery: in the kind of *montage* he was seeking, changes in filmed imagery could not occur arbitrarily—they had to be linked, it appeared, with a specific word and timed to coincide with its articulation.

After his success with *La Vie est à Nous*, Brunius was entrusted with the making of *Records 37* (1937). This time, having only a sketchy scenario, he could do what he liked with the spoken text as well as with the imagery of his movie. He made sure he would be free to use Arthur Hoérée's music in whatever way he chose. As for the spoken text, it was to be a "recitative" by Desnos, on a rough outline supplied by Brunius himself. Only when the music and texts had been recorded did Brunius set to work synchronizing images, words, music, and sounds. In the process, he refined the discoveries made during his work on *La Vie est à Nous*. For instance, he became convinced a cut should be synchronized with a certain syllable, not merely with a certain word.

Although devoted to the surrealist cause, Brunius was still working entirely within the framework of the commercial cinema on *La Vie est à Nous* and *Records 37*. Thus technical experimentation in the latter testified to the applicability of his methods to the commercial documentary. We see no sign of it, though, in Brunius' other commercial documentary films, *Voyage aux Cyclades* (1931) and *Venezuela* (1937). Nor does it appear to have influenced any other director of commercial documentaries, even though, as he affirms in *En Marge du Cinéma français*, the best parts of *Records 37* "represented a new cinematographic genre, absolutely different from the documentary as it had been conceived up to then and as it is con-

Buñuel, *Un Chien andalou*

Buñuel, *L'Age d'Or*

Buñuel, *L'Age d'Or*

Buñuel, *L'Age d'Or*

Buñuel, *Las Hurdes*

Buñuel, *Las Hurdes*

Brunius, *Violons d'Ingres*

Brunius, *Violons d'Ingres*

Benayoun, *Paris n'existe pas*

Benayoun, *Paris n'existe pas:* Simon (Richard Leduc) and
Félicienne (Monique Lejeune)

Benayoun, *Paris n'existe pas:* Simon (Richard Leduc) and
Angela (Danièle Gaubert)

Buñuel, *Viridiana*

Buñuel, *Viridiana*

Buñuel, *Viridiana*

Buñuel, *El Angel exterminador*

Buñuel, *El Angel exterminador*

ceived even today" (p. 133). In the context of Brunius' remarks, "today" meant the late forties, his essay having been completed in September 1947. Had he written his book just prior to its 1954 publication in French, he would no doubt have added a word about a purely non-commercial experiment taking the very direction explored through *Records 37*. This was *Revue surréaliste* by the surrealists Georges Goldfayn and Jindrich Heisler.

The first issue of *Revue surréaliste* comprises four brief films, amounting to no more than fifteen minutes in all. Heisler's death terminated the venture before a second issue could be prepared. But although accumulation of evidence is slight, it deserves notice. *Revue surréaliste* occupies a halfway position between Brunius' efforts and those of Jean-Louis Bédouin and Michel Zimbacca, *L'Invention du Monde*, which *En Marge du Cinéma français* would surely have mentioned, had Brunius written it during the fifties.

There is no evidence of direct influence from Brunius on Heisler and Goldfayn. Yet if they were ignorant of what he had tried to do, we face a curious coincidence in concept and execution. The authors of *Revue surréaliste* noticed how sound and image may contradict as well as complement one another while yet remaining limited by one another to a noteworthy degree, if conceived as going together. They approached sound and picture separately, dealing with each independently, without regard for the other. The result, according to another surrealist, Gérard Legrand (writing a "Petite Préface au Sur-Cinéma" in the sixth number of *L'Age du Cinéma*) was "multiplication" of the elements used in the film: "a film to the power of two." Using "ready-made" material as Brunius spoke of it—in this case scenes borrowed from old films—Goldfayn and Heisler destroyed the pre-established sequence of elements to be used, by rearranging the order of showing these. They concentrated next upon rearranging yet again the scenes selected. When they had four lengths of film—one cannot really call these sequences, since none of them is more consequent than the others—they turned them over to a third person, whom they left completely free to add a sound track, including words, noises, and music, according to his fancy.

Spared obligations consonant with commercialism, Heisler and Goldfayn were able to carry Brunius' proposal a step further. They were quite free to use whatever visual material they cared to select. Better off than Brunius in his commercial documentaries, they were spared the obligation to justify selection and arrangement of their material through verbal commentary. In fact, addition of another element, in the form of a sound track, made reconciliation between image and reasonable expectation less likely, not more. After all, the sound track in their *Revue surréaliste* became essentially a subjective interpretation carried out upon material supplied by chance. The net result is therefore something like a palimpsest, from which care has been taken not to erase one statement in favor of another. We are to read both statements and draw our own conclusions. As our participation is solicited in this fashion, we are made to comprehend better than before why surrealists take pleasure in quoting Lautréamont's dictum: "Poetry will be made by all, not by one."

Michel Zimbacca had already made a film called *Square du Temple* in 1949 when he joined Jean-Louis Bédouin on *L'Invention du Monde* [*Invention of the World* (1952)], for which the surrealist poet Benjamin Péret provided the spoken text.[39]

The technical file states the object of their twenty-five-minute movie in these terms: "Following the evolution of primitive thought, as we can picture it from the different plastic creations revealed by time." The artifacts featured in the film were selected from among the holdings of museums in Europe, Australia, and the Americas. The Musée de l'Homme in Paris supplied recordings of music from Japan, Mexico, and Bali. The sound track utilizes also Australian aborigine chants, Iroquois Indian chants, Voodoo tom-toms, Bahian drums. After assembling this material, Zimbacca and Bédouin noted, in a synopsis drawn up later when their film was ready for showing,[40] how man "alters and recreates everything he chooses to represent." They concentrated upon myths and symbols as expressions of "all the mind's desires and interrogations" transmitted by "the imagery of natural necessity." Taking up the thread of these myths and symbols, as it could be traced through the form and decoration of household utensils, etc., and in magical signs and rites, they proceeded to examine totemism and the role of the mask in primitive society.[41] From here they advanced to an analysis of action ("In the beginning was action")—the drama of life and death—and to a concluding section, concerned with the couple: "The couple doubles up to the infinite and becomes god and goddess, with multiple arms and a thousand attributes, unquenchable source of life."

As summarized above, *L'Invention du Monde* would appear to have little about it to mark this movie as a surrealist documentary, beyond pooling of their resources by three surrealists. To appreciate its originality, one has to understand why neither Zimbacca nor Bédouin found it necessary to prepare a written scenario. Bédouin explains matters this way: "The film was conceived as a poem in pictures and it was the analogies discovered between the pictures [*images*] which entirely dictated the editing [*montage*] and the very articulation of the sequences. Instead of writing the scenario down, Zimbacca and I *drew* it entirely, using tracings."[42] Commenting in 1951 upon what they were doing, he and Zimbacca declared they had undertaken the experiment of making a surrealist documentary "outside the latest-style classification of ethnography and in perfect disregard for aesthetic ratings."[43] In *L'Invention du Monde* we are invited to participate in the form of analogical play in which surrealist poets so often ask us to join. It plainly reveals this game as designed to question the stability of the everyday world, while it tends toward unveiling a world presently hidden from our eyes. Hence this statement by Zimbacca and Bédouin in *L'Age du Cinéma*:

> *L'Invention du Monde* admits, as its basic hypothesis, the perenniality in the human mind of certain forms of association which permit us, as soon as poetic consciousness is awakened to one of them, to embrace by analogy all the others, and to be carried right away to the source of mythical thought. [. . .] In these conditions, only the poetic influx can *open* these forms and these symbols, considered as so many clusters of meaning closed in upon themselves. Only this can bring forth their multiple prolongations to organize them at last in a responsible chain reaction.

Explaining the hypothesis upon which their movie rests, the directors explain also what role they reserve in it for the text supplied at their request by Benjamin Péret. Bédouin has taken care to stress that Péret's text is "in reality a sort of long poem that becomes comprehensible [*s'éclaire*] really only when accompanied by the image."[44] If, as Bédouin is convinced, the merit of *L'Invention du Monde* lies in manifesting the relationship between surrealist thought and the "vision of the world of so-called 'uncivilized' or 'primitive' peoples,"[45] then the virtue of Péret's poem must lie in appealing to verbal magic as an eminently appropriate accompaniment to images of magic significance passing before the camera. The press release of *L'Invention du Monde* asserts fittingly, "Benjamin Péret here restitutes by his commentary the poetical images of primitive conception, founded on analogy, and at the same time delineates the sense and origins of the presented documents." It adds, "By lending his voice to some of them, Benjamin Péret has reproduced their ritual significance, and by impersonating spirits and forces, expresses the dramatic side of the screenplay."

In fact, Péret's text does two things. First, it explains and informs, after the fashion of the commercial documentary's commentary:

> Fixing in stone the prey he covets, the animal he wishes to tame, man affirms his power.
> But to model nature according to his desires he first has to exorcise it.

Second, it interprets, providing the form of interplay between spoken word and visual image that is an essential contribution of surrealism in the documentary mode:

> My crest is a double crenelated rainbow traversed by lightning.
>
> . . . .
>
> Eyes take flight with the image that has risen out of matter, as the flower blossoms so that its seed may fall to germinate, grow, flower, fall, germinate, grow, flower, fall, germinate, grow, flower, . . .

It seems a far cry from Buñuel's interpretation of the word "domestics," in *Las Hurdes,* to the poetic accompaniment provided *L'Invention du Monde* by Péret. And yet, without attempting to limit the scope of surrealism in the documentary by seeking to standardize its manifestation, one can draw a few general conclusions from the evidence examined above.

It is not the exotic nature of materials brought together in *L'Invention du Monde* that makes this movie a notable example of adaptation of the documentary mode to surrealist purposes. Rather, it is, we find, the relevance of subject matter to the surrealist outlook controlling its directors' approach to those materials.[46] For this reason, the aims pursued by Bédouin and Zimbacca through their presentation of primitive societies are not far distant from those of Brunius in *Violons d'Ingres,* where the immanence of surrealism is illustrated by examination of subversive forces working against the reality principle, in the everyday world of bourgeois, materialistic France.

One can feel confidence separating surrealist documentaries into categories only if distinctions are drawn on the level of film technique. The necessity for attention to distinctions of this kind disappears, though, once the *sense* of the end product has been grasped, once we perceive how every documentary of surrealist inspiration disengages its audience from unquestioning acceptance before the idea that reality is unchangeably fixed in its depressing or horrifying forms. This counts most of all, whether the response elicited is one of revulsion or wonder. Like Brunius, Buñuel, or Borde, the maker of surrealist documentaries would always gladly say with Péret, in *L'Invention du Monde*, "I am going to contemplate the other face of the world."

As Breton speaks of it in his first manifesto, the beauty of the surrealist poetic image is directly proportionate to its novelty. Its originality lies therefore in departing from banality, not in fidelity to familiar features of our world. We call the latter real because the elements we are accustomed to find in the world we know, in an order that presents no novelty, are incapable of occasioning us any surprise. Hence image-making is deemed poetic, in surrealism, only when it makes us aware that the poet's way of looking at things has routed our expectations about what really exists. The salutary function of the surrealist documentary film, in other words, is to challenge, through its imagery, the immutability of the real as ever hostile to man's desire. This is why the declaration made by Zimbacca and Bédouin regarding the opening of forms and symbols by means of "the poetic influx" provides such an important clue to the surrealist documentary-maker's basic aims. As the title *L'Invention du Monde* testifies, man really creates his own world, and does so less by turning away from ambient reality than by infusing objective phenomena with poetic virtue.

Embezzlement of the Familiar

Eroticism plays an important role in the work of the Dane Wilhelm Freddie. It is so aggressively present in his painting that several of his canvases have found their way into the Copenhagen Criminological Museum. His sculpture *Sex-paralysappeal* (1936) was confiscated by the police in 1937 and not returned to him for almost a quarter of a century. The paintings he intended to show at the 1936 International Surrealist Exhibition in London were not allowed past British Customs. In the circumstances it is only to be expected that eroticism will mark his film *Spiste horisonter* [*Eaten Horizons* (1950)].

In *Spiste horisonter*, two men dressed as peasants are eating off a table. Their table is a nude woman. When one of them puts down a loaf of bread it proceeds to an intimate examination of the woman and finally disappears from sight. The men then cut a hole in their table, and set about eating her with spoons.

If we consider the visual material assembled in the film on its own, *Spiste horisonter* is reminiscent of the cannibal orgy Brunius

produced for his own amusement. But there are enough differences
to make it fruitful to compare a piece of film never publicly shown,
and never meant to be seen by an audience, with a complete short
movie destined for public viewing, and indeed shown during the
Festival of Short Films in Paris, in 1951. Essentially, Brunius obtained his effects by joining together ready-made elements never
designed to be utilized as he was to use them. Hence the disturbing
impression created by his brief sequence comes directly from enrichment of its humorous content by blatant gratuitousness: it has
and looks for no justification outside the shock it administers to the
reasonable eye. On the other hand, *Spiste horisonter*, filmed by Jør-
gen Roos under Freddie's direction, resulted from premeditation.
Chance encounter of unrelated materials, from which Brunius made
something unforeseen, gives way here to deliberation. As this confronts audiences with the need to know the meaning lying behind
what they are seeing, the spectator listens carefully while he
watches.

The visual imagery of *Spiste horisonter* is accompanied by a
spoken text, written by Freddie himself. The word guides our response to the image in this movie, just as much as the image exerts
control over our interpretation of the word. In fact, the scenario of
Spiste horisonter places special emphasis under the interdependence
of word and image; and from the very beginning:

> *1st picture* I dare not touch her with my fingers, but I am
> thinking, let pins fasten her body to the perspective void
> which contains all the joy of anticipation. The power which
> is in her raised arms shall be decisive of the character of
> those actions which are conjured up by the words "Puba,
> PUBA, PUBA: see the miraculous, three fetters nailed fast
> with frontal rivets."

> *2nd picture* These confident words of the Nestor of Infinity
> bring here [*sic*] without fear closer to Luna, the Moon, and to
> the abode of the moon in the unknown, which with fingertips
> trace the magic sign, which is the picture of torture—and of
> delight.[47]

One does not have to read through the entire scenario, in which each
of the nineteen "pictures" is accompanied by a verbal parallel, to
grasp what Freddie has in view. The result will differ from the
proses parallèles Breton wrote for Joan Miró's *Constellations* (1959)
in one important respect. Whereas Breton's prose texts were inspired
by Miró's graphics, admission of the precedence of the visual ele-

ment over the verbal is not a necessary prelude in *Spiste horisonter* to understanding the relation established and maintained between them. At the beginning of the film, the spoken text creates a magic atmosphere which heightens our responsiveness to the events about to take place. Later, the eighth picture is interpreted by the statement going with it: "A woman fashioned of the most rosesoft marble and with her fine veins close under the fragrant skin of glass, is an alter [*sic*] of desire, where breasts, warm as old gold, function as a dock for my, oh so heavy, bread-ship." Later still, the fourteenth picture is presented to the accompaniment of this explanatory exclamation: " 'Shadow, give me your tongue and throat, and let me fill you, this is a Sacrament'." And yet our interpretation of *Spiste horisonter* is not dictated by what we hear alone. At times the words uttered are purely magical invocations ("Puba, PUBA, PUBA," "VANA IMAGO!," "BAEL, ASTAROTH, FORRAS," and "ARDOR"), drawing their strength from the visual material passing before our eyes as we listen to them. When finally the movie comes to a close, it is on a joyous note of wonder that words are not enough in themselves to communicate:

> *18th picture* Without apprehension I stand in the white airless hall, where the laughter of children cascades down to me from the smooth walls, as letters of the alphabet from the dancing bell—letters which form words, sentences, meanings—whose pictures become the fittings of the walls, disappearing hastily, making me naked,

> *19th picture* and the bread, the big, vital and rich bread, describes in the ecstasy of its victory that circle of love, the radius of which is the worldbed, into which the volcano strews its pearls.

Everything we hear increases our wonder at what we see. It does not purport to reconcile visual imagery in *Spiste horisonter* with good sense, any more than imagery makes sense of the words. Meanwhile, indications we took to be clues—mention of a Sacrament and presumably an allusion to the rituals of the Black Mass (a nude woman being substituted for the altar, while two celebrants officiate)—are found in the end to be misleading. Although he eschews the gratuitous rebuff to reason in Brunius' cannibal orgy, Freddie resists any attempt to restrict the meaning of his film within the limitations of our expectations. *Spiste Horisonter* does not stop at inverting Church ritual, any more than it is confined to placing before us erotic elements defying the taboo of nudity. The woman it shows us can no longer be seen as the symbol of defiance against the Church and its teachings once, as table-altar, she turns out, against reason, to be edible. This is evidence that Freddie's surrealist view of life demands submission of the reality principle to the pleasure principle, under pressure from desire.

Do you like women? asks the title of Jean Léon's film *Aimez-vous les Femmes?* (1964) as casually as one might ask if you like oranges. One shot involving a nude woman recumbent in the middle of a dining table at which a group of black-hooded figures are sitting gives special point to the innocent question, already posed implicitly in Meret Oppenheim's *Le Festin* [*The Banquet*].[48] This is a question Freddie posed before either Oppenheim or Léon, reminding us the proof of the pudding is in the eating, and catching us between horror and amusement, so as to upset our moral and sentimental balance.

Characterizing Wilhelm Freddie as a film-maker, Benayoun speaks of "a bulimia for the absolute."[49] Exact definition of the significance to be attached to the final proof of man's all-consuming appetite in *Spiste Horisonter* is less to the point, perhaps, than noting the care Freddie has taken to leave his movie open to interpretation. We are reminded of Lewis Carroll's Alice and of her responsiveness to the injunction "Eat me." And—since the woman-altar of *Spiste horisonter* has been *entered* by bread—possibly of the colloquialism for pregnancy: "She has a bun in the oven." Yet no single association has any priority over any other. Instead the multivalence of Freddie's film helps eat away the horizons delimiting our view of the world.

In *Spiste Horisonter* multivalence results from careful avoidance of facile symbolism. The same thing is true Marcel Mariën's *L'Imitation du Cinéma* [*Imitation of the Cinema* (1959)].

For the background to the Belgian Mariën's thinking about movies we can consult two articles of his, published in the magazine *Les Lèvres Nues* edited by him. The first of these protests against film directors' unwillingness to aim "higher and further than nature." It complains, also, of the injurious effect of realism in films touching upon legend, dreams, or the marvelous.[50] Its argument is illustrated by reference to three recent films, Emilio Fernandez's *La Red*, André Cayatte's *Avant le Déluge*, and *How to Marry a Millionaire*. The second of Mariën's articles is more extensive. In it, like surrealists before him, he identifies the mediocrity of the cinema with its ever-increasing technical resources, and with the crushing burden imposed upon films by the introduction of sound.[51] Sound, he claims, reduces movies to the level of translating literature and so militates against the free use of cinematographic language (p. 11). If we want to extend the language of the cinema, he contends, we need "experimentation with the images themselves, the isolated images torn from the external narration, to which people wish to constrain them: and, today, with the complex of images and sounds that make up the substance of the cinematographic work" (p. 12).

Although well aware of economic restrictions exerting their influence on the cinema, Mariën does not see these as insurmountable obstacles. On the contrary, he asserts, "it always remains possible to draw *from any subject* an honorable film," defining "honorable" as "subversive or at least comic." All one needs is ability to treat familiar material in an unusual manner—by borrowing footage from the commercial cinema, for instance, and adding new dialogue. The essential thing is to have the film-maker rid himself of the "psychological conditioning" left by novels—literature at its worst. With such a scenario as his new-found liberty enables Mariën to imagine, he believes one can proceed to revitalize the movies just as Brunius foresaw, by editing without regard for demands imposed by the obligation to respect consecutive dialogue.

Taking pains to make clear that his attention to editing owes nothing to respect for artistry in the cinema and even less to desire for "true-to-life" cinema, Mariën insists upon his preoccupation with "disarticulating the subtle tissue of images, sounds, gestures, and words" (p. 14), as he holds to his aims: "reaching a new world" and "inventing a new man" (p. 15). Already we sense what sort of interpretation will be appropriate for the title of the film Mariën presents as his *L'Imitation du Cinéma*. Imitation is to open up a way to invention—the production of something "higher and further than nature." As such, it relates to a concern manifest throughout Mariën's discussion of films: "It is a matter of dealing a mortal blow at the present-day notion of the personality, as it is given us by historical reality and by the wretched infantile representation of that reality." Hence his confident deduction: "It is enough, today, it will always be enough,—once the crack in the rock has been discovered—to defy the Holy Inquisition, that is to say not to respect the rules of the game."

Mention of the Inquisition in Mariën's article of 1955 seems to suggest that the primary function of *L'Imitation du Cinéma* is to parade an anticlerical spirit which, by the way, the film's director has never troubled to conceal. But Mariën cared enough to contest this conclusion, in a text prepared for reading before an audience seeing his film in Antwerp on May 15, 1960. By that date, *L'Imitation du Cinéma* had caused a stir already. Accused of seeking scandal for scandal's sake in a forty-minute movie having as its theme a young man's crucifixion complex, Mariën riposted that to believe his film rested on "traditional anti-religious motivation" would mean "falling into the trap of appearances." He went on to observe, "I simply used the objects of Christian religion for, let's say, humorous ends, and I don't doubt that I am entirely within my rights."[52] What is done with these objects in *L'Imitation du Cinéma*—and principally with the Cross—is scandalous, he asserts, only to those incapable of witnessing the "embezzlement of familiar objects" without taking offence. He goes on to argue that such people protest because they are unable to "avoid confusion between the thing and the sign" —the confusion attacked by Wilhelm Freddie.

Whether or not we take at face value Mariën's comment regarding the scandalous subject matter of his film—and we have to give him credit for forewarning his listeners to be on their guard— there is no doubt he spoke without prevarication when claiming his movie to be scandalous in quite a different respect. "This scandal is situated on the plane of the aesthetics of the cinema; it results mainly from the exceptionally poor way it is put together," he said. "It seems, indeed, that there is a close and as though inevitable connection between the subject of the film and its deficiencies, that the one required the other, and vice versa." The important point, to begin with, is that Mariën's movie is an "outline," a "rough draft," the "first version of a work which cannot be completed" because of lack of financial resources. *L'Imitation du Cinéma* was shot without retakes, as two intermingled though distinct films, differing in spirit and function.

The first film carries the plot. This has to do with a young man, "something of a juvenile delinquent in appearance," whom a priest upbraids when he finds him reading a girlie magazine on a park bench. Tearing up the young man's reading material, the priest replaces it with a copy of Thomas à Kempis' *Imitation of Christ*. Reading the book assiduously, Mariën's hero becomes obsessed with crosses, even going so far as to cut his French fries in the shape of the Cross. As though in confirmation of à Kempis' warning that the Cross is everywhere, awaiting us, he begins to see crosses all around him, while his obsession develops to the stage where he yearns for crucifixion. An interlude with a prostitute passes the time while a carpenter is at work on a made-to-measure cross, which the young man finally succeeds in transporting to his home. Here, the priest having proved more of a hindrance than a help when it came to realizing the hero's ambition, the young man is left alone to attempt self-crucifixion. Discovering before long that he is one hand short for the successful completion of his plan, he settles before an open gas jet, in the attitude of Christ crucified.

All the incidental details of this first film stress Mariën's humorous intent. The young man's visit to a shop specializing in religious articles, for a start. Here, unable to purchase a cross large enough to bear his weight, he buys sixty francs' worth of small crosses, which he carries off in a paper bag. Later, the prostitute with whom he kills time wears a crucifix as "a tool of the trade," she explains, adding "It's a matter of putting people at their ease, of breaking the ice." It appears she once made a vow to the Virgin, hoping to save her sick son's life. Although the child succumbed to illness, she still keeps her vow of never charging her thousandth client. "Does it not fall to the cinema always to choose the exceptional moment?" Mariën asks in his script, as the prostitute exclaims, "You're in luck, honey, you just happen to be the last of the series. Today you screw for nothing!"

This small miracle is not characteristic of the young man's experience. On the contrary, after stealing his companion's crucifix as he leaves for the carpenter's, he has some difficulty cycling home with a heavy wooden cross on his shoulder. A flat tire obliges him to complete the trip on foot. All the same, despite slipping on banana peel and colliding with someone carrying a ladder (each ends up with the other's burden, before realizing what has happened), the hero does manage to get his cross home. Unfortunately, the carpenter having inadvertently sawed through his foot rule while cutting the timber for the cross, the young man finds its dimensions quite inadequate for his purpose. The only solution possible now seems to be the one proposed by the priest, who kindly offers to nail the young man's feet to the floor. No sooner said than done:

"Does it hurt?"

"No, I don't feel anything at all."

"That is grace, my son!"

In fact this false miracle is attributable not to grace but to the priest's inaccurate aim: he has driven nails between the youth's toes, instead of into them.

Further effects of this kind were considered, among them the arrival of the hero's cross by freighter, among a whole cargo of crosses, unloaded on the shoulders of a multitude of longshoremen, against the background of a strike threatening to hold up operations. But none of these could be implemented. And even in the form shown to the public, *L'Imitation du Cinéma* bears ineradicable marks of extreme technical indigence, reflecting the circumstances under which it was made. Lack of funds compelled Mariën to use a camera incapable of shooting long sequences. He had to be content with inadequate lighting and resort to adding the voices without benefit of post-synchronization. Time was against him, also. Filming had to be completed in ten days, with unprofessional actors whom Mariën could allow no time to rehearse. Practical necessity thus reduced his film to a mere succession of photographs, "slightly animated here and there," as he admitted.

Because the original outline had called for one or two allusions to the technical poverty of the movie (e.g., the priest carries on him a amateur film-maker's handbook), Mariën now decided to make no serious effort to rescue it. He undertook instead to aggravate its weaknesses, "justifying them by accumulation and excess." In this way was conceived the second film in *L'Imitation du Cinéma*.

This film begins immediately after the first, being a repetition of it, at a slower rhythm. At this stage, crude errors of continuity, born of insufficient preparation or simple haste, are "corrected" in the dialogue. For example, when the prostitute takes off underwear she obviously could not have been wearing in preceding shots, she remarks, "That's odd, I don't have the impression I was wearing a slip a moment ago. I'm sometimes absent-minded . . . " In other places in the film, where psychological inconsistency cannot escape notice, it is now exaggerated. This increases the audience's feeling of detachment from events. The prostitute, for instance, is shown to have come to her profession "by way of philology," thanks to her study of Greek and Latin classics. She keeps up her interest in "the physics and metaphysics of her profession," we are told, reading Stekel, Pavlov, Krafft-Ebing, Gurvitch, Moreno, and even Grévisse's *Le Bon Usage*. As for the hero, despite his obsessive motivation, we see him continually yawning, as though bored by everything that goes on.

One other noteworthy disconcerting effect sends us back for an explanation to Mariën's article in the seventh number of *Les Lèvres Nues*. In 1955, Mariën spoke of the script girl's regrettable role in ensuring that, from one shot to the next, an actor moving from one room to another should not be seen wearing a different necktie, or with a different complexion (p. 11). Now, in preparing the second film in *L'Imitation du Cinéma*, Mariën noted:

> *Shot 437*—Walking alongside a wall, the priest, carrying a case in his hand, is about to turn a corner.

> *Shot 438*—The actor playing the part of the priest, but in street clothes, appears turning the corner (link with the move-

ment in the last shot), carrying a suitcase, which he shifts from one hand to the other, while heading straight toward the camera lens.

Shot 439—The priest moving away, his back to the camera, shifts his case from one hand to the other, so that it is in the hand in which he was carrying it in N° 437.

To make doubly sure the spectator does not "enter into" the story (this being, in Mariën's view, the pernicious principle of cinemato-graphic continuity) an additional ending is provided, showing the actor who played the priest, dressed in street clothes, leaving a movie house as though after seeing a film.

The concluding shots of the movie are devised to add to the spectator's perplexity by "discouraging him from forming too readily and with too much assurance his opinion on all things." The criticism implicit in this statement of Mariën's is directed as much against those who reject the teachings of the Church as against those who accept them. André Souris reveals why, when discussing the music he selected for *L'Imitation du Cinéma*.[53] In keeping with the theme of the movie, the musical selections Souris utilized—ranging from Wag-ner's *Parsifal* for the religious theme, to a Rumanian fisherman's song for the titles and the epilogue, to ritual native music for the erotic theme—were all divested of their original affective associations so that they could play a role as accompaniment for the visual material in Mariën's film. Souris sharply condemns the "melomania" of one spectator who expressed indignation at the disrespectful use of *Parsifal* during the sequence when lethal gas escapes from a jet. He argues that this spectator had been guilty of detaching the music from the movie, where it is just one element (a ready-made element) among several. Just as a musical extract from *Parsifal* ceases to be Wagner's, in *L'Imitation du Cinéma,* so the Cross ceases to be what the Chris-tian or the anti-Christian sees in it.

Promoting perplexity in their audiences, Mariën and Souris aim at detachment by disarticulating the public's associative re-sponses. The images brought together in *L'Imitation du Cinéma* are liberated from the "external narration" to which they would be subordinated in a film devoted to telling a story after the fashion of the novel. More than this, they are freed from mental and emotional overtones that would exercise a retarding influence upon the audi-ence's capacity to react to them. The subversive impulse underlying all surrealist experimentation with film can be seen as the vital driving force of *L'Imitation du Cinéma* once we perceive how much Mariën has in common with Wilhelm Freddie. Just like Freddie, he wishes not merely to leave his film open to interpretation, but to make sure the spectator is denied the reassuring convenience of closing it upon a familiar symbol.

Artaud, planning "La Coquille et le Clergyman," and Buñuel making *Un Chien andalou*, took care to leave their public full latitude in making a connection here, drawing a parallel there, from the cinematic visual imagery provided. Hence a Freudian interpretation of parts of *Un Chien andalou* is permissible, although not mandatory. Alert to the audience's instinct for finding the easiest way out from a mentally and emotionally disturbing situation, Freddie and Mariën take care to close the exit doors the public reserves for emergencies. Of these exits the ones marked "Church teaching" and "Freudian teaching" are apparently the most accessible. Therefore, while *Spiste horisonter* and *L'Imitation du Cinéma* are screened, they are sealed off first.

In his article "Un autre Cinéma" Mariën affirms that experimentation dealing with elements as concrete as images and sounds has nothing to do with "a given philosophical context" (p. 17). He foresees success in such experimentation as dependent upon elimination of the philosophical background against which we habitually see and hear. Here we uncover the motives underlying his presentation of a scene depicting sexual intercourse in *L'Imitation du Cinéma*, which provoked the Belgian Centre Catholique d'Action Cinématographique to demand that his movie be banned. The sequence alternates an evocation of the sexual act (done without undue insistence, as it happens) and shots that are innocent enough in themselves. These include a woman's hand helping a man's insert a key in a lock and a candle flanked by two eggs. As Mariën notes with satisfaction, obscenity comes, in every instance, not from the picture itself but from the association aroused by its appearance.

So as to establish a balance between vulgarity and decency, Mariën took advantage of Freudianism, deliberately cast as a mantle over the offensive section of his movie to make it more acceptable. A kind of safe-conduct for the film-maker, the word "Freud" had an inevitable disadvantage, all the same: that of influencing interpretation of the imagery it was being used to authorize, and so restricting it. For this reason, Mariën placed immediately after the phallic candle a short sequence showing a bearded professor lecturing in front of a large labeled portrait of Freud, which lights up "solemnly" as he turns to point to it. Reproducing the photograph of the candle and eggs in the special number of *Les Lèvres Nues* on his film, Mariën underlined the point he wanted to make by references to Freudian teaching in *L'Imitation du Cinéma*. He printed the still over a quotation from *The Imitation of Christ* to the effect that it is difficult to give up old habits and go beyond what we see. Within the movie itself, Mariën conveys his meaning by showing Freud's portrait disintegrating and finally dissolving in a whirling pattern of gray and white shapes to prove that, far from seeking endorsement in Freudian theory, he has no wish to illustrate it. By ironic treatment of Freud, who finally disappears in a gyrating blur, Mariën aims to liberate his film from an interpretation which, it now becomes clear, he has allowed us to formulate just long enough for him to be able to communicate material that only respect for Freud persuades the general public to find respectable.

Mariën resembles Freddie, then, in casting us adrift upon an ocean of images, after taking pains to obliterate from the sky the Pole Star by which we have been accustomed to navigate. It is up to us, from now on, to find our own way.

From Mariën's *L'Imitation du Cinéma* to Robert Benayoun's *Paris n'existe pas* [*Paris does not exist* (1969)] seems a long step. *L'Imitation du Cinéma* is typical of surrealist film productions executed on a minimal budget, with all the odds against success. In contrast, *Paris n'existe pas* is a ninety-five-minute feature movie in Eastmancolor. Written in 1966, shot in August and September of 1968, and completed in February 1969, it was made with the aid of funds advanced by the Centre National du Cinéma, covering one third of the budget. It was shown with notable success at festivals in Cannes, Locarno, and San Francisco.[54] It won the 1969 Prix Arts, Sciences et Lettres, and has been praised by such technicians of the cinema as Joseph Losey and Louis Malle. It is a commercial success, enjoying general distribution in France and abroad. Yet although everything would seem to conspire to make *Paris n'existe pas* the object of suspicion in their eyes, the surrealists have praised this movie, called by its author-director "a deliberately surrealist attempt" in film.[55]

Benayoun admits readily that, while "surrealist in spirit, climate, mood, and content," *Paris n'existe pas* does not attempt to include "a complete surrealist credo." He prefers to call his "a very personal film, done by a surrealist, in the most romantic tradition of a few surrealist autobiographical books," insisting, "it cannot be taken as exemplary of what should, or can be done in that field."[56] His modesty is refreshing, his emphasis instructive, and his achievement notable.

Benayoun characterizes his movie as "a time-travel fantasy with distinct Breton allusions and a treatment of *hasard objectif* themes."[57] It deals with a young painter, Simon Dévereux, living in Paris with his mistress. A succession of disturbing phenomena and events leads Simon to doubt the reality of familiar spatial and temporal surroundings. He embarks on an exploration of the past. This precipitates an encounter with a young woman, Félicienne, to whom he becomes so attracted as to end up sharing his time between her and his present-day companion, Angela. Finally Simon returns to a normal existence, apparently recovered from some momentary delirium. His experience could be put out of mind, but for tangible proof that he really visited the past: an old photograph in which he himself figures. Nothing indicates at the end of the movie that his choice in favor of the present, and of love in the present, will be definitive.

The phrase "time-travel fantasy" really serves simply to identify the framework of a film within which Benayoun proposes to make a statement of strictly surrealist value. Gérard Legrand, who cites *Peter Ibbetson* and Frank Lloyd's *Berkeley Square* as models to which Benayoun renders homage,[58] might well have mentioned also Lewin's *Pandora and the Flying Dutchman* as yet another film in which care is taken to dispose of the facile assumption that the dream world and reality are quite separate. For at the end of *Paris n'existe pas* Simon's photograph provides visible evidence that Benayoun shares Breton's belief in dream and reality as communicating vessels. As in William Dieterle's *The Portrait of Jenny* (1948), what counts is the possibility of contamination of the real by the imaginary. This, surely, is one of the key ideas Benayoun speaks of having wished to introduce:

> My concern, when I wrote *Paris n'existe pas* was above all to bring forward a number of key ideas. I said to myself: for my first film I must do something that is essentially cinematographic, find a form of story that cannot be adapted as a novel, a play in the theatre, or a radio play, in which everything is based on the image, or on successions of images. I therefore found a visual system that came before the subject, and afterward I made up the story in terms of the rhythm of the images which I wished to introduce, which I wanted to see live on the screen.[59]

As Benayoun goes on to discuss his visual system he proves his full agreement with Mariën and Freddie and his intention of embezzling the familiar:

> Its principle is a simple one, that of double vision. At will, my hero can see in the past everything that lies directly in front on him but this vision is practically limitless in the

measure that he moves through time. On this basis, an immense number of possibilities present themselves to him. He can go backward, forward; he works, if you like, like a tape recorder with variable speed. There are also his projections of the future, which are involuntary; he cannot regulate them. He can fix the rhythm of his vision of the past, on the other hand, and even stop at a particular second . . .

Less interested than Alain Resnais in the privileged moment (*Je t'aime, je t'aime* was made about the same time as *Paris n'existe pas*), Benayoun was concerned mainly with the different phases which make time "display vectorial activity," either backward or forward: "That is what I wanted to analyze, cut into slices, and immobilize at will." The choice of a painter as the central character of his movie is not accidental. Simon will acquire a novel mode of artistic expression, as Benayoun seeks out a new form of cinematic language: "Not only does Simon Dévereux put himself on stage in the ideal scenic situation he has chosen but, at the same time, I put myself on stage with him."

For both Benayoun and Simon, the problem of creation is faced and has to be solved in visual terms. To each of them solutions must come from learning to deal with life, not simply from successful confrontation with aesthetic difficulties. Asked in an interview if his painter is a surrealist, Benayoun has specified he "is a surrealist in life." Simon's situation in front of a canvas is that of a surrealist poet practicing automatic writing—trying to "cross a certain threshold of the imaginary." Throughout the first third of the film, we in the audience remain unsure whether he is merely possessed by his own memories of the past. It takes some time to realize he has gone further than he would be able to remember, back in fact to a period before his own birth.

Simon Dévereux's contact with past time does not rest upon the authority Proust's Marcel so clearly needs to recapture time in *À la Recherche du Temps perdu*. The hero of Proust's novel reconquers his past thanks to the sensory stimulation of taste, which opens for him the locked door of memory. But in *Paris n'existe pas* "everything belongs solely in the domain of vision." Meanwhile Simon finds himself incapable of touching anything encountered during his exploration of the past. Yet Félicienne, the woman who occupied his apartment before him, is not a projection of fantasy, as a ghost would be, but a flesh-and-blood person, all the more fascinating to him because he cannot touch her.

The symbolic significance of Félicienne ("she represents somewhat the intangible ideal" for Simon) is easy enough to perceive. However Benayoun refuses to stress symbolic function to the exclusion of other possible interpretations of her presence and conduct. He does not expect his audience to dismiss the young woman as a mere figment of the hero's imagination. Indeed, when questioned about a hint in his movie that Simon may be using drugs, Benayoun confessed this hint is given deliberately, as "a red herring," making Simon himself believe, at first, that Félicienne exists only in a hallucination to which he has fallen victim.[60] In doing this, Benayoun takes one step among several to dispose of the reassuring deduction on the part of those watching his film that the hero simply *thinks* he has made contact with the past. The precautions taken in this direction are essential to emphasizing the theme of temporal parallelism in *Paris n'existe pas*.

One precaution calling for special mention is the attention given music in *Paris n'existe pas*. The subject matter appeared to call for two sorts of musical theme: contemporary life (imaged in modern rhythms) and the call of the past (in something nostalgic and spellbinding), as well as identifiable themes for Simon, for his mistress Angela, and for Félicienne. "I wanted then," Benayoun has explained, "since the whole film is based on temporal parallelism, the style of the music to be if you will contrapuntal." Independently of this, there had to be musical effects destined to link up with, and not underline, certain ultra-temporal phenomena in the screenplay—"Simon's aberration-effects," as he and his film editor Jean Ravel called them. Evidently the keynote had to be ambiguity and ambivalence. Benayoun's expression of admiration for the work of his composer, Serge Gainsbourg, leaves no doubt about his satisfaction with the contribution made by music in his movie.

In addition to composing the music, Gainsbourg plays the part of Simon's friend Laurent Sébastien, the "young Faust" of *Paris n'existe pas*. The character of Laurent (with whom Gainsbourg so identifies that he can say, quite simply, "He's me") testifies further to Benayoun's concern for evading simple answers to the questions raised in his movie. This young Faust does not take himself seriously. As Benayoun has pointed out, "If Laurent believed in the theories he expresses, he would be a bore." Stressing the importance to him of making a film which, "even in its theoretical aspect," furnishes no explanation, Benayoun indicates that Laurent, whose theories on time are a "crazy" mixture of Berkeley, Hume, Donne, Borges, and Schopenhauer, advances these "a little facetiously."

Benayoun admits to sharing his hero's belief that each of us must communicate "his personal world," or "share a view of things."

In the film, the admission that Simon is his creator's spokesman takes the form of a private joke. Throughout a good third of *Paris n'existe pas* Richard Leduc, playing Simon Dévereux, wears clothes belonging to Robert Benayoun.[61] All the same, communication of a personal world and sharing a view of things are still speculative acts. Neither pretends to be authoritative. Moreover, it is clear from the way Benayoun speaks of them that each of these acts resists both classification and limitative explanation of the events with which life confronts us. We face a problem, therefore, when we hear Benayoun asserting "imagination liberated from all constraint, as Breton has established, also becomes a liberating element and serves revolution in its own way." Is not his film, we wonder, with its attentiveness to imagination, a mere plea for escapism?

Benayoun provides answers to this question in a number of ways. The most direct of these finds expression through the scene in which Simon leaves his apartment for the first time after becoming conscious of a new outlook on things, to engage in discussion with some politically minded friends. In view of the date when *Paris n'existe pas* was shot, the discussion, centered on the student riots of May 1968, might appear purely circumstantial. In fact, when it was written with the rest of the screen-play in 1966, the scene alluded to the Algerian war. Yet updating political events brought no change in the opinions expressed by Dévereux or in Benayoun's motivation in introducing them:

> In that scene, I wanted to sum up the old surrealist quarrel about Love and Revolution. We know it was a false problem,[62] and that the surrealists refused to sacrifice the one to the other of these notions which are meant to live side by side in scandal.

Audiences are not expected to see in Simon Dévereux a young man diverted from the path of revolution because beguiled by some unattainable fanciful ideal. Benayoun makes this very clear with his assurance:

> when the time comes, he will be in the streets with his friends. But for the moment, he is prey to a poetic experience which will open new horizons to him. In his mind, as in that of a true surrealist, any poetic experience cannot but be progress for the cause of revolution.

The theoretical positions defended by Dévereux in Benayoun's name make us attentive to certain effects by means of which the director of *Paris n'existe pas* solicits support for his views. These effects are calculated to marshal evidence of a kind that film audiences will find persuasive.

Only visually can Simon Dévereux cross "the threshold of the imaginary." His inability to make physical contact with Félicienne reduces his erotic relationship with her to one of voyeurism. Benayoun wishes to go further than this, though. He wants to show how Félicienne's existence intrudes upon Simon's sexual relations with Angela, for example. Yet the danger remains that, contemplating Simon's behavior from the safe distance of the auditorium, we may be persuaded of nothing more than that we are witnessing a crisis to which Dévereux alone is subject and which does not implicate us. To avert the risk of distance cultivating detachment, Benayoun takes a precaution not mentioned so far: he incorporates documentary material into his movie.

Once we grant that Benayoun has the privilege of extending Simon's experience outside the apartment where he first becomes aware of what is happening to him, utilization of material from the Toulouse Film Library would appear to call for no special comment, so long as we notice these stock shots were discovered after the screen-play had been written and after Benayoun had decided upon the period most appropriate to his purpose. The practical advantages of using contemporary film documents (dating from 1929, to be precise) over attempting to recreate the period on a studio lot are obvious. Nevertheless, Benayoun's statement upon his reasons for choosing a point in time twelve years before the birth of his hero (and incidentally, of the actor playing Simon) shows something more: the importance he attaches to the date selected and the value he sees in materials resurrected from that precise moment in time:

> It seemed to me that the imaginary could be established more easily in an everyday dimension, that for example explored by the surrealists. I think it has much more force when it affects familiar things, calls for a very simple shift. Finally, one must be frightened too; it must be just as striking an impression to perceive that one can move about in the preceding half hour as in the three centuries gone by. It is just as taxing for the imagination, and as exciting.

Following the lead given by Mariën and Freddie, Benayoun concentrates as they have done upon taxing the imagination by exciting it. However, whereas they sever the links supplied by affective associations rendering certain things and concepts familiar, Benayoun introduces evidence taken directly from the past with the purpose of discrediting confidence in the stability of the present.

Using the documentary to support his case, he defies us to situate the dividing line between truth and falsity with any degree of assurance.

Generally speaking, the cinema draws no distinction between film material reflecting the present and material imaging a period no longer with us. Because the camera has no sense of time, it can attain effects denied the theatre, where every décor is an arranged imitation. Whereas in the theatre all is false but seems true because we wish to see it so, in the cinema all appears equally true, whether we wish it or not. This is especially the case when evidence adduced by the cinema has the authenticity of historical documentation. Buñuel, we know, has traveled this road before Benayoun. So has Brunius. Hence one thinks of Brunius' discoveries about the importance of synchronizing word and image in the documentary, when reading Benayoun's remarks upon his use of film documents in *Paris n'existe pas*. Noting that he had foreseen the use of film documents in brief flashes, Benayoun explains:

> In elaborating my screen-play, and afterward in the work I did with Ravel, I had to determine in advance the length of these blinks, this fluttering of the eyelids which links up one time with the other. That is to say, it was necessary to find a pulsation, so that the old rooms could be identified subliminally with the modern rooms, according to a thrust, a progression. In the same way, with the editing of stock shots we had to fix a rhythm which little by little imposed its dictate upon us. The period didn't submit, it defended itself, and we learned to respect its primordial integrity.

Stress upon the two capital elements in this process—subliminal suggestion and respect for the documentary elements used in its application—seems most significant here. Manipulation of audience response by judicious use of a cinematic technique (to which Benayoun, by the way, was one of the first in France to draw attention)[63] finds authority in surrealist belief; specifically in the reliance all surrealists place in the revelatory role of objective hazard in human affairs. *Paris n'existe pas* is an eminently fitting title for a movie that erases the present-day city by means of images of a Paris which no longer exists.

From the moment when the titles are seen against the background of Giorgio de Chirico's painting *L'Énigme de l'Heure (The Enigma of Time)* Benayoun never loses his main theme from sight. Meanwhile, the conclusion suggested by a study of his use of documentary elements is in keeping with his approach to the movies as a mode of surrealist initiation, conducted on the level of visual response. The appeal of sophisticated technical effects never diverts the director's attention from his prime concern. This is why his movie ends on a flashback lasting one minute (twenty-four images a second, one thousand five hundred in all—for the technically minded) made up of still shots resuming Simon's life with Angela. These are arranged in carefully thought-out order and presented at a regular rhythm, after the recommendations of Robert Breer, the pioneer of film animation. Introducing pictures of drawings and engravings by Bernard Childs (whose paintings are those attributed to Simon in the film), and postcards from Simon's apartment, Benayoun and Ravel "invented a progression, and chiseled that little final nightmare" testifying to Benayoun's passion for arranging images.

Thinking about this passion and the impetus it provides in *Paris n'existe pas*, we can appreciate how reluctant Benayoun would be to admit in the end that Simon's vision must have been a fleeting one. Yet ninety-nine percent of the film had been written, apparently, before a suitable ending suggested itself to its author, who has commented:

> What I was reaching was the disintegration of the power gained. My hero understood that he had been endowed with a quite transitory faculty which, all of a sudden, was ceasing to work. But it worried me a lot to finish like that, because nothing irritates me so much, in the cinema or in books, as the cliché: "It was a dream." For me the dream is something much too important to be limited, minimized; and daily life, we know, can be illuminated, guided by knowledge of the unconscious. It is a rule of life, in a surrealist, to keep an attentive eye on his dreams. In short, I wanted at all cost to give the film an open conclusion, and to refuse explanation. My ending explains nothing, I like stories that get under way again just as they are finishing.

Hence the need for Simon to bring back proof of his voyage of discovery into the past—photographic proof, we notice. Hence, too, the enigmatic meeting—a reminder of the de Chirico canvas—with a woman who could be Félicienne but whom Benayoun refuses to show at the age Félicienne would have to be by 1968.

At the end of *Paris n'existe pas* Benayoun introduces a woman whom some of his audience, fully prepared to accept the visual evidence placed before them, will gladly recognize as Félicienne, even though others will be persuaded by a process of rational deduction to conclude it cannot be she. Allowing the former to witness "an irruption of poetry" to which the latter are bound to remain insensitive, Benayoun expresses profound disbelief in the need to make poetic experience consistent with reasonable projection. With due discretion he has remarked, "One can imagine enough things for me to hold my tongue. I am not going to close that door, it must be left swinging."

"A swing-door is in us," Simon Hantaï and Jean Schuster have remarked, "leading to the memoryless spaces of the metahuman condition."[64] How better to prepare to explore these spaces than by accumulating funds through embezzlement of the familiar?

Luis Buñuel: The Surrealist as Commercial Director

Writing in the tenth number of *Cahiers du Cinéma* in 1927, Luis Buñuel commented, "Rare are they who are to accomplish their mission in the rhythmic and architectonic gearing of the film." Two years before, Paul Nougé had remarked, while discussing the potential of the movies, "If the cinema were no more than people want to make us believe, perhaps we should have to despair."[1] Fortunately for the surrealists, Buñuel was to demonstrate before long that despair was not inevitable and that, with the right qualifications, one could feasibly undertake the mission with which surrealism entrusts the movie director, despite the restrictions imposed upon the film by commercialism.

After making *Las Hurdes*, Buñuel did not direct another movie for quite some time. He was executive director for a few films made in Spain, and involved in two documentaries. Then, coming to the American continent, he was given the opportunity to make an anti-Nazi documentary for the New York Museum of Modern Art in 1938. Subsequently he made propaganda films for United States distribution. In 1942, accusations of atheism leveled at him in *The Secret Life of Salvador Dali*, combined with frustration at being unable to work with any degree of real independence, led him to resign. The year 1945 found him working as a producer at the Warner Brothers studios in Hollywood. Here he made a lot of money, but no films. He took a year off, leaving for Mexico where he directed his first commercial feature, *Gran Casino* (1947). Thereafter he directed a number of movies in Mexico, including one of his most widely respected, *Los Olvidados* [*The Young and the Damned* (1950)].

138

Gran Casino is a musical movie devoid of interest. Buñuel has made no excuses for it, dismissing it as "a silly film" with only a few redeeming scenes. It certainly seems to owe nothing to the inspiration from which *Las Hurdes* came. Little more can be said for *El Gran Calavera* (1949), adapted from a play by Adolfo Torrado. Of this comedy, filmed in a mere two weeks (no worse than many of its kind and better than most), he remarked that it was "without one scene of interest." And indeed nothing here, either, suggests in the director anything but ready willingness to accept and conform to commercialism's every demand. Making his earliest Mexican films, Buñuel apparently counted himself lucky to be working as a film-maker once again, and it looked as though he had turned his back for good on surrealism until he made *Los Olvidados*.

What is interesting in *Los Olvidados* therefore is not that it earned two prizes, including one at the 1951 Cannes Festival, but that it provides clues for an answer to the important question: in what measure has Buñuel managed to reconcile the requirements of the commercial cinema with the spirit of surrealism?

Ado Kyrou judges the film harshly,[2] admitting that he feels entitled to do so because it falls short of the standard Buñuel set himself in *Las Hurdes*. Comparison in such terms as Kyrou wants to impose is unfair, however. *Las Hurdes* had been shot in complete disregard for the conventions of the commercial cinema, while Buñuel was responsible to a producer when making *Los Olvidados*. Less is to be gained from stressing that a note of compromise can be detected now and again in his later film—the sequence relating to the reformatory, mainly—than from noting what signs he gives here of still being the director to whom we owe *Las Hurdes*.

It might appear that Buñuel was making a major concession to commercial tastes when consenting to treat in *Los Olvidados* the melodramatic theme of the life of slum children in Mexico City, one of whom corrupts the innocence of another before both fall victim to their environment.[3] True, melodrama is a particularly popular mode in the Mexican film industry. Yet we should be oversimplifying in suggesting that, while filming in Mexico, Buñuel accepted melodrama as a necessary evil. His subsequent career has shown that a case might well be made for his predilection for the melodramatic form as a vehicle especially adapted to conveying themes strongly attractive to him. At all events, there is no doubt Buñuel is prepared to treat any subject at all so long as it can be made to serve as a window on the surreal. Interviewed by Simone Dubreuilh in *Les Lettres françaises* as late as October 11, 1956, he affirmed, "I accept an adaptation only if I think I can, from one moment to another, express myself, say something of my own, slip in between two images."

Nevertheless, in *Los Olvidados* commercial demands curb his natural inclination. To what extent they do so can be estimated by comparison of the effects he achieves here with what he would have liked to produce.

Certain viewers may be persuaded that only in a celebrated dream sequence does the surrealist viewpoint find uninhibited expression in *Los Olvidados*. And they appear to be on safe ground, when contending this is the case. During his interview with Bazin and Doniol-Valcroze published in *Cahiers du Cinéma* in June 1954, Buñuel himself admitted, "I don't make the films of my choice; I choose from among several subjects proposed the one that might suit me, that I can rework. I can introduce—by means of a dream— some irrational elements, but never anything symbolic." However he places the images assembled in the dream passage of *Los Olvidados* on an equal footing with those drawn from the hideously ugly world where his young dreamer lives. There is nothing accidental at all in the dream being as real to Pedro as the waking world. The same can be said about the experience of Buñuel's hero in *Robinson Crusoe* (1952), whose erotic daydreaming brings to life a woman's dress, billowing in the wind where he has set it up as a scarecrow. Neither in *Los Olvidados* nor in *Robinson Crusoe* is surrealism kept at an acceptable distance from what is customarily called realism. Instead Buñuel sets off a subversive process of contamination which his later work reveals as far from accidental or gratuitous. In his commercial films, Buñuel firmly declines to depict a world limited by conventional realism, even when he seems to be depicting reality in its most sordid aspects. In theory, as much as in practice, he goes so far as to reject the commonly accepted definition of realism. During the fifties, for example, he took a stand against neo-realism in the cinema.

Speaking at the University of Mexico on poetry and cinema, Buñuel asserted in 1953, "Neo-realist reality is incomplete, official and above all reasonable; but poetry, mystery, all that completes and enlarges tangible reality, is completely absent from its works." On these grounds, Buñuel, who defined the essential characteristic of the cinema as "mystery and the fantastic," found neo-realism unduly limited in its ambitions. It does not interest him, he explained during a later interview granted Elena Poniatowska for the *Revista de la Universidad de Mexico,* in January 1961: "Because reality is multiple and because for many different men it can have a thousand diverse meanings. I want to have an integral view of reality. I want to enter the marvelous world of the unknown. The rest I have to hand, daily." Just as he has confessed to Bazin and Doniol-Valcroze, "Surrealism was a big lesson in my life and also a big marvelous and poetic step," so he declared to Elena Poniatowska, "A good film must have the ambivalence of two opposed and related things. This is why I should very much like to film Juan Rulfo's *Pedro Páramo*, because what attracts me in the work of Rulfo is the movement from mystery to reality, accomplished almost without transition; that mixture of reality and fancy pleases me a lot, but I don't know how to bring it to the screen."

Behind statements of this kind lies a notion of cinematographic reality to which Buñuel alluded during an interview accorded Guy Allombert for *Image et Son*, in October, 1960: "I put into my films what I feel like putting into them. [. . .] But I demand that the cinema be a witness, a review of the world, one which says all that is important about the real." It might appear that Buñuel was leading up to some theory of cinematographic technique calculated to surmount the limitations of conventional realism. This seems especially likely when one recalls that in the tenth number of *Cahiers d'Art* he had observed, "Technique is a necessary quality for a film as for every work of art, indeed for an industrial product!" But his 1927 comments had been intended to introduce this significant assertion: "One must not believe, however, that this quality determines the excellence of a film. There are qualities in a film which can be of more interest than technique." Buñuel's continued fidelity to a viewpoint on the cinema expressed in the twenties is attested in his reply to a remark made by François Truffaut, interviewing him for the magazine *Arts* on July 21, 1955. When Truffaut suggested his Mexican films are technically superior to most French films, Buñuel responded: "Oh! yes? Technique poses no problems for me. [. . .] I detest unusual angles. I sometimes work out a superb and very clever shot with my cameraman; we polish everything up, we are finicky and when it comes to shooting we guffaw and destroy everything so as to shoot simply, with no camera effects."

In the circumstances, it is fair to assume Buñuel approves when surrealists remember *Los Olvidados* for the glimpses it offers of reality drawn directly from life, yet appearing not to be of this world. Perhaps the most striking instance of effects to which we find him most sensitive is provided by the scene in which a gang of boys knock a legless beggar off his trolley, leaving him on the sidewalk, gesticulating in rage and looking like a repulsive insect. Here pity for a mistreated cripple takes second place to horror at the offensive creature examined by the camera, just as it examined the scorpions of *L'Age d'Or*. Naturally, as in *Las Hurdes,* surrealism in *Los Olvidados* means protest against social conditions and against our apathy before them. But the images of the world with which it confronts us strike us at a lower level and in a more sensitive region. We are not accustomed to having a crusading film-maker aim such low blows at our complacency. During his lecture at the University of Mexico Buñuel paraphrased Octavio Paz's statement, "It is enough for a man in chains to close his eyes for him to have the power to burst open the world," declaring, "It would be enough that the white eyelid of the screen can reflect the light which belongs to it to blow up the universe."

Departure from conventional standards of moral indignation in *Los Olvidados* signifies that the moral responsibility expressed throughout Buñuel's work is of the revolutionary kind advocated in surrealism. The director's approach is revelatory of an attitude from which he has never varied. While conceding the mediocrity of his commercial movies prior to *Los Olvidados*, he asserted in an interview with Elena Poniatowska, "But I have always followed my surrealist principle: 'The necessity to eat never excuses the prostitution of art.' Out of nineteen or twenty films I have made three or four frankly bad ones, but in no instance have I contravened my moral code." Drawing attention on the same occasion to his rejection of conventional morality, he affirmed, "Obviously, I've made bad films, but always morally worthy ones." Invited to define morality as he understood it, he responded, "Bourgeois morality is for me immorality, against which one must fight. Morality founded on our very unjust social institutions, like religion, patriotism, the family, culture; in brief, what are called the 'pillars' of society."

From Buñuel's moral standpoint, *Robinson Crusoe,* with its sensitivity to class distinction and racism (that is, as he elects to show us Crusoe and Friday), bears comparison with *El Bruto* [*The Brute* (1952)]. Here the hero is shot down by the police after he has turned against his father and broken his neck, upon discovering in him the personification of imposed authority and exploitation of the oppressed. Moreover both these movies are in harmony with *Los Olvidados*. They also harmonize with *Nazarin* (1958), which Buñuel assured Elena Poniatowska was entirely in accord with his moral principles. As he intimated to Bazin and Doniol-Valcroze, "I try never to do anything unworthy or reassuring. One must not make people believe that everything is for the best in the best of worlds."

Conventional appeals to indignation in audiences convinced of the validity of conventional moral and social standards have never meant anything to Buñuel. There is self-righteousness in such audiences' expectations. They count upon the film-maker's respect for these, and rely on him not to go beyond them, when inviting his public to voice protest against the misery he depicts. Attacking self-righteousness of this kind in *Los Olvidados* just as in *Las Hurdes,* Buñuel eliminates condescending pity for the legless cripple—cripples are always suspect, anyway, in the world he presents. This, in part, is why the villain of his melodrama is, as later in *Viridiana,* a blind man.

Armed with a club, a stick with a projecting nail, the blind man in *Los Olvidades* has all the deviousness of his trade as beggar, and (being a child molester) few of the moral virtues society prides itself upon inculcating. When he has been beaten by the gang and struggles to his knees, his sightless eyes stare into those of a hen. We are meant to learn no lesson from the brutal punishment meted out to a man who is at the same time one of society's victims and one of its predators. Buñuel's emphasis upon the exchange of a blind glance with a mindless one makes this clear. It forewarns against misinterpretation of a statement he made *Le Monde* on June 1, 1961: "I belong to a Catholic family, and from the age of eight to fifteen I was brought up by the Jesuits. In my case religious education and surrealism have left traces for a lifetime." His work lends itself naturally to surrealist interpretation, once we understand how religious teaching—normally quite incompatible with surrealist teaching—has left its mark upon his movies.

"Thanks be to God, I'm still an atheist." The remark is typical of Buñuel.[4] Its paradoxical character testifies to an ironical approach to religious matters and specifically to the teachings of the Church in which he was raised. References to religious faith and to what it demands we believe and accept are to be found in most of his films. They never appear without ironic overtones. Like the eyeball-to-eyeball shot of the blind man and the hen, these express Buñuel's determination not to be blind to what all must see. He made his point clearly enough as early as *Las Hurdes,* stressing the injustice of a world in which faith disseminates the belief that the righteous receive their just reward.

Opposition to the Church and ironical treatment of its lessons aligns Buñuel throughout his life with the surrealists. His next movie after *Los Olvidados, Susana* (1950), concerns a young woman who, after being brutalized in jail, prays to God to work a miracle. She is duly released from captivity, only to disrupt the life of a decent family by the exercise of her considerable sexual talents. It finally becomes necessary to call in the police, who carry her off to prison once more—with or without God's approval, one is not quite sure. Religious solutions have never held any validity for Buñuel. Meanwhile social problems have always held his close attention. In conversation with André Bazin and Jacques Doniol-Valcroze he declared, "For me *Los Olvidados* is indeed a film of social struggle. [. . .] I observed things which moved me and I wanted to transpose them to the screen but always with that sort of love I have for the instinctive and the irrational which can appear in everything. I have always been attracted by the unknown or strange side that fascinates me I know not why." Speaking of cuts he was obliged to make when shooting his script, Buñuel explained to Bazin and Doniol-Valcroze:

> Into the most realistic scenes, I wanted to introduce some mad, completely disparate elements. For instance, when Jaibo is going to beat up and kill the other boy [Pedro], a camera shift reveals, in the distance, the framework of a high eleven-story building under construction. I wanted to put an orchestra with a hundred musicians in that building. One would have seen it in passing, vaguely. I wanted to put in many elements of that kind, but it was absolutely forbidden.

Had Buñuel been given his way, Durgnat would have been obliged to reconsider the statement in his *Luis Buñuel* that *Los Olvidados* derived in part from the "Marxist neo-realism with violence" for which De Santis' *Riz amer* [*Bitter Rice* (1948)] provided a precedent (p. 60). We, on the other hand, should have less reason to stress the effects Buñuel was prevented from creating in this movie, if he had not been subjected to similar interdictions two years later, when making *Robinson Crusoe*.

From *Gran Casino* and *El Gran Calavera* to *Los Olvidados*, then from *Los Olvidados* to a creaking vehicle like *Susana* (his worst film, Buñuel has remarked)—and the very same year, by the way: the remarkable variation in quality in Buñuel's film work done in Mexico is disconcerting to note. However it gives some indication of the pressures imposed upon him. For the first time he was working within the frame of commercialism, which called for popular success more insistently than it demanded lasting achievement. In 1951 Buñuel made two more faceless movies, *La Hija del engano* and *Una Mujer sin amor*, the latter an adaptation of Maupassant's static novel *Pierre et Jean*. The following year it was *El Bruto*, about which he has commented that the script (written by Luis Alcoriza and himself) was "quite interesting, but they made me change it all, from top to bottom. Now it's just another film, with nothing extraordinary about it."[5] Nothing extraordinary, one would agree, except for a typical

Buñuel touch: placing a picture of the Holy Virgin in the slaughter-house where the hero works.

One might say that, shooting his movie in only eighteen days, Buñuel had no right to expect to do better. But the time factor is secondary here. More important is that a pattern was emerging from Buñuel's effort to enliven the commercial cinema with elements which had a special meaning for him and for the surrealists. Exact-ing from him serious concessions, commercial production conditions were in danger of emptying Buñuel's films of their most personal elements, depriving them not only of originality but of vitality. Buñuel had reached a crucial moment in his career. He now had to make up his mind which way to go. *Subida al cielo* [*Ascent to Heaven* (1951)] indicates which direction seemed to him to promise most.

Written and produced by Manuel Altolaguirre, *Subida al cielo*, which took the prize as the best avant-garde feature at the 1952 Cannes Festival, concerns a bus trip taken by a young man whom family business obliges to leave his bride on his wedding day. On the surface, this is so commercialized a cinematographic effort (a compendium including travelogue, life, death, copulation, and some fine fare for Freudians)[6] that it would appear best to forget it. Kyrou's tactic is to see another film, more palatable to him, in place of the one passing before him. Those curious about Kyrou's version of *Subida al cielo* can read it for themselves.[7] What is more interest-ing to us is to see him advance the hypothesis that Buñuel's *Subida al cielo* may be "an ultra-personal film" concealed beneath the sur-face, made "in total disinterest" for the public, while the director delighted in the idea that "he alone *knows* what his film represents."[8]

Kyrou's treatment of *Subida al cielo* could be set aside as of questionable value, but for evidence that Buñuel consistently ap-proached the problem of making films in Mexico, within the restrict-ing confines of commercialism, as though asking himself how he could evade these. Of course, he was largely unsuccessful at first. For this reason, whatever we conclude about his early Mexican movies, we can never be harder on them than Buñuel himself. Whether a change of strategy is to be noticed in *Subida al cielo* or not, it is evident Buñuel learned this from his first encounter with commercial demands: they could not be ignored, nor could they be denied with impunity. They had to be circumvented.

From the surrealist standpoint, Buñuel's memorable films are those which give the producer his money's worth while the director keeps something back for his own satisfaction, through communi-cation of a *vision surréaliste* he will not consent to surrender. It is characteristic of the movies of his maturity that in every case he succeeds in bypassing objections at odds with his own preferences. It is worth noticing, therefore, that after *Subida al cielo,* he had a hand in writing every one of the scripts he has filmed, with the exception of *La Ilusión vieja en tranvía* (1953).

Buñuel has brought to the screen adaptations of a number of novels. From Defoe's *Robinson Crusoe* he turned to an old surrealist favorite, Emily Brontë's *Wuthering Heights,* for the subject matter of his *Cumbres Borrascosas* (1953). Subsequently came versions of Roblès' *Cela s'appelle l'Aurore* (1955), Galdós' *Nazarin* (1958), Mirbeau's *Le Journal d'une Femme de Chambre* (1964), and Kessel's *Belle de Jour* (1966).

It seems strange at first Buñuel should elect to treat subjects like these, since his lecture at the University of Mexico included the statement that the screen "displays the moral and intellectual void in which the cinema wallows; indeed the latter confines itself to imitating the novel or the theatre with this difference that its means are less rich for uncovering psychology." Buñuel considers the filmmaker invites trouble when trying to compete with the novelist; he believes too such competition is unworthy of any director. He subscribes to the surrealist belief that literature is of dubious significance: "What is the use of all this visual ornamentation," he asked, when condemning neo-realism, "if the situations, the motives animating the characters, their reactions, and the very subject matter are all based on the most sentimental, most conformist literature?" The theme of Mirbeau's *Le Journal d'une Femme de Chambre* is anything but sentimental, to be sure. None the less, the paradox is not fully resolved unless one notices how, in the process of transposition, novelistic material acquires color and texture which mark it as distinctively Buñuelian.

Such is the case with *El* (1952), shot from a script by Buñuel and Alcoriza after a novel by Mercedes Pinto. In this movie the central figure (*He,* in the title) is a man of about forty, comfortably off, unmarried and inexperienced in sexual matters. Fascinated by the glimpse of a woman's foot during a church service, he falls in love with its owner whom he courts and then marries. Gradually succumbing to jealousy, he finally attempts to strangle a priest and is consigned to a monastery. Here, when visited by his former wife, her husband, and their son, he claims to have found happiness.

Buñuel's contempt for the ambitions of directors who try to make of a movie the excuse for psychological penetration gives us confidence to expect that he is not primarily concerned with presenting a case history. As Francisco is presented in *El,* his story is

the tragic history of a man insufficiently equipped to respond without reserve to mad love. Mad love nevertheless succeeds in turning
his outlook on life upside down, leading him finally to attack the
representative of religious imperatives he wishes to suppress. Torn
between desire and guilt feelings, Francisco collapses beneath the
burden of the conflict they release within him. As was the case during the scene of destruction in the bedchamber of *L'Age d'Or*, inability to cope with his situation is betrayed by violent acts and
gestures.

In the end, Francisco's reward is nothing better than voluntary delusion. Thus aberrant behavior is not subjected to clinical
examination in *El*, but is shown to be merely a sterile substitute for
fulfillment in a man who has been so preconditioned that he is unworthy to meet the challenge of love.

Buñuel has declared that his movie is devoted to studying
exacerbated jealousy in an individual whom the director scrutinizes
as he would "an insect, beetle or anopheles." When we read this
declaration among his replies to Bazin and Doniol-Valcroze, we do
so knowing how attentive Buñuel has always been to the cruelties of
the world, as revealed by the study of entomology. And we know,
too, how much pleasure he takes in directing attention to aspects of
reality which shock preconceptions based on his audience's limited
experience. Hence *El* takes us to the vertiginous brink of the un-
thinkable as it shows Francisco entering the room where his wife
is sleeping, after arming himself with a length of rope, some cotton
wool, disinfectant, scissors, and needle and thread.[9]

During his talk with Bazin and Doniol-Valcroze, Buñuel confessed:

> I don't like to go to the movies, but I like the cinema as a
> means of expression. I find there is no better means of show-
> ing us a reality we do not touch with our fingers every day.
> This is to say that through books, through the newspapers,
> through our experience, we know our exterior, objective
> reality. The cinema by its very mechanism opens a little
> window on the prolongation of that reality. My aspiration as
> a film viewer is to have the movie *uncover* something for me
> and this happens very rarely.

Intent upon indicating the prolongation of reality which is surreality, Buñuel is perpetually concerned to uncover something. *El*
is typical of the work of a man who has affirmed, "In practice I am
not at all sadistic or masochistic. I am so only theoretically and I
accept these elements only as elements of struggle and of violence."

Francisco is condemned to struggle and violence by his own incapacity to surmount the barriers erected between him and the enjoyment of love by his education. His differences from Buñuel himself are fundamental, as one appreciates immediately upon reading his creator's response to a surrealist questionnaire on love, dating from 1929: "I would willingly sacrifice my liberty to love. I have already done so."

Horror betrays frustration in *El*, under pressure from religio-social education. Its use is by no means intended to edify the spectator. There is nothing surprising, then, in finding Buñuel treating a parallel theme in comic vein, with *Ensayo de un crimen* [*The Criminal Life of Archibaldo de la Cruz* (1955)]. Here the hero conquers his obsessions by learning to handle them, instead of looking for relief from them through deviant behavior of the sort that drives Francisco to the brink of insanity.

From one end of this movie to the other, we watch Archibaldo being denied the chance to realize his fondest dream. Had Buñuel not warned us in advance, we might be tempted to speak of the psychological motivation of his hero's conduct, clearly visible to all. While he was still a child, we discover, a stray bullet fired during a riot killed his governess, so treating him to the delightful spectacle of blood running over her stockinged legs. Reminded of the incident when he comes upon a music box surviving from his childhood (Buñuel is making fun of Proust's laborious insistence upon the triggering mechanism of involuntary memory), Archibaldo becomes obsessed with the idea of recreating the scene that thrilled him as a young boy. From now on, his differences from Francisco are clear-cut. Francisco's life disintegrates under the force of his obsession; Archibaldo's takes direction from his. Francisco fears sensuality, even while compulsively attracted to it; Archibaldo offers no resistance as passion draws him into sensual abandon. Of individuals such as he, Desnos wrote in *Le Soir*, on February 26, 1927, "To sensual persons [. . .] belong the profound revolutionary pleasures, the legitimate perversions of love and poetry." In Buñuel's important lecture at the University of Mexico we find confirmation of the pertinence of Desnos' reference to poetry: "The cinema seems to have been invented to express the life of the subconscious, the roots of which penetrate so deep into poetry."

The comic pattern of *Ensayo de un crimen* emerges as soon as Archibaldo has been reminded of his pleasure at contemplating the body of his dead governess. As is frequently the case in comedy, the joke improves with repetition. All the same, the amusement afforded audiences rests entirely upon their capacity to respond to the black humor Buñuel is practicing, and upon their ability to free themselves from respect for the conventional standards of morality Buñuel's code contravenes.

The first incident, showing how an accident denies Archibaldo the chance to achieve his purpose, tests our moral values, as it does our sense of humor. Attended in hospital by a nun, Archibaldo learns she wishes nothing more ardently than to depart this life for the felicities of heaven. What better occasion could he hope to have to render someone a service and satisfy his own desires at the same time? A heaven-sent opportunity, one might say. Rising to it, Archibaldo generously offers to cut the young woman's throat. Running off screaming, the nurse is so panic-stricken she throws herself down an elevator shaft, thus fulfilling her dream, without letting Archibaldo fulfill his.

Is the nun's death a sign of divine interest in her case? If it is, then Archibaldo must face the fact that he enjoys fewer privileges than she. He might be tempted, of course, to say with Defoe, "What Providence has reserved for me he only knows," but for a determination he has in common with all surrealist heroes to place his trust in no one and in nothing but himself.

Breton's adjectives *convulsif* and *délirant* apply as well to *Ensayo de un crimen* as to Freda's *L'Orribile Segreto del Dottor Hichcock*. Buñuel's film has a different tone, naturally. But this difference does not place Archibaldo's conduct in a category other than Freda has chosen for his hero. Like Dr. Hichcock, Archibaldo de la Cruz is dominated by a socially unacceptable passion. His is a dream of possession, just as Hichcock's is. It is a dream refined, in his creator's mind if not in his own, by exposure to the writings of Sade. For this reason, he is no less dedicated than Hichcock to the pursuit of a desire which, if allowed full expression, could revolutionize human relationships. Within the framework of the commercial cinema, selection of such a hero entails some concession to convention. Freda accepted the convention of the film of terror. Buñuel, for his part, chooses the conventional form of comedy. The remarkable distinction of *Ensayo de un crimen* is this: Buñuel has succeeded in his movie in using comic effects not as a mere palliative, not to forestall objections, but to invalidate these, so actually reinforcing the message he wishes to communicate.

Laughter does not prompt us to condemn Archibaldo, once we have passed the first test and become aware of the pattern of his life of frustrated crime. Instead, it establishes a bond of sympathy strong enough to withstand the resistance we may feel to his methods. We are persuaded that it does so partly because of the

ineffectuality of these methods: because something always intervenes to prevent him from applying them successfully. Above all, it
does so because, respecting one of the proven techniques of comedy,
Buñuel encourages us to anticipate his hero's failure. Archibaldo
decides to rid the world of a woman far less morally admirable than
the nun with whom he had no success; she commits suicide. He
turns back to the ranks of the pious, resolving to dispose of his
fiancée; her ex-lover upsets his plans, by killing her first. Then he
meets Lavinia.[10]

Up to this point in the film it has appeared that chance opposes realization of Archibaldo's desires. But chance intervened
beneficently when a stray bullet caused Archibaldo to identify the
erotic with death. It also brought back to him the music box (discovered in an antique shop) which revived memories of the past and
with which he continues to associate magical occurrences. Chance
now offers him liberation from his obsession: Lavinia looks just like a
dress-shop dummy he has acquired, and it so happens that Archibaldo, who plans to kill Lavinia "like Joan of Arc," is a ceramist,
owning an oven large enough to receive her body.

After inviting Lavinia to his home, Archibaldo heats up his
oven. He is confident she will come because he has promised her she
will not be alone with him, taking care not to explain that only the
dummy will be present at their meeting. Lavinia will allow him to
take no liberties. She consents with some signs of amusement to surrender her underwear to the dummy, which Archibaldo has dressed
exactly as she is dressed. The rejected lover now gives his attention
to the substitute Lavinia, kissing his dummy on the lips, and caressing its body. Lavinia leaves him in the company of her effigy, which
he consigns to the flames in her place. We see Archibaldo standing
entranced before the spectacle of the wax figure writhing as the
flames consume its clothing and devour it.

It may have appeared that chance saved Archibaldo, earlier,
from committing the irreparable act of murder. But we know him to
have been convinced each time of his own responsibility for the
death of the woman in question. Indeed he accuses himself of guilt
when he goes to give himself up to his friend, the chief of police. If,
then, he feels he has really killed those he simply *wished* dead on his
magic music box, there can be no doubt that in his mind Lavinia was
substituted for the substitute Lavinia in his oven. The act of burning
her effigy, to which we are witnesses, is thus a ritual act and an act
of exorcism ("Fire is a friend which renders us a service," wrote
Breton and Éluard in their *L'Immaculée Conception*). Archibaldo's
conviction of being legally responsible sends him to confess to the

police. Yet he has no difficulty in bowing to the police chief's argument that everyone is guilty of having wished someone dead. Society, we realize, crudely draws a line between desire and its ful-fillment, gladly enough admitting the former, so long as it does not result in the latter. Receiving absolution from the law, Archibaldo is free to go, freed on a technicality his friend does not even suspect. Tossing his music box in a lake, Archibaldo spares the life of an in-sect, which for a moment he appeared about to crush with the tip of his walking stick. Then he returns to a normal life.

Earnest efforts like those of Durgnat and Grange to explain what each of Archibaldo's "victims" represents psychologically (fig-ures of authority, reincarnation of the mother, and so on) are less relevant to understanding the end of *Ensayo de un crimen* than appreciating what has happened to Archibaldo. He has been liber-ated from his obsession by the experience of fulfilling his dream. This being a comedy, the hero can go scot-free, since he has achieved his ambition without contravening any law. But he has been liberated, really, not by being denied the chance to commit a crime but by the fact that he no longer will need to do so. This comes about because, in *Ensayo de un crimen*, Buñuel does not con-fine the irrational element he favors within the frame of a dream. The irrational begins to pervade this movie from the moment when the young Archibaldo believes he has brought about his governess' death by the use of his fetish, the music box. It reaches fullest ex-pression when the adult Archibaldo burns his Lavinia. The process of contamination of realism by surrealism, initiated in *Los Olvi-dados*, is taken to the stage where, before our eyes, the real sur-renders its rights to the surreal. We know the dummy is really only a wax model. But while it is burning we, like Archibaldo, see it twist and turn in the flames as a human body would. So, as affective re-sponses displace reasonable evidence, our interpretation of what is happening is identified with his, and we comprehend how he is released from his obsessive thoughts. To anyone who has truly shared Archibaldo's experience in front of the oven, it is no surprise to see the man who threatened the life of a nun shortly afterward spare that of a praying mantis.

With *El* and *Ensayo de un crimen* Buñuel establishes a promising basis for an approach to the commercial cinema. He shows he feels no discomfort in handling plots which would embarrass a director more touchy about his reputation. He shows, too, he is not averse to offering a little ironic encouragement to those among his audience who demand proof of psychological motivation before they grant characters in films their serious attention. But he intimates above all that he will never consent to let his movies be limited by the imaginative inadequacies of those with whom he is prepared to make only minimal compromises. With every justification, Claude Beylie has remarked that any attempt at a literal interpretation of Buñuel's work is sure to run into difficulties, pointing out that the "phantasms" in which Buñuel's heroes take pleasure "have no other explanation, really, than the unbridled fancy of their creator."[11] It is exactly this unbridled fancy which gives *El* and *Ensayo de un crimen* their surrealist quality, making them acts of protest against the reality principle.

Buñuel's next film, faithfully adapted from Emmanuel Roblès' novel of class struggle and socio-political commitment, *Cela s'appelle l'Aurore*, is less impressive. It clearly evidences Buñuel's fidelity to the moral code he is determined never to forget. The themes it develops in this connection are never in doubt: the problems posed by social conflict and solidarity among men. But one may wonder, with Kyrou, where the surrealist point of view is, in a movie to which, nevertheless, no surrealist can object. It seems one must answer by acknowledging that the surrealist viewpoint takes second place in *Cela s'appelle l'Aurore* to a somewhat rigid demonstration of a theory, which is not Buñuel's own, even though his respect in presenting it indicates he approves of it. *El* and *Ensayo de un crimen* succeed because of what they suggest without quite stating. Made in France in 1955, *Cela s'appelle l'Aurore* is less successful because it suggests no more than it states.

The same may be said of *La Mort en ce Jardin* (1956), adapted from a novel by José-André Lacour and filmed in Mexico. As for *La Fièvre monte à El Pao* (1959), after Henry Castellou's novel, it is, in Buñuel's own terse phrase, "not a good film." Its relative failure, despite the moving spectacle of Gérard Philippe in his last screen role, has two causes. The first of these is the effect of concessions the director was obliged to make before demands imposed by his Franco-Mexican producers. The second is a related factor. Like *Cela s'appelle l'Aurore* and *La Mort en ce Jardin*, *La Fièvre monte à El Pao* takes up a political theme, treating it explicitly and with few of the undertones and overtones which give *El* and *Ensayo de un crimen* their poetic magic. Presenting a subject which necessarily follows the inevitable progression of a mathematical equation, Buñuel finds it difficult to "slip in between two images." Logically accepting precedence of the theme he is developing over all else, he abstains from bringing to its presentation more than a few of the touches which, elsewhere, set his signature on his films.

The three movies just mentioned form a trilogy occupying a place apart in Buñuel's work. Looking chronologically over the films he completed during the fifties, one notices these three concentrate on a single aspect of *Los Olvidados* at the expense of other features much more personal to him. Since the last of the trilogy was preceded in 1958 by *Nazarin,* the possibility suggests itself that *La Fièvre monte à El Pao* convinced Buñuel his best prospects lay in the direction he had left in order to make *Cela s'appelle l'Aurore.* Certainly, *Nazarin* is distinctly superior to the movie that followed it, while the latter's weaknesses highlight the strengths of Buñuel's adaptation of Galdos' novel.

Nazarin took a Special Jury Prize at the Cannes Festival. It provoked a critical reaction which Buñuel's interview with Jean de Baroncelli, the following year, reveals him to have been far from anticipating. Telling of a priest who humbly sets out to follow the teachings of the Christ to the letter, this movie almost won the International Catholic Cinema Office Prize, so well was it received by the Church. After seeing it, many people found themselves wondering whether Buñuel was not returning to the faith in which he had been raised. Questioned by Jean de Baroncelli on this reaction to his latest movie, he replied characteristically in *Le Monde,* on December 16, 1959:

> Everyone is free to find in my films what pleases or suits him. Personally I was dumbfounded when I read certain reviews: where do people get what they write! I like *Nazarin* because it is a film that has allowed me to express certain things I feel strongly. But I don't believe I have repudiated or abjured anything at all.

These views are given fuller development in the interview granted Elena Poniatowska, for the *Revista de la Universidad de Mexico* at the beginning of 1961. Questioned about his assertion that *Nazarin* accorded perfectly with his moral code, Buñuel replied affirmatively when asked the following: "The Nazarin who fails? The Nazarin who can do nothing with the Church? The Nazarin without his cassock going through the fields followed by two hysterical women?"[12] To Buñuel, emulation of the Christ is clearly a vain and fruitless ambition. Reminding Elena Poniatowska that the Christ was crucified after being condemned, he countered, "Do you not consider that a failure?" Then he asked the question which is fundamental to his *Nazarin:* "Do you believe it is possible to be a Christian in the *absolute* sense of the word?" To his interviewer's reply, "Yes, divesting oneself of everything, moving away from the world," Buñuel responded roughly:

> No! No! I'm speaking of the *world*, of this earth where we are now. If the Christ were to return they would crucify him over again. One can be *relatively* Christian, but the *absolutely* pure, innocent person is condemned to failure. He is beaten before he starts. I'm sure that if the Christ came back, the high priests, the Church, would condemn him.

Convinced the Christian "in his pure *absolute* form, has nothing to do on this earth," Buñuel presents his Nazarene as a man doomed to failure and frustration. Quite rightly, Carlos Rebolledo has pointed out that Nazarin is a figure directly evocative of Cervantes' Don Quixote.[13] The parallel between Cervantes' hero and Buñuel's is valid to the extent that Buñuel treats his Nazarin as a man possessed by a delusion preventing him from seeing the world as it is, a man who persists in giving events a focus that has to be recognized as false. Whether or not his audience recognizes Nazarin's error matters little to the director. He gladly accepted the word "ambiguous," when Elena Poniatowska applied it to his movie, seeing nothing pejorative in the adjective. He even added this enlightening comment: "I agree. The style is ambiguous and that's why it interests me. If a work is self-evident, it's finished for me."

Ambiguity is to be regarded, Buñuel implies, as a necessary skill. Experience in the commercial cinema obviously has taught him to prize and has trained him to develop it, as a means of eluding supervision and censorship at the same time.

Nazarin marks an important step in the direction Buñuel takes during the sixties, demonstrating that, for him, ambiguity is not simply visual but ethical and moral too. He confided in Georges Sadoul for *Les Lettres françaises* (June 1, 1961), "I'm fond of the character in *Nazarin*. He's a priest. So what? He could just as well be a hairdresser, or a waiter. What interests me is that he sticks to his ideas, that they are unacceptable to society and that, after his adventures with prostitutes, thieves, etc., they lead him to irrevocable condemnation by the forces of order." Buñuel likes his Nazarene because he is condemned to failure by the purity of his motives and the idealism holding him on his self-destructive course. The film *Nazarin* illustrates its director's belief that the absolutely pure Christian has no place in this world. "Why?" asked Elena Poniatowska. "Because," answered Buñuel, "there is no other way than that of *rebellion* in a world that's in such a mess." Hence Buñuel uses Christ, in the person of Nazarin, to prove his point that the Christ did not have the answers to the evils of our world.

As we are prompted to revolt against the unfairness of the fate reserved for Nazarin, we are placed on the road of rebellion which Buñuel first took when he filmed *Las Hurdes*. It is the road we find him traveling in *Los Olvidados* and in his political trilogy; the road he follows also in *El* and *Ensayo de un crimen*, where he arranges "elements of struggle and of violence" to illustrate the moral lessons he believes life necessarily must teach.[14] This is the road the movies he will make during the sixties will show him to be resolved never to leave.

Interviewed by Guy Allombert in *Image et Son*, Buñuel declared in 1960, "No more dreams! I've had enough of plagiarizing myself and I've no desire to do over again the films I've already made." It is relatively easy to see how a movie like *The Young One* (1960), Buñuel's only English-language feature, adapted from Peter Matthiessen's *Travelin' Man*, meets the requirements laid down here. No less than the political trilogy of the fifties, *The Young One* speaks directly, relying for effect upon its theme alone—racism—to trouble our complacency and awaken our conscience. Buñuel's next film *Viridiana* (1961), is more complex.

Talking over *Viridiana* with Yvonne Baby in *Le Monde* on June 1, 1961, Buñuel commented, "I didn't try to blaspheme, but, of course, Pope John XXIII knows more about that than I. Chance led me to show impious images; if I had pious ideas perhaps I'd have expressed them too."[15] He went on to point out, "*Viridiana* follows my personal tradition since *L'Age d'Or*, and, thirty years apart, those are the two films I have made with the greatest liberty." He took care to remind his interviewer, "I have been more or less successful with my films and I've made banal ones to earn my living. However I've always refused concessions and defended the principles I cared about." While he still can say, as he did of *Nazarin*, that in *Viridiana* everyone is free to find whatever pleases or suits him, it is more difficult for audiences to misinterpret the latter in the way some misjudged the former.

To make his new film Buñuel went back by invitation to Spain. He was required to make only minor modifications before the script, written in collaboration with Julio Alejandro, was approved for shooting. When finished, *Viridiana* was promptly banned by the Republican government, after proving to be the most brilliant demonstration up to then of Buñuel's skill at mocking the principle of censorship while apparently submitting to the censor's requirements.

First thoughts about devoting a movie to the "unappreciated" saint, Viridiana, a contemporary of Francis of Assisi, were linked in Buñuel's mind with this image: "A young woman 'drugged' by an old man: thus she is at the mercy of someone who, in other circumstances, could never have held her in his arms. I thought that this woman must be pure, and I made her a novice." Evidently, he was more interested in precipitating the situation just described than in recounting or transposing the life story of a saint. Only associatively did he arrive at the idea of making his heroine a novice—and only then, it is plain, because the scandalous potential of the image is enhanced by choosing a victim whose innocence is above question. Hence, as he himself has indicated, genesis of this film followed a familiar pattern: "I proceed each time in this way, and the movie then springs forth like a fountain." He is referring to a fountain of images which, in the case of *Viridiana*, literally bring one another forth. As he explained to Yvonne Baby:

> The idea of the beggars came after, because I found it natural that they be given shelter by a former nun on her property. Then I said to myself I'd like to see these beggars eating in the dining room of a manor house at the big table covered with an embroidered tablecloth and candles. Suddenly I realized they were posed as in a picture, and I evoked Leonardo da Vinci's *Last Supper.* Finally I associated the Halleluia Chorus from Handel's *Messiah* with the beggars' orgy and dance, more striking that way than underlined by a rock and roll rhythm. This effect pleased me. In the same way, I wanted to introduce Mozart's *Requiem* at the moment of the love scene between the old man and the young woman and to place the gentle orison of the Angelus against the workers' labor.

Reviewing Buñuel's protestation that he did not set out to blaspheme in *Viridiana,* we see from the above why this was so: the associations from which his movie grew were of a nature to render conscious effort in this direction superfluous. However, his film is divested of its complexity, if treated as the simple demonstration of an antireligious thesis.

Asked about *Viridiana* by Georges Sadoul in May 1961, he declared, "I have never had the intention of writing a scenario *with a thesis,* demonstrating for example that Christian charity is useless and ineffectual." He added, "Basically I wanted to make a funny film—no doubt corrosive, but spontaneous—through which I express erotic and religious childhood obsessions."[16] Then he went on to remark, "It amused me that my heroine, in honor of her patron saint, should carry around a little case from which she takes the cross, the crown of thorns, the nails, etc." Evidently, it amused him no less to act upon the attractive idea of entrusting the part of Viridiana to Sylvia Pinal, whose reputation rested upon her performance in comic roles.

Invited to tell Yvonne Baby which images were found most offensive in his movie, Buñuel replied:

> The crown of thorns on fire, although to burn is not to profane. I have been criticized for showing a knife in the form of a cross. One oftens finds them in Spain and I've seen a lot of them in Albacete. My sister who is very pious one day met a nun who used these little knives to peel potatoes. So it was not I who invented the "switch blade" Christ. Only photography brings out the joke and the surrealist character of an object manufactured innocently or by mass production.

Like Mariën in *L'Imitation du Cinéma,* Buñuel draws comic effect in *Viridiana* from exploiting his audience's inability to dissociate certain symbols from religious belief. The joke we have just heard him mention is a mischievous one then. In fact, the word he uses in French, translated here in one of its senses as "joke," is *la malice.*

Viridiana's fetishes (the cross, the crown of thorns, the hammer, the nails) are as much a sign of her delusion as Archibaldo's music box was. Like the box, they have to be taken into account in our evaluation of her conduct, because for so long she believes implicitly in them. In the end, she consigns the crown of thorns to one of the elements (fire), as Archibaldo, similarly released from delusion, consigned his to another (water). Meanwhile Don Jaime, the uncle at whose home her Mother Superior insists Viridiana spend a few days before taking her vows, has his fetishes too. Juxtaposition of the image of Viridiana piously kneeling before the emblems of her faith with that of Don Jaime grotesquely rigged out in his dead wife's shoes indicates clearly how Buñuel judges his heroine's state of mind, at the beginning of the movie.

In view of the care taken in *Viridiana* to control response to its material by methods such as these, Buñuel's reply to some of Yvonne Baby's questions about the film must be treated circumspectly:

> People have reproached me with cruelty. Where is it in the film? The novice proves her humanity, the old man, a complicated character, is capable of kindness toward men and toward a mere bee [which he saves from drowning in a bucket of water]. His son is rather likable, and the beggars— of a type that is classic in Spain—can manifest their vulgarity

without cruelty. Only the blind man is mistrustful, hypocritical, vicious, like those affected by such an infirmity. For that reason my blind men always have moments of viciousness.

Once again, Buñuel declines responsibility for having presented a thesis in *Viridiana*, any more than in other films. "I insist," he says to Yvonne Baby, "I have tried to demonstrate nothing and I do not use the cinema as a pulpit from which I should like to preach." And he tells Georges Sadoul, "In my film not one of the heroes is vicious. Viridiana is purity itself. Her uncle is not a sadist and a debauchee, but a good fellow and even an idealist. [. . .] He punishes himself terribly for a moment of weakness in which he didn't do much wrong." Even so, when we read statements of this sort, we find ourselves protesting, as Buñuel himself did through *Las Hurdes*, "Yes, but . . ."

The pure Viridiana personifies Christian charity. But none of those whom she shelters either understands her behavior or—as one great orgiastic scene demonstrates—feels any inclination to imitate it. Her uncle is kindly enough, yet not so kindly as to resist the temptation to drug her one evening, after persuading her to don the wedding dress worn by his late wife. True, he does not rape her, but she later believes he has done so, consequently losing faith in her purity. Don Jaime then punishes himself, committing suicide the following morning, when he discovers Viridiana has packed and left, to go back to the convent. But he punishes himself by an act the Church condemns as sinful, hanging himself from a tree in the garden. And why does he do so? Because he believes he has lost Viridiana, perhaps? Or is it out of shame at having been tempted to violate her? Or because he has discovered his incapacity to see the act through, and to do as much wrong as he had hoped? Whatever conclusions we draw, we have to agree he has wasted his chance, according to Buñuel, for whom the solution to moral and ethical problems must be found on "this earth where we are now."

Is Viridiana herself really closer to the Christian ideal of purity than her uncle? We wonder about this, as we ask whether she is so revolted by his conduct because it supposedly has deprived her of her virginity or because, under the influence of the drug, she did not enjoy consciousness during defloration. The alternative explanation mentioned here might appear unpardonably malicious but for Buñuel's skill in suggesting Viridiana has a strong instinct for sex which her pious feelings do their best to conceal and control. We are alerted to the existence of her instinct very soon in the movie. As Viridiana undresses before going to bed, she displays charms which can hardly be ignored. Of course, the undergarments brought from the convent do not set her body off to best advantage. But there is no mistaking an awareness in movement and gesture, even though the performance of disrobing is gauche. Indeed, Buñuel incorporates a joke into this scandalous sequence, by covertly bidding us remember we are watching a novice stripper.

No sooner have we had time to react to this scene than Viridiana is shown sleepwalking. She heads for her uncle's room. Here she throws knitting and needles into the fireplace before spreading ashes on his bed, next to the wedding veil worn by her aunt who, we know, died before her marriage with Don Jaime could be consummated. Subsequently responding to the pleasures of living in the country, she expresses a desire for milk, while watching operations in the dairy. To anyone who remembers the shot in *Los Olvidados,* showing milk running down the thighs of a little girl, it is no surprise when, reaching out to grasp a cow's udder upon an invitation to draw milk for herself, Viridiana recoils, unable to complete the apparently innocent gesture.

Later still she is overpowered by two of her beggars, one of whom sets about trying to rape her. This time Viridiana is awake and able to put up a fight. But in the struggle we see her grasping the handles of a skipping rope. Originally this was bought by Don Jaime as a gift for his servant's little daughter so he could enjoy the sight of her legs and feet as the child used it. Thereafter it was used by Don Jaime to hang himself, and now it serves as a belt for the rapist beggar. In view of the phallic shape of the rope's handles, there can be no doubt Buñuel meant his remark to Georges Sadoul to be understood ironically: "My heroine finds herself more of a virgin at the dénouement than she was at the beginning." Exactly the same might be said of Archibaldo de la Cruz, if this statement were adapted to his case. He is at least no less innocent at the dénouement of *Ensayo de un crimen* than he was at the beginning. Yet we know Archibaldo has sinned in thought; and we have reason to believe Viridiana has done so too.

Wherever we look, ironical overtones are cast upon what we see. For instance, the blind man is surely the most repulsive character in *Viridiana.* Yet this does not prevent Buñuel from according him the central position in the "Last Supper" photographed with original obscenity by an old hag who throws up her skirt to reveal a "camera" all her own. Who could believe for a moment that pure accident has led the blind man to take a seat in the center of the table when his disciples share with him a last meal before they are disbanded?

As for Don Jaime's illegitimate son, Jorge, we can gladly concede that, by the side of the blind man, he appears quite a likable human being. None the less, as a natural son, professionally trained and worldly wise, he represents everything that conflicts with what Viridiana's education has made her. To whom else can she turn, now that her world has collapsed and the police—arriving too late on the scene—have finally restored order? With this question in mind, we come to the closing sequence of *Viridiana*. The original script sketched the scene as follows: Jorge and the maid Ramona are playing cards (evidently after making love) when Viridiana arrives. Delighted, Jorge dismisses Ramona, closing the door after her. The film was to end with the maid stooping down to peer through the keyhole. Like father, like son—Jorge wants to make the woman his father desired his mistress. Like mother, like daughter—Ramona's curiosity leads her to spy on Viridiana's sexual initiation, as her little daughter's curiosity led *her* to climb a tree to watch when Don Jaime began to undress the defenseless body of his niece (a sequence shot in part from the point of view of the child). No wonder the Spanish censor protested, demanding an alternative ending!

Unperturbed, Buñuel set about providing an alternative acceptable enough to pass without demur. He succeeded in devising a new version which, beneath its air of innocence, turned out to be even more scandalous: when Viridiana arrives, Jorge simply invites her to join the card game. She accepts. Does she know how to play the game? She could hardly have learned it in the convent. We can be sure Jorge holds himself ready to initiate her into its mysteries. In fact, we hear him tell her, as he puts a record on the phonograph, that he knew they would play together, one day. As he shows us a *ménage à trois* established, Buñuel uses rocks and roll music to underscore the scene when the saintly Viridiana finally sits down opposite her cousin, played by Francisco Rabal, whom Buñuel had chosen earlier to play the saintly Nazarin.

Upon the surface, *Viridiana* proceeds at unhurried pace until the scene of orgy and destruction, and in the end reverts to languor, so persuading the unwary that life has resumed as before. However the real drama of its heroine's conversion from faith to life is played out beneath the surface. Probing the meaning behind the movie, we are persuaded without difficulty that Viridiana's readiness to join the world and accept its usages is a sign of redemption. In contrast, Francisco's withdrawal from the world to a monastery marks his damnation. Our last glimpse of Viridiana suggests she has found her place. Our last memory of Francisco, in *El,* is the spectacle of an odd figure in monk's habit, unable to walk straight along the path he takes when moving away from the camera. It would be regrettable to leave the theatre having missed the conclusion Buñuel intends us to draw. However, it would be no less unfortunate to treat *Viridiana* and *El* as films of didactic intent. It is preferable to let some aspects of these movies escape us rather than impose a rigid interpretation liable to divest them of their precious quality of ambiguity. For this reason, the most important lesson *Viridiana* has to teach us is to be cautious, when we come to examine the film that follows it, *El Angel exterminador* [*The Exterminating Angel* (1962)]. Of this film Buñuel observed in *Positif No. 58*, "I am a little tired of the cinema. I don't want to set about making films to earn money. I shall make a film every three years, when I feel like it, and only on subjects I feel like handling, absolutely irrational subjects like that of *The Exterminating Angel*."

When the irrational dispenses with comedy as this is generally understood, directly attacking intelligence, the temptation is strong to see in its use some symbolic intent the reasoning mind can assimilate and digest comfortably. However, the intention from which *El Angel exterminador* derived was to impede digestion, not assist it. In giving rein to an impulse to explain every aspect of Buñuel's film by reasonable standards, one only distorts it. It is far better to heed the curious warning issued at the very beginning of the movie.

The scene of the arrival of dinner guests at the expensive home of a wealthy host is repeated twice, treating the audience to the spectacle of supposedly normal people behaving apparently abnormally, yet without giving any sign of noticing what they are doing. Out of consideration for the public, the manager of a Parisian movie house showing *El Angel exterminador* asked for some kind of introductory statement. Buñuel supplied the following: "If the film you are going to see seems to you enigmatic or incongruous, life is that way also. It is as repetitive as life, and similarly subject to many interpretations. The author declares he has not wished to play upon symbols, at least consciously. Perhaps the best explanation of *El Angel exterminador* is that, reasonably, it does not have one."

With *El Angel exterminador* Buñuel openly brings surrealism in its most aggressive form into the commercial cinema, doing so by a process of cinematic creativity very close indeed to the one he utilized at the beginning of his career. As he himself stresses, he seeks no conscious symbolism in *El Angel exterminador*. This being the case, many of the views advanced about the film may be discounted; Philippe Durand's explanation for the presence of a bear in the movie, for instance,[17] or Michel Estève's.[18] Commentators like these two appear unmindful that a bear appears to audiences as a heavily-built, thick-furred plantigrade quadruped; because that is just what it is. Buñuel would be the first to agree the unaccountable presence of such an animal, wandering through the house in his film, could have some obscure significance. But this is a long way from confessing he means it to suggest something for which he, as the movie's director, can be held accountable. Is it not enough that a bear, an exotic menacing creature of the genus *Ursus,* suddenly appears in an elegant residence where it obviously does not belong?

Advancing his estimate of the meaning of the bear, Durand affirms complacently, "I do not believe I am betraying Buñuel's thought." He does betray something, though: his assumption that the image of the bear is to be considered one step in an argument Buñuel has in mind to place before us. Durand's interpretation is of dubious value because it rests upon the belief that systematic explanation of the images in Buñuel's movie, considered in sequence, will uncover some thread of thought which the director supposedly requires us all to take up like Theseus in the Labyrinth. Exactly the same is true of Maurice de Gandillac's interesting parallel between the movie and certain Biblical details to be found in Exodus and Revelation.[19] While his exegesis is permissible, and obviously takes momentum from the film's title, the important point, surely, is the one he neglects to make: reference to the Bible furnishes only an incomplete explanation for events occurring in *El Angel exterminador.* If Buñuel really wishes to entice us to look to the Scriptures when unraveling his movie, we are confronted, in the end, with a situation to which the Bible cannot supply the key. One can approach *El Angel exterminador* profitably only by bearing in mind Buñuel's firm belief that "ambiguity reigns high and low over all our acts and all our thoughts."

As the guests arrive at a house located on a street called Providence, the servants are mysteriously leaving. Their reasons will remain entirely hidden from us; only their urgency to get away is clear. Retrospectively, though, their conduct leaves us wondering whether they had received some forewarning or enjoyed some inexplicable privileges. Before long, we discover that those remaining in the house are unable to leave the drawing room, let alone escape from the building. Roman Catholics, Freemasons, and even adepts of black magic are all equally powerless to break the spell confining them, against reason, within the four walls of one room. Release from incarceration comes not from faith nor from free-thinking rationalism, but through an apparently nonsensical act of exorcism. One of the prisoners (she is played by Sylvia Pinal) sacrifices her virginity and subsequently (is this her reward?) realizes that re-enactment of the scene during which all were listening to a Paradisi sonata will lift the spell. Liberated at last, all repair to a church to keep their vow to give thanks. There, no sooner has a Te Deum been sung than congregation and clergy alike are immobilized, and seem unable to leave.

Did Providence cause three sheep to wander into the house, to be captured, put to the knife, and eaten by a group of people whom hunger is driving in the direction of cannibalism? Are we to understand here—urged on by Maurice de Gandillac—an illusion to the Paschal lamb? Or a reference to the Christ as Agnus Dei? Then what are we to make of the final scene showing everyone imprisoned in church, while only a flock of sheep are at liberty to wander where they will, as revolution breaks out in the streets?

The collapse of any theories we may have nurtured about the symbolism of sheep in *El Angel exterminador* is representative of what becomes of any impulse to explain Buñuel's film in a reason-able manner. Meanwhile his calm acceptance of the idea that certain things in life resist explanation is brought home to us time and again. In this connection, in fact, the ironical encouragement given us to grasp at illusory explanations is a noteworthy feature of Buñuel's method. The lamb, for instance, is blindfolded before being slaugh-tered to satisfy hunger. To satisfy thirst, a water main is burst, with a gesture reminiscent of Moses smiting the rock in Horeb "that the people may drink" (Exodus 17:6). Yet if we are to identify the lamb with the one slain and eaten at the Passover, or with the Lamb of God, if we equate the discovery of water with divine intervention, then we must admit at the same time that the Old Testament Moses and the New Testament Christ lead their followers away from sal-vation. And who can be sure the exorcism will work twice, or even that it will work at all, in a church? Should symbolism be present, its function is to trap the spectator into conclusions entailing denial of the very interpretive process which has led him to descry sym-bols in *El Angel exterminador*.

The only tangible evidence connecting the circumstances de-taining everyone in church with those which, earlier, held many of them prisoner in the house on Providence Street is blatantly inappli-cable, by sensible standards. A quarantine flag is displayed outside the house, although we know those inside are not separated by mere sickness from the crowd outside the grounds. Who placed the flag there? Is the same person responsible for affixing the same flag to the church door, as soon as everyone is inside? One thing is clear: asso-ciations we usually would make upon catching sight of a quarantine flag are patently inapplicable in the anti-reasonable circumstances Buñuel presents.

El Angel exterminador bears comparison with *Los Olvidados,* at least as the latter was planned. In *Los Olvidados* Buñuel wanted to highlight realistic violence by disturbing use of irrational elements. In *El Angel exterminador,* he tackles things from the opposite end. He uses violence, realistically depicted, to underscore the irrationality of his film, in order to indicate that the irrational is not simply an escape route from reality.

As the characters imprisoned in the house become more and more desperate, they lose the veneer of social grace and revert to instinctive behavior patterns. From now on, everything they do and everything happening to them has the effect of testifying to the power of the mysterious force holding them prisoner. Their instinctive conduct bears witness to the influence of irrational forces. Irrationality is authenticated by realistic technique, as inexplicable confinement gives the director his chance to open a window upon "the prolongation of reality," not upon its distortion. At the same time, realistic horror becomes the precipitate of the irrational, as self-preservation disrupts social relationships, leading to scenes which Buñuel, ever contemptuous of the "visual ornamentation" of neo-realism, observes dispassionately, training upon his characters the eye of an entomologist.

Bemused by all that eludes rational explanation, the reasonable viewer may be forgiven for failing to see *El Angel exterminador* as a funny film. His situation is very similar to that of someone whose faith makes it difficult for him to see anything amusing in what happens to a novice nun in a movie called *Viridiana.* Buñuel willingly runs the risk of being misunderstood by people like these, because the alternative to ambiguity is so abhorrent to him. Instead of expressing himself more directly as he grows older, Buñuel elects to utilize increasingly equivocal methods. To take an example, the device of repetition is used in much more complex fashion throughout *El Angel exterminador* than in *Ensayo de un crimen.* The audience is permitted to anticipate the recurrence of situations casting light both on Archibaldo's predicament and his mental and emotional make-up. In the later film, comic effect derives from the audience's unpreparedness to see guests arriving twice and, at the end, being imprisoned for a second time. And it rests no less upon their ignorance about why things occur more than once.

Presumably impervious to the comic aspect of *El Angel exterminador,* Michel Estève refers to it ponderously as "le huis-clos de la condition humaine," treating it as suggestive of the hell evoked in

Jean-Paul Sartre's play *Huis Clos* (1944). Nothing, though, could be further from the condescending didacticism of Sartre's theatrical text than the mood and tone of Buñuel's movie. Sartre's play illustrates a thesis, never leaving us confused about why its characters are confined to a circular pattern of unproductive immobility. Its author's whole purpose in introducing us to them is to warn against dangers his existentialist philosophy makes him regard with revulsion. This, after all, is the function of Sartre's play, to try an exemplary case *in camera* (the exact meaning of the title, generally rendered as *No Exit*). In contrast, Buñuel has no wish to try a case. All that he shows takes place in open court, on camera. No doubt we are at liberty, if we choose, to extend Estève's conclusions and treat *El Angel exterminador* as an existentialist drama. And we are just as free, if we would rather, to try reconciling our conclusions with Maurice de Gandillac's suspicion that Buñuel was following the Bible, not Sartre, when making his film. But if we do exercise our privilege to understand *El Angel exterminador* in ways such as these, we must not be surprised to hear Buñuel say, as he did to Elena Poniatowska, "It's mystery that interests me. Mystery is the essential element in every work of art. I shall never tire of repeating this."

Joseph, the enigmatic gardener-coachman of Octave Mirbeau's *Le Journal d'une Femme de Chambre* (1900), is the kind of complex fictional character to appeal to Buñuel. The contradictions in his make-up reflect the socio-religious background of the age in which he lives. Devious, elusive, a rabid anti-Semite, he is a brutal figure. Célestine, the chambermaid whose diary we are reading meets him at about the time of the Dreyfus case, upon coming from Paris to a bourgeois home in the provinces. As drawn to her as she is to him, Joseph proposes marriage. He wants Célestine to accompany him to Cherbourg, where he is going to open a café in which she will be the main attraction. In the meantime, he declines to have sexual relations with her, not out of respect for her—she lost her virginity at twelve—but because, being a pious man, he regards premarital sex as sinful. His piety does not deter him, though, from killing ducks by the old Norman method of driving a long pin into their skulls and twisting it slowly. The more they suffer, he explains placidly, the better they taste.

Célestine suspects Joseph of having raped and murdered a little girl, and he is evidently guilty of the crime. Yet when he has purchased his café, he refuses out of respect for the ruling classes to precipitate a quarrel with his employers, even though this would permit him and Célestine to leave without raising suspicions about his part in the theft of the family silverware. But he will put the silver to good use, no doubt, upon getting to Cherbourg. Mirbeau describes him in these terms at the end of the novel: "More violently than ever, he is for the family, for property, for religion, for the navy, for the army, for his country"[20]—for the pillars of society Buñuel abhors.

When we compare the film Le Journal d'une Femme de Chambre [The Diary of a Chambermaid (1964)] with the novel, it seems reasonable enough that Buñuel should disregard the discursive chapters recalling Célestine's experiences in other houses where she has worked, and concentrate upon the relationship between her and Joseph. But before long we discover that he alters the plot materially, having the chambermaid marry a retired army officer, her employers' hated neighbor, while Joseph replaces her with a blonde, as siren in Cherbourg. The final scene shows Joseph approvingly watching a crowd of political demonstrators surge by his establishment, shouting the name of the man who, as Paris prefect of police at a time subsequent to the action of this movie, closed the Studio 28 theatre for showing a movie called L'Age d'Or: "Vive Chiappe! Vive Chiappe!"

These strictly narrative changes are not the only modifications for which Buñuel is responsible. If we examine the character of Mirbeau's Célestine, we find her to be little better than Joseph. In fact, the sexual attraction she feels toward him is based for the most part on excitement at the thought that he may be a rapist and a murderer. She marries him firmly convinced of his guilt and prepared, she confesses in the last sentence of her diary, to do anything he asks, however criminal. Célestine's literary ancestry may be traced, obviously, through the naturalist novel in France after 1850. She reminds us of the heroine of the Goncourts' 1864 novel Germinie Lacerteux, hopelessly enslaved to an all-devouring infatuation for a man who is nothing but an insensitive monster. Buñuel's Célestine is a more complex individual. She possesses a sense of irony and even a sense of humor, both displayed in a scene with the head of the household which, by the way, has no counterpart in Mirbeau's main theme. The old man is a fetishist who requires her when in his presence to wear samples from his impressive collection of button boots. As she complies, her expression of amused incredulity earns her a certain amount of sympathy. So does her attitude toward Joseph. She is interested in him only out of desire to prove him guilty of his crime against little Claire. Hence her approach is unemotional. It highlights the vulgar cynicism of a man who seeks a wife so he can exploit her to his material advantage. And it sets off the psychological quirk of a prospective pander rendered impotent by religious beliefs, symbolized—like Viridiana, Joseph has his fetish objects—in the crucifix and other signs of faith visible in his room.

Turning to the background against which the main action of the film is placed, we have the impression at first that Buñuel's movie is faithful to the mood of Mirbeau's narrative. Sex is ever-present. In the old man it takes the form of deviation. In his daughter, who runs the house, it occasions revulsion: she complains to her priest of her husband's burdensome demands, demands she is evidently unwilling or unable to meet. As for her husband—played by Michel Piccoli, who was Father Lizardi in *La Mort en ce Jardin*—he is so desperate that he is not averse to spending a few minutes with a drab servant girl, whom he pushes roughly into one of the outhouses on the estate. When Célestine gives herself to Captain Mauger, she does so for practical reasons, so as to climb the social ladder. Even her willingness to go to bed with Joseph is a form of prostitution, since her motive is to uncover the truth about the crime against Claire.

Buñuel is not simply following Mirbeau's lead, however. He is faithful to the code which has always been his. His film condemns those who deny love (the wife), those in whom it takes aberrant forms (her father), those who equate it with the exercise of feudal rights (her husband). It condemns also those who debase love for commercial gain (Joseph), or for social advancement (Célestine). Thus no adult in *Le Journal d'une Femme de Chambre* enjoys Buñuel's unequivocal approbation. The director reserves tenderness and affection for Joseph's victim, expressing these with a reticence typical of his treatment of children. He seems inclined to believe the child is especially close to the mysteries of life and death, to hidden horror and menace. His *Los Olvidados* shows a pretty little girl perched on the knees of the repulsive blind beggar, who palpates her thighs. When the bus cannot be shifted from the river mud, in *Subida al cielo*, another little girl manages to charm a team of oxen into pulling it to dry ground. Archibaldo de la Cruz discovers the magic powers of his music box while still a boy. Ewie, *The Young One*, is only fourteen years old. Ramona's daughter Rita is witness to Don Jaime's abortive attempt upon Viridiana's virtue. Subsequently, she reports seeing "the big black bull coming in through the ceiling."

In Mirbeau's novel Célestine is not acquainted with Claire. She merely hears of the child's fate from one of her friends. By the time the matter is mentioned in her narrative, we have read half her diary. In Buñuel's film, Claire is introduced early enough for Célestine to become fond of her and to be stimulated to horror, not perverse fascination, by what happens to her. But the physical presence of an eleven-year-old girl does much more than help explain the chambermaid's motivation in seeking to bring Joseph to justice. *Le Journal d'une Femme de Chambre* shows Claire going off into the forest like Little Red Riding Hood. When next we see her, snails from the jar she carried are crawling over her blood-streaked thighs, as she lies dead in the underbrush. The origins of this image are speculative.[21] But the impression it creates is striking. As for its interpretation, this is of considerable relevance to our understanding of the movie and of its differences from the novel that inspired it.

Frédéric Grange affirms apropos of *Le Journal d'une Femme de Chambre*, "Buñuel has often denied his surrealist origins but never as in this film."[22] Crediting Buñuel with an instinct for self-criticism supposedly manifesting itself for the first time late in life, Grange apparently finds it expressed through the selection of "the most weak and degenerate character" in *The Diary of a Chambermaid* as "the champion of mad love and desire." This character goes unnamed in Grange's text. However, whether we are to understand a reference to M. Monteil, to his father-in-law, or to his servant Joseph, the conclusion Grange advances appears of dubious value. It betrays voluntary blindness, in defense of an unfounded thesis, or naïveté about Buñuel's way of communicating with his audience.

Why should a film director not imply positive answers by way of negative statements? Whichever of the characters we select for examination in Buñuel's *Le Journal d'une Femme de Chambre*, we find his conduct, or hers (we can choose Célestine, if we wish), reflects in no way at all the concept of life which Buñuel joins the surrealists in defending. Passion impels the lovers of *L'Age d'Or* to scandalous behavior. In *Los Olvidados*, it causes Pedro's mother to flout conventional standards when she accepts his friend Jaibo as her lover. Passion turns a son against his father, in *El Bruto*. In *Cumbres Borrascosas* it drives Buñuel's Heathcliff to violate his Cathy's tomb. In each case, then, passion—the expression of mad love—betokens rebellion against one form of restraint or another, affirming liberty in the face of conformity. Passion of this sort is absent from Buñuel's *Le Journal d'une Femme de Chambre*, because each character in whom the sexual drive is strong seeks purely selfish ends. Indeed, Célestine's case is such a striking one because hers is simulated sexual attraction, first to Joseph and then to the man she agrees to marry. Sex indulged selfishly is shown to be unproductive of viable results. Instead of challenging social usages and moral conventions, it simply confirms the status quo: Joseph escapes the punishment he deserves, while Célestine acknowledges the existence of a social hierarchy she does not question, when she takes steps to ensure herself a more advantageous place in it.

As unaffected by contact with the adults among whom she lives as the little girl in the elegant brothel of *Belle de Jour,* Claire is the only person who does not merit punishment, for one reason or another. Buñuel makes her the victim of sex, punishing her unjustly. In the same way, in *L'Age d'Or,* he immolated a thirteen-year-old girl to another form of sexual abnormality. In both cases, innocence causes the victim to be singled out in a situation where survival of the fittest means survival of the guilty.

It is here that Buñuel departs most radically from his source material. After suggesting that most of us can find extenuating circumstances when rape is discussed, Mirbeau's Célestine remarks casually, "for rape is still love" (p. 144). Buñuel's code precludes such indulgence. His ideal of love cannot admit the crude identification of love with blind sex so easily. In an interview published in *Les Lettres françaises* on May 12, 1960, he said, "Look (in *The Young One*), Miller, a naturally brutal character, shows a certain imagination in love: while he could have taken Ewie by force, he acts almost 'against his nature': he is tender, he gives her presents, he falls in love." The gamekeeper Miller, in *The Young One,* follows the same calling as Joseph, in Buñuel's *Le Journal d'une Femme de Chambre.* Hence the contrast between them can hardly be accidental. Rejecting the callous acceptance reflected in what Mirbeau's Célestine says, Buñuel rejects with it the permissiveness of the hypocritical society where she lives. So criminal assault, in revolting circumstances leading to murder, is the most sensational form of debasement to which he shows love subjected in *Le Journal d'une Femme de Chambre.* In the process, the meaning of Mirbeau's novel (its dedicatory letter to Jules Huret speaks of "the sadness and comedy of being a man") is replaced by a meaning of Buñuel's own. Instead of "slipping in between two images," this time Buñuel introduces a capital image to communicate a *vision* expressing a code surrealism has helped develop and keep alive in him. It is unfortunate, of course, that in some parts of the world the image of a dead raped child with snails exploring her thighs has been considered so shocking as to call for excision. Long before making *Le Journal d'une Femme de Chambre,* Buñuel learned the censor is not capable of either understanding his moral values or dealing with them.

Buñuel's next movie was a forty-two minute short subject that earned him a Special Jury Prize at the Venice Film Festival. Called

Simón del desierto [*Simon of the Desert* (1965)], it makes its audiences witness the temptations undergone by the fifth-century anchorite Simeon Stylites. In one scene, the devil appears in the guise of a shepherd with a lamb on his shoulder. The saint takes him for Jesus. In another scene, he interrupts the anchorite's prayers by appearing in the form of a young woman dressed as a turn-of-the-century schoolgirl, "to give himself a more intense sexual attraction" when teasing Simón. To anyone inclined to accuse him of being inconsistent in using a child as a temptress here, after depicting little Claire as the incarnation of innocence, Buñuel would reply no doubt that it pleases him to have a viewer of his movies feel disconcerted by apparent contradictions. As he assured Yvonne Baby, in 1961, "I try so far as possible to avoid my own commonplaces."

The shot of the schoolgirl riding away naked on a big white pig is entirely in keeping with the atmosphere of *Simón del desierto,* where sexual attraction is closely related to the theme of temptation. During a conversation with Manuel Michel reproduced in *Les Lettres françaises* in 1960 Buñuel remarked, "Nowadays everyone wants to lure the audience with scenes of nudity, with sensuality. The bourgeois public which flocks to the movies craves for them in the measure that it condemned them twenty or thirty years ago. They are very easy to do and in the measure that they correspond to the general spirit, providing them signifies bending to general conformism." These words indicate well enough how pointless it would be to look for evidence of conformity to fashion in the work of Buñuel. It would be a grave mistake indeed to see the film that followed *Simón del desierto* as Buñuel's contribution to commercialized film eroticism.

His 1966 movie, *Belle de Jour,* deals with a well-to-do young woman who takes up employment under a high-class procuress, for whom she works under a nickname suggested by the fact that she is available only in the daytime. Although this film brings together a number of actors Buñuel has used before (Michel Piccoli as Husson, Francisco Rabal as Hippolyte, and Georges Marchal, who was in *Cela s'appelle l'Aurore* and *La Mort en ce Jardin),* the leading roles go to three performers with whom Buñuel has not worked previously. Catherine Deneuve plays Séverine, Jean Sorel her husband (Pierre), and Pierre Clementi her gangster lover (Marcel). Séverine's relationship with the former, marred by frigidity, and her relations with the latter, to whom she seems able to respond without reserve, create a situation resolved by a highly melodramatic dénouement. Bursting into his mistress' house, Marcel shoots Pierre, and then is himself shot down by police in the street. Developing a plot that is anything but subtle, the director allows himself a private joke of the kind he likes: the theft demonstrating Marcel's professional skill takes place in the office building of the producers of *Belle de Jour,* on the Champs-Élysées. Touches of this nature remind us pointedly that, with Buñuel, the storyline is far from being the major preoccupation when a subject is selected for cinematographic treatment.

In none of his commercial ventures prior to *Belle de Jour* did Buñuel seek to raise questions in the minds of those seeing his film about the viability of the melodramatic framework in which it was cast. He always left his audience free to be more or less attentive—according to their inclination—to the narrative, developed in some cases with more concern to convince than in others. As he explained to Georges Sadoul for *Les Lettres françaises,* in 1961:

> The world being what it is where we live, I do not make my films for the "public", I mean the public in quotation marks. If this "public" is conventional, traditional, perverted, this is not its fault, but society's. And it is very difficult, very rare, to be able to make a film that pleases at the same time the "public" (in quotation marks) and friends, people whose opinion matters to you.

The element of melodrama is more pronounced in Buñuel's early commercial movies than later. As his reputation with the critics and his knack of earning festival awards was reflected in increased box-office appeal, earning him greater independence, his films used less melodramatic features. But this fact does not detract from the significance of the step he takes in *Belle de Jour.* Here for the first time Buñuel openly turns against the convention used so often to mask his originality as a film-maker: he explodes its conventionality. The end of *Belle de Jour* has Pierre, crippled by Marcel's bullet, paralyzed in a wheel chair, the object of Séverine's solicitude. The enigmatic friend, Husson, persuades the young woman that Pierre should be informed of the circumstances under which she made Marcel's acquaintance at Madame Anaïs' establishment, where we have seen her report for work beautifully dressed in clothes designed for the movie by one of the leading couturiers in Paris. Husson takes it upon himself to enlighten the husband before leaving. Now Séverine goes in to Pierre, who appears to die, presumably because Husson's news is more lethal than Marcel's revolver shot. Then, miraculously, he rises from his chair, not only healed but apparently with his devotion to his wife undiminished.

Anyone who has managed to disregard certain disconcerting features of *Belle de Jour* because he is confident the plot will explain them away in the end, is going to be disappointed. More than this, he is bound to find his trust in the plot as the film's *justification* undermined by its ironical dénouement. In *Belle de Jour* things do not "come out right in the end"; they do not come out at all.

As we ask what Buñuel wishes us to make of *Belle de Jour*, an apparently minor detail takes on unexpected significance. It has to do with an Asiatic client who comes to the brothel during Belle de Jour's working hours, carrying a little wooden box which emits an unidentifiable buzzing sound, like that of an insect, when the lid is raised. Ever since the beginning of his commercial career Buñuel has used fetish objects in his films. They lend themselves without difficulty to interpretation. In fact, interpretation of them is a necessary step to comprehending the outlook and behavior of those to whom they belong. In *Belle de Jour*, however, we never see the Asiatic's fetish. We observe that, whatever it is, it horrifies every one of the girls employed by Madame Anaïs with the exception of Belle de Jour, who agrees to accommodate the smiling courteous client. But we are denied the chance to watch what goes on between them, even though the brothel provides an extra service in the form of peepholes through which voyeurs can witness activities taking place behind closed doors. The incident involving a fetish box which leaves Belle de Jour wrapped in thought and little else, after the departure of her client, is significant for what it conceals, rather than reveals. It is representative of the whole film, leaving us free to choose between possible interpretations of what we have seen and not been permitted to see.

In *Belle de Jour* every care is taken to blur the distinction between Séverine's fantasies and things the audience may reasonably believe actually happen to her. From the opening shot, the movie epitomizes confusion in this regard. Séverine is seen driving away from a large country house, her husband beside her in an open carriage. In a forest clearing she is dragged from her seat, tied and gagged, her back ritualistically bared. Then she is beaten with a whip before one of the coachmen rapes her, upon her husband's orders. Not until the scene is over do we feel entitled to interpret this occurrence as a sexual daydream. Subsequently, incidents which strike us as of the same nature are accompanied by the sound of bells like those attached to the harness of the horses drawing the carriage in the first sequence. Thus it is a simple matter for audiences to identify and draw inferences from the auditory clue provided on these occasions. Not all viewers will be so prompt, though, in noticing something else. In retrospect, the calm expression on Séverine's face while she is being flogged appears to signify she is only imagining being mistreated. And yet she wears a very similar expression after the departure of the Asiatic whose mysterious needs she has just satisfied in Anaïs' apartment. This similarity becomes significant when we consider Séverine's experience in the forest side by side with her encounter with the Asiatic client.

Once it is over, we readily assign the scene in the forest to the realm of fantasy. Then we congratulate ourselves on identifying a clue supplied by the director, when certain other scenes are ushered in by the sound of harness bells. Hence we feel entitled to take these for fantasy also. As for events occurring in the brothel, we are persuaded to lend these credence as actual experience because, back home after her first visit, Séverine is seen burning underwear selected in advance for her initial experience in vice. Revulsion appears retrospectively to authenticate the sequence during which Séverine met her first client as Belle de Jour. Consequently, it seems to suggest that everything occurring in Anaïs' apartment really does take place. But if this is true, why do we see the same look on Séverine's face when she is in the hands of her imaginary coachman and when she has just spent some time with her flesh-and-blood Asiatic? Such a question might appear hardly worth asking, if the apparently small detail under discussion were the only sign in *Belle de Jour* of the director's desire to establish a parallel between what we are sure is pure fantasy and what we are willing to accept as real experience. This is not an isolated incidental detail, however. One whole scene in particular adds its testimony to Buñuel's aversion for separating dream and reality. It concerns Séverine's encounter with Georges Marchal, playing an aristocrat.

They meet at a fashionable Parisian café, where Séverine lets herself be picked up with singular promptitude. One is tempted to suspect Anaïs has arranged an assignation and to conclude, therefore, that Belle de Jour's meeting with an aristocratic client is taking place in the world of reality. However we are not permitted for long to draw a clear line between the real and the imagined. If Belle de Jour is really meeting a client found for her by Anaïs, why do we see during this sequence the carriage we assumed existed only in Séverine's daydream? If, on the other hand, we are now to revise our opinion and believe the carriage really exists, then why do we hear harness bells, and see the vehicle pass in the street below Séverine's window, during the final scene of the film which common sense advises us to treat as pure fantasy?

Belle de Jour's client likes to lie in a coffin with a young woman crouching close by. Unequivocal evidence provided during Séverine's visit to his home reveal the principal motif during this sequence as masturbation. There seems some justification, therefore, for considering the whole of *Belle de Jour* as a fantasy, some kind of fairytale the heroine is telling herself. Viewing Buñuel's version of Kessel's novel in this light, we need not trouble ourselves overmuch, when we come across details in the movie that strike us as difficult to explain rationally, or hard to countenance on the plane of psychological motivation.

Moreover the subtleties of the process contaminating reality by surreality elude us so long as we are reluctant to see *Belle de Jour* as illustrative of the surrealist thesis that dream and reality are communicating vessels. This film exemplifies the conviction that reality and surreality are not at odds, but bound up with one another in human consciousness. Everything in *Belle de Jour* centers on the consciousness of Séverine/Belle de Jour, whose conduct proves her unwillingness—inability, perhaps—to keep apart the dream where her sexual fantasies are acted out and the world where she lives in frustration at her husband's side. Whether we are watching something true or false is far less significant, under these conditions, than whether it seems real or unreal to the heroine. It matters less whether Séverine does work for Anaïs and meets Marcel, or simply imagines doing so, than whether she desires the kind of experience prostitution can offer. The scale of values is imposed less by the reality or imaginary nature of events than by the intensity of experience, drawn either from the outside world or from within.

Buñuel's success in presenting Séverine's experience confirms that mystery continues to be, for him, "the essential element in every work of art." His success grows out of a remarkable capacity for bringing to light the surrealist virtualities of human existence. Michel Piccoli, who has had occasion to observe him at work more than once, has commented, "He is a film-maker who does not belong in his world because he has never been able to understand the constraints of the commercial cinema. Or else he pretends not to know them."[23] This characteristic makes Buñuel fascinating to a professional film actor like Piccoli. It makes him no less fascinating to all surrealists.

Conclusion

When Marguerite Bonnet advanced the confident conclusion that the whole history of surrealism's relations with the cinema is "in reality, that of a great hope betrayed,"[1] she oversimplified matters. She presented the history of surrealism's relationship with the movies in an unduly pessimistic light. More than this, she diverted attention from important features of the relationship which help sharpen our understanding of surrealism, its demands, and consequences.

It is a fact that regret marks Breton's review of the surrealists' involvement with films, in his article "Comme dans un Bois." And it is no less true that Péret also has hinted at real disappointment, in a statement from which the opening sentences run, "Never has any means of expression registered so much hope as the cinema. Through it not only is everything possible, but the marvelous itself is brought close to hand. And yet never has such a great disproportion been observed between immense possibilities and derisory results."[2] For all that, like Breton's, Péret's dissatisfaction at seeing the cinema generally fall short of giving surrealists all they have expected of it, points to a number of factors Mlle Bonnet would have been well advised to take into account. These factors reveal where Péret sensed the disproportion he mentions, showing why he and Breton were equally aware of it.

From the beginning, the surrealists' conception of the film was idealized in at least two ways, each with significant consequences for the history which Mlle Bonnet discusses summarily. For a start, it tended to underestimate how much the majority of film directors respect the visible world about us. As a result, most surrealists have been unduly optimistic about commercial moviemakers' willingness to take such liberties with everyday reality that they find themselves unwittingly collaborating in the surrealist

175

revolt. Then, too, advocates of surrealist principles have been generally inclined to grant the technical conditions of film-making less than full measure, when estimating the cinema's capacity to meet their requirements. For the first of these reasons surrealists were destined from the beginning to be dissatisfied more often than pleased with movies sponsored under commercial or vanguard aegis. For the second reason they have persisted in believing in films, long after the weight of discouraging evidence might well have undermined their idealism, leaving them convinced it lacks firm foundation. In spite of everything, surrealists look upon the film as potentially one of the most efficacious means available for communicating feelings, attitudes, and ideas that meet with their approval.

When they come to make films of their own, ingrained mistrust for aesthetic pretension and contempt for the reality principle, in the cinema just as much as elsewhere, engenders in surrealists indifference to many of the technical demands respected during cinematographic production by directors who treat these as fundamental to their art. When a surrealist shoots a movie, his dearest hope is to provide a succession of cinematic images, free from dependence on theatrical plot, stimulating the imagination to explore in directions that surrealism teaches him to regard as promising. As a movie-goer, he is particularly attentive when he can detect cracks in the apparently solid face of the real. As a film-maker, he takes special pleasure in making his audience aware that such cracks exist and are not to be ignored.

If its validity for surrealism is to be above suspicion, the film must never be considered an end in itself, any more than surrealist painting is. It should always remain a means, a pathway to attaining goals that will take their value entirely from surrealist theory. Only under these conditions, surrealists are persuaded, can watching movies become an act proving conclusively that the surrealist viewpoint bears witness to a state of mind capable of rendering reality submissive to needs imposed by the imagination, to the detriment of reason. So long as the surrealist testimony of films can find a sympathetic and perceptive audience, the cinema will hold a particular and vital attraction for surrealists, a recurrent fascination which no momentary disappointments will be able to eradicate.

Notes

Unless otherwise indicated, the place of publication for all books in French is Paris.

Introduction

1. See the article "Comme dans un Bois" (1951) in Breton's *La Clé des Champs* (1953), pp. 241–246.
2. Ibid.
3. *Le Surréalisme au Cinéma* (1953), édition mise à jour (1963), p. 83. All references are to the 1963 edition.
4. *En Marge du Cinéma français* (1954), p. 115. An English version of Brunius' essay appeared under the title "Experimental Film in France" in Roger Manvell ed., *Experimental Film* (London, 1949). In translation, Brunius' text was prudently toned down, its violence reduced. Quotations given here are all taken from the French version.
5. Herbert Read was unsuccessful in his attempt to launch the word 'superrealism' as a translation for *surréalisme*. See "Realism and Superrealism" and "A Further Note on Superrealism" in his *A Coat of Many Colours* (London, 1945).
6. *Manifestes du Surréalisme* (Jean-Jacques Pauvert, n. d. [1962]), p. 28. All references to Breton's manifestoes are to this edition.
7. In this connection see J. H. Matthews, "Du Cinéma comme Langage surréaliste," *Études cinématographiques,* N° 38–39, 'Surréalisme et Cinéma,' 1, 1ᵉʳ trimestre, 1965 (hereinafter called *É. C.* 1), 65–74.
8. Breton's use of the adjective "new" does not take on its full significance unless it is related to the surrealists' admiration for Guillaume Apollinaire as promoter of a "new spirit" in poetry. Cf. Apollinaire's article "L'Esprit nouveau et les Poètes," *Mercure de France,* 130 (1918), 385–396. For the influence of Apollinaire's concept of the *nouveau* on surrealism, see the chapter on Philippe

Soupault in J. H. Matthews, *Surrealist Poetry in France* (Syracuse, N. Y. 1969), pp. 17–30.

9. "Signe ascendant" (1947) in his *La Clé des Champs*, p. 112.

10. Cf. J. H. Matthews, "Intelligence in the Service of Surrealism: Breton's *Anthologie de l'Humour noir*," *Books Abroad*, 41 (1967), 267–273, and "Paul Nougé: Intellect, Subversion, and Poetic Language," *Symposium*, 24, 4 (Winter 1970), 365–379.

11. *É. C.* 1, p. 29.

Surrealism and the Commercial Cinema

1. After serialization from 1925 onward in the Paris surrealist magazine *La Révolution surréaliste*, Breton's articles on surrealism and painting were collected in book form under the title *Le Surréalisme et la Peinture*, first published in 1928.

2. "Souvenirs d'un Témoin," *É. C.* 1, p. 13.

3. *Les Champs magnétiques* (1967 reprint), p. 15.

4. "Cinéma frénetique et Cinéma académique," *Le Soir*, March 5, 1927.

5. "L'Aube du Surréalisme et le Cinéma: Attente et Rencontres," *É. C.* 1, p. 90.

6. *Amour-Érotisme et Cinéma* (1957), édition mise à jour (1966), p. 17. All references are to the 1966 edition.

7. *Curiosités esthétiques* (Lausanne, 1956), p. 328.

8. "Painting is a Wager" (reprinted from *Cahiers du Sud*), *Horizon*, 7 (1943), p. 178.

9. "King Kong," *Minotaure*, Nº 3 (1934), p. 5.

10. Carlos Clarens, *Horror Movies: An Illustrated Survey* (London, 1968), p. 117. The London edition is a retitled, revised, and enlarged version of Clarens' *An Illustrated History of the Horror Film* (New York, 1967).

Terror

11. "La Pensée et Une et indivisible," *VVV*, Nº 4 (February 1944), p. 10.

12. For the surrealist conception of black humor see Breton's *Anthologie de l'Humour noir*. The most accessible edition is the last, published by Jean-Jacques Pauvert in 1966. It contains, incidentally, a passage from Sade's *Juliette* illustrating the relationship between black humor and the horrible.

13. In *Positif*, No. 53 (June 1963), p. 88. The editorial board of the magazine *Positif* includes, besides Ado Kyrou, the surrealists Robert Benayoun and Raymond Borde.

14. The significance which surrealists attach to this sign of social non-conformity is not difficult to estimate when we recall that, after celebrating during the eighth international surrealist exhibition (Paris, 1959–1960) the "Execution du Testament du Marquis de Sade" (see J. H. Matthews, 'The Right Person for Surrealism,"

Yale French Studies, 35 ['Sade'], 1965, 89–95), Jean Benoit prepared for the eleventh exhibition (Paris 1965) a costume dedicated to France's most famous necrophile, Sergeant Bertrand. A color photograph of Benoit's *Le Nécrophile* appears in the catalogue, *Écart absolu,* of the exhibition held at the L'Œil Gallery.

15. "Cinéma frénétique et Cinéma académique," *Le Soir,* March 5, 1927. The dominant image of this key passage—Perceval's search for the Grail—is one that fascinates surrealists, who frequently use it in reference to their own search for the marvelous (see J. H. Matthews, "Julien Gracq and the Theme of the Grail in Surrealism," *The Romanic Review,* 58 [1967], 95–108). At the end of the passage, Denos cites the title under which Paul Leni's *Das Wachsenfiguren Kabinett* [*Waxworks* (1924)] was released in France.

16. *The Exploits of Elaine* serial was known in France—presumably out of deference to Eugène Sue—as *Les Mystères de New York.* Louis Gasnier's serial was particularly exciting to the early surrealists. Later, Kyrou was to prefer *The Perils of Pauline.* Desnos and Breton, however, were never to forget the impression made on them by the Elaine series. *Fantômas,* meanwhile, haunts Desnos' prose narrative *La Liberté ou l'Amour!* (1927). As for Musidora, her presence in Feuillade's *Les Vampires* serial was a perpetual source of pleasure to the future surrealists. See Michel Sanouillet, *Dada à Paris* (1965), p. 72. See also the play *Le Trésor des Jésuites* published by Breton and Aragon in 'Le Surréalisme en 1929,' a special surrealist issue of the Belgian magazine *Variétés,* 1929, pp. 47–61.

17. Cited in Brunius, p. 82. *Caligari* was written by Hans Janowitz and Carl Mayer who objected, to no avail, when the film's director framed their script between a prologue and an epilogue representing the story as being told by a madman. Details are to be found in Clarens, pp. 28–31, where the script is summarized.

Comedy

18. For further details see J. H. Matthews, *An Introduction to Surrealism* (University Park, Pa., 1965), pp. 110–116.

19. Jindrich Heisler, rather than Max Ernst, is cited here as a significant practitioner of surrealist collage technique, since Heisler's use of contemporary photographs—in contrast with Ernst's liking for material drawn from old magazines, textbooks, etc.,—relates the effects more closely to the modern cinema. *Rrose Sélavy* is a series of 150 poetic statements, all created by granting sound associations precedence over sense associations (see Matthews, *Surrealist Poetry in France,* pp. 56–57).

20. Bearing in mind Breton's plea in the *Manifeste du Surréalisme* for "des contes encore presque bleus," one might call this sequence, out of respect for Émile Zola, a "Nouveau Conte à Nichon."

21. Charlie yields to the compulsion which decent gallery-goers must resist before the nipple-like press-button protruding from Ernst's painting *Deux Enfants sont menacés par un Rossignol* [*Two Children Are Threatened by a Nightingale* (1924)].

22. A defective translation of this text by Mary Caroline Richards, who appears to have a doubtful command of French verb usage, is to be found in Antonin Artaud, *The Theater and Its Double* (New York, 1958), pp. 142–144.

23. *Le Dessin animé après Walt Disney* (1961), p. 38. Benayoun's comment on the place of humor in cartoon films makes further discussion of that mode of filmed comedy superfluous. One might add, however, that Breton had the highest regard for Harold Muller's animated movie *It's a Bird* (1937).

24. *Le Surréalisme au Cinéma*, p. 27.

Love

25. *Amour-Érotisme et Cinéma*, p. 230.

26. *Nadja* (1928), revised edition (1963), pp. 33–34.

27. *Entretiens* (1952), p. 110.

28. *Le Surréalisme au Cinéma*, p. 131.

29. See *Médium: Informations surréalistes*, May 1953. Out of respect for the autonomy of the cinema, Breton was opposed to the cinematographic adaptation of literary works. However, like Artaud, he was fascinated by "Le Rideau cramoisi" in Barbey's collection of stories *Les Diaboliques* (1874). In *Le Surréalisme au Cinéma* (p. 191), Kyrou attributes the failure of Breton's project to adapt the same Barbey text to fear on his producer's part. Breton's reservations about Astruc's version of the same tale suggest that his producer might well have had grounds for concern.

30. Benayoun has written an *Érotique du Surréalisme* for J. M. Lo Duca's series "Bibliothèque Internationale d'Érotologie" (1965). A remarkable volume, Benayoun's is nevertheless incomplete. See the review by J. H. Matthews, *Books Abroad*, Winter 1965.

31. Cf. Desnos' article "L'Érotisme," *Paris-Journal*, April 20, 1923: "It is in this cinematographic eroticism that we should seek, today, consolation for all that can be disappointing in the factitious life of most people."

32. Clarens, p. 120, remarks, "The makers of *King Kong* went so far they carried the Beauty-and-the-Beast premise to absurdity—the acute disparity of size between Ann and Kong puts any erotic rapport completely out of the question." It would appear that Clarens understands erotic rapport to mean sexual intercourse.

33. *Le Surréalisme au Cinéma*, p. 85.

34. *Amour-Érotisme et Cinéma*, p. 45.

35. *L'Amour fou* (1937), p. 113.

36. *Le Surréalisme au Cinéma*, p. 177.

37. *Amour-Érotisme et Cinéma*, p. 117.

38. *Études cinématographiques*, N° 40–42, 'Surréalisme et Cinéma,' 2, 2ᵉ trimestre, 1965, p. 168.
39. Gherasim Luca, Gellu Naum, Virgil Teodoresco, Trost, *Éloge de "Malombra"* (Bucharest, 1947).
40. Soupault's review appeared in *Littérature*, N° 6, August 1919. See *É. C.* 1, pp. 85–86.
41. See Matthews, *An Introduction to Surrealism*, pp. 129–132.

Surrealist Film Scripts

1. Letter dated November 14, 1918. See *Lettres de Guerre de Jacques Vaché* (n. d. [1949]). Although he did not live long enough to participate in the surrealist venture (and quite possibly would have valued his independence too much, if given the opportunity to do so), Vaché exerted a capital influence over Breton. In view of Desnos' reference to the cinema as a perfect opium and of Breton's Sunday outings in Vaché's company, it is relevant to note that Vaché committed suicide in 1919, by taking an overdose of opium.
2. *É. C.* 1, p. 30.
3. Cited in Michel Décaudin, "Les Poètes découvrent le Cinéma," *É. C.* 1, pp. 79–80.
4. On *La Liberté ou l'Amour!* see J. H. Matthews, *Surrealism and the Novel* (Ann Arbor, 1966), pp. 59–73.
5. Cf. J. H. Matthews, "Mechanics of the Marvellous: The Short Stories of Benjamin Péret," *L'Esprit créateur*, 6 (1966), 23–30.
6. Desnos' title defies translation. It derives from the phrase "chercher midi à quatorze heures" (literally: 'to look for midday at two in the afternoon') which means looking for difficulties where there are none, or missing the obvious. Desnos substitutes 'midnight' for 'midday.' "Minuit à quatorze heures" appeared in the twelfth number of *Les Cahiers du Mois* in 1925.
7. "La Femme 100 Têtes," *Documents*, N° 4, 1930.
8. "Réponse à une Enquête," in his *Œuvres complètes*, Vol. III (1961), p. 74.
9. "La Vieillesse précoce du Cinéma," *Les Cahiers jaunes*, N° 4, 1933.
10. "Sorcellerie et Cinéma" (undated). Published in part in the catalogue of the *Festival du Film maudit* in 1949, it is given in full in *Œuvres complètes*, III (see p. 81).
11. "Le Cinéma et l'Abstraction," *Le Monde illustré*, N° 3645, October 1927.
12. Ibid.
13. "Distinction entre Avant-Garde de Fond et de Forme," in *Œuvres complètes*, III, p. 84.
14. Cited in Kyrou, *Le Surréalisme au Cinéma*, p. 189.
15. "Project de Constitution d'une Firme destinée à produire des Films de court métrage, d'un Amortissement rapide et sûr," in *Œuvres complètes*, III, p. 90.

16. Feuillade's serial captured Desnos' imagination (see *Paris-Journal*, April 6, 1923; *Journal littéraire*, November 15, 1924; *Journal littéraire*, May 2, 1925; and especially *Le Soir*, February 26, 1927). It was adapted from the writings of Souvestre and Allais, which also inspired Ernst Moerman's *Mr Fantômas*, made in Belgium in 1937. Moerman's film displays distinctly surrealist characteristics. Its actors were permitted no virtuosity in their performances, so as not to prejudice the movie's oneiric atmosphere. Technical sophistication was banned throughout the shooting of this silent feature, made outdoors, on a severely limited budget.

17. *Monsieur Phot (seen through a Stereoscope): Scenario for a Film*, Flushing, N. Y., 1933.

18. *Une Étude sur Raymond Roussel* (1953); *Le Mécanicien et autres Contes* (prefaced by a text of Breton's, dated August 1949) (1953).

19. In *Le Surréalisme au Cinéma*, Kyrou praises "Fidélité" as "the perfect example of the surrealist scenario, owing nothing to what has been done up to the present" (p. 193). His view of Ferry's as "the best cinematographic text I know" led Kyrou to select it to be the second volume (1953) in the collection "Ombres blanches" he edited for publication under the imprint Arcanes.

20. *Trois Scénarii*, Brussels, 1928.

21. *É. C.* 1, p. 47.

22. Benayoun's volume of one-act plays *La Science met bas* (1959) does not fall into this category. Some of these plays have been successfully produced in a Paris theatre. I refer to other texts of his, so far unpublished with the exception of "Trop c'est trop," given in the seventh number of *La Brèche: Action surréaliste* (December 1964), 47–48, over the subtitle *pièce injouable*. None of Barbé's plays have been published to date.

23. Published anonymously in the Belgian surrealist magazine *Les Lèvres Nues* in December 1955, "D'Or et de Sable" is reprinted in Nougé's *L'Expérience continue* (Brussels, 1966), pp. 175–176.

Surrealist Film-Makers

Original Barbarity

1. Cited by Brunius, p. 49.

2. *Entr'acte* was presented as an entr'acte during a performance of Picabia's ballet *Relâche* (music by Erik Satie) at the Théâtre des Champs-Élysées, during the Swedish Ballet program on December 4, 1924. The scenario of the film was subsequently published in Milan by Cilanco Viazzi (Poligono Società Editore, Nº 1, 1945, in the Collection "Biblioteca Cinematografica").

3. *É. C.* 1, p. 18.

4. As a man who had acted in movies (notably as a Franciscan in Dreyer's *La Passion de Jeanne d'Arc*), Artaud was not entirely ignorant of the practicalities of film-making.

5. Artaud, *Œuvres complètes*, III, p. 312.
6. Ibid., p. 73 ("Réponse à une Enquête").
7. *É. C.* 1, p. 43.
8. Man Ray, *Self Portrait* (Boston and Toronto, 1963), p. 270.
9. Cf., *152 Proverbes mis au Goût du Jour* by Paul Éluard and Benjamin Péret (1925) and Desnos' *Rrose Sélavy*.
10. These stills are reproduced in the magazine *Cahiers d'Art* (1935) under the title "Essai de Simulation de Délire cinématographique."
11. See Breton's untitled foreword to Man Ray's *La Photographie n'est pas l'Art* (1937).
12. See *É. C.* 1, p. 45.
13. Arthur Knight, *The Liveliest Art* (New York, 1957), p. 106.
14. "Notes on the Making of *Un Chien andalou*," in Frank Stauffacher, *Art in the Cinema* (San Francisco, 1947).
15. Carlos Rebolledo, *Buñuel* (1964), p. 1. This volume appears under Rebolledo's name, even though the first two parts were written by Grange.
16. "Le Comportement des Personnages et la Psychanalyse," *Études cinématographiques*, N° 20–21, 'Luis Buñuel,' 1, 4ᵉ trimestre, 1962, pp. 101–102.
17. In *The Secret Life of Salvador Dali* (New York, 1942).
18. Raymond Durgnat, *Luis Buñuel* [London and Berkeley, (1967)] is among these. Durgnat's, the only book to have appeared on Buñuel in the English language, is most disappointing. See the review by J. H. Matthews, *Surrealist TransformaCtion*, N° 2, 1968, p. 52.

The Moral Path

19. In Rebolledo, p. 102.
20. Jacques Doniol-Valcrose and André Bazin, 'Entretiens avec Luis Buñuel," *Cahiers du Cinéma*, N° 36, June 1954.
21. Adonis Kyrou, "*L'Age d'Or*, Centre et Tremplin du Cinéma surréaliste," *L'Age du Cinéma*, N° 4–5 (August-November 1951), special surrealist number, pp. 4–5.
22. This surrealist declaration is reproduced in *L'Avant-Scène du Cinéma*, N° 27–28, July 1963.
23. "Many spectators interpret their embraces as a brutal assault by Gaston Modot on Lya Lys, reminding us of Freud's observation that children glimpsing sexual intercourse between their parents often imagine that Daddy is savaging Mummy. The misinterpretation of this scene is so natural that one can hardly call it a misinterpretation, and the confusion links with other themes in the film" (*Luis Buñuel*, p. 40).
24. *Le Miroir du Merveilleux* (1940), reprinted in 1962.
25. *Les 120 Journées de Sodome*, Œuvres complètes du Marquis de Sade, XIII [Au Cercle du Livre précieux (1967)], p. 8.
26. No commentator has pointed out that Buñuel misspells the name of the castle where Sade situates the action of *Les 120 Journées de*

Sodome. Grange, who, for reasons best known to himself, refers his readers to Sade's *Justine* (in Rebolledo, p. 30), speaks of the "Château du Celigny" (p. 43). Kyrou writes "Selligny" (*Le Surréalisme au Cinéma,* p. 216)—a spelling hardly consistent with the location of Silling Castle in the Black Forest. He leaves us wondering whether his comments on the appropriateness of the final section of Buñuel's film were made on trust, rather than after comparison of the movie with Sade's text.

The Documentary

27. "The Films of Luis Buñuel," *Sight and Sound,* 23, 3, January-March 1954.
28. In Rebolledo, p. 50: "Buñuel, with *Las Hurdes,* moves away from surrealism definitively; there is no mistaking this."
29. "Entretiens avec Buñuel." The version of this interview with Doniol-Valcroze and Bazin, given as "Conversation with Buñuel" in the Spring 1955 issue of *Sight and Sound,* distorts the sense of the French, "J'avais une vision surréaliste," by translating "I had a surrealist vision." As for the last sentence cited here, it is offered in the following mutilated form: "And surrealism made me look at reality in a completely different way."
30. Raymond Borde and André Breton, *Pierre Molinier* (1964), no pagination.
31. Letter to the author, July 31, 1963.
32. *Les Inspirés et leurs Demeures* (1962). The deluxe edition of this work carries three unpublished texts by writers associated with surrealism: Benjamin Péret, Gherasim Luca, and Claude Tarnaud.
33. See the statement by Cheval reproduced in Ehrmann, pp. lx–lxii.
34. These phrases are cited in Ehrmann, p. lx. In 1959 Kyrou's film about Cheval, *Palais idéal,* used as a commentary Cheval's own statements, spoken by Gaston Modot, who had played the hero in *L'Age d'Or.*
35. Preface to Ehrmann, *Les Inspirés et leurs Demeures,* p. xi.
36. This question is discussed in detail in André Labarrère, "La Musique dans les Films de Buñuel," *Études cinématographiques,* 'Luis Buñuel' 1, 135–144.
37. On Roussel's use of language see Matthews, *Surrealism and the Novel,* pp. 41–45.
38. Since *comme* means 'as' also, whole phrases may be linked in novel fashion by this method, e.g., these lines from Jehan Mayoux's "J'aime Maïs," in his *Au Crible de la Nuit* (1948):
Et l'arbre est transparent comme une bouée rougit de la rencontre
D'une guitare et d'un marteau dans une mongolfière
[And the tree is transparent as a buoy blushes at the meeting
Of a guitar and a hammer in a montgolfier].
39. A volume reproducing the text of Péret's poem, in Italian, and illustrated by stills from the movie has been published as *L'Invenzione del Mondo* (Milan, 1959).

40. The information summarized in this paragraph is borrowed from the press release provided in English when *L'Invention du Monde* was shown at the Edinburgh Festival.
41. Bédouin subsequently wrote a book on *Les Masques* for the "Que sais-je?" series, 1961.
42. Letter to the author, April 26, 1963.
43. See the special 1951 issue of *L'Age du Cinéma* on surrealism. *L'Invention du Monde*, by the way, was distributed by "Age du Cinéma" Productions.
44. Letter to the author, May 27, 1963.
45. Letter to the author, February 28, 1963.
46. The bibliography evidencing the character of the surrealists' interest in primitive societies is considerable. Those interested in this question could begin by consulting Péret's *Anthologie des Mythes, Légendes et Contes populaires d'Amérique* (1959).

Embezzlement of the Familiar

47. Translated by Wm. Peterson in Steen Colding et al., *Wilhelm Freddie* (Copenhagen, 1962), where the scenario of *Spiste horisonter* is accompanied by a few stills.
48. A woman lying nude in the Galerie Daniel Cordier during the 1959 International Surrealist Exhibition, her body serving as a table from which one could help oneself to food. See the photograph reproduced in *La Brèche: Action surréaliste*, N° 6 (June 1964), facing p. 16.
49. "Une Boulimie de l'Absolu," in Steen Colding et al., pp. 73–74.
50. "Le Feu sous la Cendre," *Les Lèvres Nues (Brussels)*, N° 2 (August 1954), p. 23.
51. "Un autre Cinéma," *Les Lèvres Nues*, N° 7 (December 1966), p. 8.
52. "L'Esprit avant l'Escalier," *Les Lèvres Nues*, Summer 1960, special number (*hors série*) on *L'Imitation du Cinéma*. The scenario of Mariën's film also appears in this eight-page pamphlet, together with some details regarding the hostile reception accorded the film.
53. "Imitation de la Musique," *Les Lèvres Nues*, Summer 1960, pp. 7–8.
54. See, for instance, *The San Francisco Examiner*, October 28, 1969, and *The San Francisco Chronicle*, October 29, 1969.
55. Letter to the author, November 15, 1969.
56. Ibid.
57. Ibid. On the surrealist conception of objective hazard see Matthews, *An Introduction to Surrealism*, pp. 99–116.
58. "Cité pleine de Rêves," *Positif*, N° 105 (May 1969), p. 2.
59. Bertrand Tavernier and Jean-Paul Török, "Entretien avec Robert Benayoun," *Positif*, N° 105, May 1969. All subsequent direct quotations about *Paris n'existe pas* are taken from Benayoun's replies to Tavernier and Török, pp. 4–20.
60. It is Félicienne, not Angela, whom we see reading Gide's *Paludes* and du Maurier's *Peter Ibbetson*.

61. During his interview for *Positif*, Benayoun played on the meaning of the word *endosser* (to 'slip on' clothing and to 'shoulder responsibility for'), when affirming that Simon's comments upon painting express, in the main, his creator's views on the cinema: "J'endosse pour le cinéma la plupart des répliques de Simon Dévereux sur la peinture."

62. Benayoun is speaking of the moral predicament in which the surrealist would be placed, if he had to choose between his obligation to love and his loyalty to the cause of revolution.

63. I refer to subliminal perception, as James Vicary has experimented with it for the purposes of commercial advertising in movie houses. See Benayoun's article "Celui qui murmurait dans les Ténèbres," *BIEF: Jonction surréaliste*, Nº 2, December 15, 1958.

64. This quotation introduces the chapter "A Swing Door" on dreams in Matthews, *An Introduction to Surrealism*, pp. 62–80.

Luis Buñuel

1. "Vers le Cinéma," from a February 1925 prospectus announcing the film performances at the Cabinet Maldoror in Brussels. The text was countersigned by two other Belgian surrealists, Camille Goemans and Marcel Lecomte, whose names do not appear after the text in *Histoire de ne pas rire* (Brussels, 1956), p. 33.

2. *Le Surréalisme au Cinéma*, pp. 224–227.

3. The title of *Los Olvidados* means literally "The Forgotten." *The Young and the Damned* is a version less unfaithful to the theme of the film than English translations sometimes are. Buñuel's later movie *The Young One* was released in England as *Island of Shame*, presumably to avoid confusion with a musical starring Cliff Richard, made there under the title *The Young Ones*.

4. Jean de Baroncelli reported that, when making this statement, Buñuel had a mischievous gleam in his eye (See "Brève Rencontre avec Luis Buñuel," *Le Monde*, December 16, 1959). Michèle Manceaux cites the same phrase, without appearing aware of any ironic intent, in "Luis Buñuel: Athée grâce à Dieu," *L'Express*, May 12, 1960.

5. Cited in Durgnat, p. 76.

6. See, for instance, Jean Bastaire's reading, "Une Chronique buñuélienne; Subida al cielo," *Études cinématographiques*, Nº 22–23, 'Luis Buñuel,' 2, 1ᵉʳ trimestre, 1963, 239–240.

7. See *Le Surréalisme au Cinéma*, pp. 227–230.

8. *Ibid.*, p. 227.

9. Anyone believing Buñuel is hinting at something so monstrous as to lie outside human experience will consult with profit H. Salamanca Alba's article on the case of Edelmira B., in *Mito* (Bogotà), Nº 15, August-September 1957. The article is accompanied by a photographic document proving that Edelmira's husband, Mar-

celino, was driven by jealousy not merely to sew up his wife's vulva but also to add a lock, which Francisco evidently is prepared to forego.

10. Durgnat's account (p. 96) of Archibaldo's encounter with Lavinia, whom he apparently would rather call Laetitia, is sadly misleading and inaccurate.

11. "*El* ou le héros buñuélien," *Études cinématographiques*, 22–23, p. 184.

12. Elena Poniatowska seemed shocked at Buñuel's reply. Perhaps she had forgotten that his first movie was made in 1928, the year Breton and Aragon published their tract *Le Cinquantenaire de l'Hystérie*, celebrating hysteria as "the great poetic discovery of the XIXth century." The text is reproduced in Maurice Nadeau, *Documents surréalistes* (1948), pp. 125–127.

13. To the volume *Buñuel* published over his signature Rebolledo contributed only the seventh chapter, a scant essay on Buñuel and the picaresque novel. The parallel between Nazarin and Don Quixote is briefly drawn on pp. 170–171, reference being made to their defense of "a dead ideology."

14. Comparison of a serious political drama like *La Fièvre monte à El Pao* with *El*, and especially with *Ensayo de un crimen*, may seem far-fetched until one reflects upon the perceptive comment by Phyllis and Eberhard Kronhausen: "Sade's fantasies are primarily concerned with sadomasochism and other sexual deviations which are intimately related to his political philosophies and which must be discussed in that connection" (*Erotic Fantasies: A Study of the Sexual Imagination* [New York, 1969], p. 106).

15. Kyrou, too, reports, "Buñuel said to me that he does not insist on making 'impious' images and that if he had a 'pious' image which seemed to him interesting or attractive, he would put it in a film, and he added with little smile 'but no pious images come to my mind'" (*Le Surréalisme au Cinéma*, p. 238).

16. See Sadoul's preface to the special number of *Domaine Cinéma*, N⁰ 2 (1962), devoted to *Viridiana*.

17. Durand sees the bear as representing "Paradise lost for a corrupt class or force on the upsurge, parallel and incomprehensible to that class itself" ("L'Esprit d'Ubu-Roi," *Études cinématographiques*, 22–23, p. 234).

18. Estève cites Durand with approbation, adding his own word on the bear: "it can also be the symbol of the essentially animal world, nonconformist because it has not lived in society" ("Le Huis-clos de la Condition humaine," *Études cinématographiques*, 22–23, p. 230).

19. See Ferdinand Alquié, ed., *Entretiens sur le Surréalisme* (Paris and The Hague, 1968), pp. 427–430.

20. Mirbeau, *Le Journal d'une Femme de Chambre* (Le Livre du Club du Livre, n. d.), p. 344.

21. Buñuel, who has never forgotten attacks upon him in *The Secret Life of Salvador Dali*, may be alluding to Dali's *Taxi pluvieux*, created for the 1938 international surrealist exhibition in Paris. The *Rainy Taxi* had a clothed dressmaker's dummy sitting in the rear seat, with snails crawling over it. A photograph appears in Marcel Jean's *Histoire de la Peinture surréaliste* (1959), p. 282. It is reproduced, full page, in the catalogue of the exhibition *Dada, Surrealism, and their Heritage* (New York, 1968), p. 154 and in William S. Rubin's *Dada and Surrealist Art* (New York, n. d.), p. 285. Dali recreated his taxi for the 1968 exhibition in New York. However, the snails made off into the garden, presumably preferring a Marini original to a Dali remake.

22. Rebolledo, p. 147.

23. Cited in Ado Kyrou, *Luis Buñuel* (1962), p. 198.

Conclusion

1. "L'Aube du Surréalisme et le Cinéma," p. 83.

2. Unidentified article cited in Ferdinand Alquié, ed., *Entretiens sur le Surréalisme,* p. 424.

Index

189